STUDIES IN THE EARLY HISTORY OF BRITAIN

General Editor: Nicholas Brooks

Corpus of Early Christian Inscribed Stones of South-west Britain

To Leila, Samir, Mona and Rami

Corpus of Early Christian Inscribed Stones of South-west Britain

Elisabeth Okasha

Leicester University Press
London and New York

*Distributed exclusively in the United States and Canada
by St. Martin's Press*

Leicester University Press
(a division of Pinter Publishers Ltd.)
25 Floral Street, London WC2E 9DS

First published in 1993

Distributed exclusively in the USA and Canada by St. Martin's Press, Inc.,
Room 400, 175 Fifth Avenue, New York, NY10010, USA

Elisabeth Okasha is hereby identified as the author of this work as provided under
Section 77 of the Copyright, Designs and Patents Act, 1988.

British Library Cataloguing in Publication Data

A CIP catalogue record for this book is available from the British Library

ISBN 0 7185 1475 0

Library of Congress Cataloging-in-Publication Data

Okasha, Elisabeth.
    Corpus of early Christian inscribed stones of South-west Britain / Elisabeth
Okasha.
        p. cm.   - (Studies in the early history of Britain)
    Includes bibliographical references.
    ISBN 0-7185-1475-0
    1. Inscriptions, Christian - Great Britain.   2. Great Britain - Antiquities.
    I. Title.   II. Series.
    CN753.G7038   1993
    942.01-dc20   93-9951
                                                                      CIP

Typeset by Mayhew Typesetting, Rhayader, Powys
Printed and bound in Great Britain by SRP Ltd., Exeter

Contents

Foreword   vii
Preface   ix
Acknowledgements   x

INTRODUCTION
Section 1:   General   3
Section 2:   Previous Work on the Inscribed Stones   7
Section 3:   Classification of the Inscribed Stones   11
Section 4:   The Texts   14
             a: Language and Formula   14
             b: Script   18
             c: Layout of the Texts   28
             d: Summary of Differences Between Categories 1 and 2   30
Section 5:   Sources of Influence   31
Section 6:   Personal Names   43
Section 7:   Dating of the Inscribed Stones   50
Section 8:   Guide to the Entries   58

ENTRIES
 1 *Biscovey* 63
 2 *Boskenna* 68
 3 *Boslow* 70
 4 *Bosworgey* 73
 5 *Bowden* 76
 6 *Buckland Monachorum* 79
 7 *Camborne* 82
 8 *Cardinham I* 85
 9 *Cardinham II* 88
10 *Castledore* 91
11 *Cubert* 97
12 *East Ogwell* 100
13 *Fardel* 103
14 *Gulval I* 109
15 *Gulval II* 113
16 *Hayle* 116
17 *Indian Queens* 122
18 *Lancarffe* 126
19 *Lanhadron* 129
20 *Lanherne* 133
21 *Lanivet* 138
22 *Lanteglos* 141
23 *Lewannick I* 146
24 *Lewannick II* 150
25 *Lundy I* 154
26 *Lundy II* 158
27 *Lundy III* 161
28 *Lundy IV* 164
29 *Lustleigh* 167
30 *Lynton* 171
31 *Madron I* 174
32 *Madron II* 179
33 *Madron III* 182
34 *Mawgan* 185
35 *Nanscow* 189
36 *Parracombe* 193
37 *Penzance* 195
38 *Perranporth* 200
39 *Phillack I* 201
40 *Phillack II* 205
41 *Plymstock* 208
42 *Porthgwarra* 211
43 *Redgate* 213
44 *Redruth* 218
45 *Rialton* 220
46 *St Clement* 224

47 *St Columb Major* 229
48 *St Endellion* 232
49 *St Hilary* 236
50 *St Just I* 239
51 *St Just II* 243
52 *St Kew* 248
53 *Sancreed I* 251
54 *Sancreed II* 255
55 *Sourton* 260
56 *Southill* 264
57 *Stowford* 268
58 *Tavistock I* 271
59 *Tavistock II* 274
60 *Tavistock III* 278
61 *Tavistock IV* 282
62 *Tavistock V* 285
63 *Tawna* 288

64 *Tintagel* 291
65 *Trebyan* 296
66 *Tregony* 299
67 *Trencrom* 302
68 *Tresco* 304
69 *Treslothan* 307
70 *Trevarrack* 310
71 *Treveneague* 312
72 *Trewint* 315
73 *Tuckingmill* 317
74 *Waterpit Down* 318
75 *Welltown* 322
76 *Whitestile* 326
77 *Winsford Hill* 328
78 *Worthyvale* 333
79 *Yealmpton* 338

APPENDICES

A: Personal names   343
B: Romano-British Inscribed Stones from the South-west   346
C: Inscribed Stones from the South-west Post-dating AD 1100   347
D: Comparable Inscribed Stones from outside the South-west   348
E: Stones excluded on Grounds other than those of Provenance or
    Date   349
F: Macalister's Numbering of the Stones   350
G: Alternative Names Assigned to Individual Stones   352

Bibliography   353
Abbreviations of Journal and Series Titles   371
List of Figures   373

Foreword

The aim of the *Studies in the Early History of Britain* is to promote works of the highest scholarship which open up virgin fields of study or which surmount the barriers of traditional academic disciplines. As interest in the origins of our society and culture grow while scholarship becomes ever more specialized, interdisciplinary studies are needed not only by scholars but also by students and laymen. The series will therefore include research monographs, works of synthesis and also collaborative studies of important themes by several scholars whose training and expertise has lain in different fields. Our knowledge of the early Middle Ages will always be limited and fragmentary; but progress can be made if the work of the historian embraces that of the philologist, the archaeologist, the geographer, the numismatist, the art historian and the liturgist – to name only the most obvious. The need to cross and to remove academic frontiers also explains the extension of the geographical range from that of the previous *Studies in Early English History* to include the whole island of Britain. The change would have been welcomed by the editor of the earlier series, the late Professor H.P.R. Finberg, whose pioneering work helped to inspire, or to provoke, the interest of a new generation of early medievalists in the relations of Britons and Saxons. The approach of this series is therefore deliberately wide-ranging. Early medieval Britain can only be understood in the context of contemporary developments in Ireland and on the Continent.

In this volume Dr Elisabeth Okasha meets the long-standing need for a scholarly *corpus* of the early medieval inscribed stones of Devon and Cornwall and of the immediately neighbouring areas. These inscriptions contain precious clues to the culture, society and religion of the Britons of the South-West. Now for the first time the student of this region has the secure foundation of a consistent and scholarly treatment of their classification and of the problems of dating, transcription and analysis. It is only when seen in the context of the entire series that sensible conjectures about and interpretations of a particular stone (or group of stones) can be offered. In making these key sources comprehensible and accessible to the interested layman, student or scholar, Dr Okasha has confirmed her reputation as Britain's leading early medieval epigrapher. I am proud that this series' first venture into the south-western counties should be to provide so handsomely what has been such a keenly-felt *desideratum*.

N.P. Brooks
University of Birmingham
June 1993

Preface

The early Christian inscribed stones of the south-west peninsula of Britain are of considerable importance in view of the paucity of other evidence concerning the early history of the area. Unfortunately, since the majority of these stones stand in the open air, their condition is deteriorating, in some cases with alarming speed. After having survived for centuries, the texts of some stones are significantly less legible now than they were when I first examined them 25 years ago. While stones remain outside they will continue to deteriorate. There is thus a clear need for an up-to-date corpus, in the first place to list the stones with an accurate description of the present location of each. Secondly, and of equal importance, is to establish the actual readings of the texts today, before they deteriorate further. The readings given are based on my own examinations and drawings made between 1984 and 1987.

The major part of the corpus consists of the individual Entries, one for each stone. As well as giving a reading of the text, each Entry contains a description of the stone, its history and likely date, as well as an interpretative discussion of its text. The Introduction discusses the inscribed stones as a group with sections devoted, amongst other topics, to the scripts and formulae employed, to the personal names occurring in the texts and to criteria for dating the stones.

It will thus be seen that I have not attempted to write a history of the south-west in the early Christian era, still less a work of palaeography or a treatise on Celtic philology. My aim is both more modest and more circumscribed. It is to offer a corpus of the early Christian inscriptions of south-west Britain which is accurate in its information and reliable in its reading of the texts. It is hoped that the corpus may be of use to others, to historians, palaeographers and philologists, whose interests lie in the areas it covers.

Acknowledgements

I acknowledge with gratitude the considerable financial support received which enabled me to undertake the fieldwork for the corpus and to acquire the photographs. This support came from The Twenty-Seven Foundation Historical Awards, c/o The Institute of Historical Research, University of London, from the Marc Fitch Foundation and from the Research Fund of the Faculty of Arts, University College, Cork. I also received awards from the Sir Arthur Quiller-Couch Memorial Fund, c/o Cornwall County Council, and from the Devonshire Association for the Advancement of Science, Literature and Art.

Many people have given me considerable help during the time that I have been working on the corpus, to all of whom I offer my grateful thanks. I should like to thank all those who gave me permission to study the stones under their jurisdiction, both private land-owners and the incumbents of churches. Several people helped me to locate and examine individual stones and this is acknowledged in the appropriate Entry. The following have helped me in various ways and I am most grateful to them all: Jill Butterworth, Richard Gilbert, Rev. Roger Gilbert, Frances Griffith, Dr Ann Hamlin, Dr Isabel Henderson, Dr Máire Herbert, P.J. Hynes, John Maunder, the late E.N. Masson Phillips, Sandy O'Driscoll, Dr Jennifer O'Reilly, O.J. Padel, Professor R.I. Page, Dr Susan Pearce, R.D. Penhallurick, Ann Preston-Jones, Lady Honora Rashleigh, Professor A.C. Thomas, David Thomas, Jean Thomson, Leslie Webster and the librarian and staff, especially Angela Broome, of the library of the Royal Institution of Cornwall. I am most grateful to Ann Preston-Jones for preparing the distribution map, Fig. I.1. My special thanks are due to Anne FitzGerald for preparing the typescript with painstaking care. It is a great pleasure to thank Joyce Greenham who, with dedication and zeal, toured Cornwall to take photographs for me. Finally I should like to thank my husband for his helpful criticism and enthusiastic encouragement, without which this work would not have been completed.

INTRODUCTION

Section 1: General

At the beginning of the early Christian period the south-west peninsula of Britain formed the kingdom of Dumnonia. Much of the early history of this area remains unclear since the historical and archaeological source material is not extensive and is not always easy to interpret.[1] In these circumstances, the group of inscribed stones from the area is of correspondingly greater importance. The stones are also significant as evidence for literacy in the south-west; they are, indeed, the only evidence for literacy before the ninth or tenth century when the scanty manuscript evidence for Old Cornish commences.[2]

The term 'early Christian' is used here to denote the period from the end of Roman rule to the Norman Conquest, from around AD 400 to around AD 1100. The evidence for the dating of individual stones within this period is given in Section 7. In Roman times the south-west was the area of the *Dumnonii* and after the Roman withdrawal was under Celtic rule. From as early as the seventh century the Anglo-Saxons began to penetrate Devon and they probably gained control over the whole peninsula during the ninth century or, perhaps, in the early tenth century following the military successes of Athelstan.[3]

The corpus comprises 79 inscribed stones; the distribution of most of the existing stones is shown on the distribution map (fig. I.1). The map shows that, while the inscribed stones come from the general area of Cornwall and Devon, there is some clustering. There are, for example, a number of stones from the Penwith peninsula, a cluster around Cardinham and four on Lundy Island. The six stones containing ogham texts are all from an area covering north Cornwall and south Devon. Altogether there are 58 stones known from Cornwall, 20 from Devon and 1 from Somerset, from near the border with Devon. Ten of these 79 stones are now lost. They are included in the corpus on the evidence of descriptions and, in some cases, drawings, made before the stones disappeared. A few of the existing stones are now totally illegible and they too are included on the evidence of earlier drawings and readings. Comparable inscribed stones occur in Wales (*see* Section 5) and there are also a few others from outside the south-west; Appendix D lists eight similar stones from Dorset, Hampshire, Shropshire and the Channel Islands.

---

1. See, for example, Pearce (1981) 165-8, 175-7; Preston-Jones & Rose (1986) 135-55; Todd (1987) 236-8.
2. For the manuscript sources of Old Cornish, including vernacular names in Latin manuscripts, see Jackson (1953) 59-62.
3. For a recent discussion of the Anglo-Saxon penetration into the south-west, see Todd (1987) 267-75.

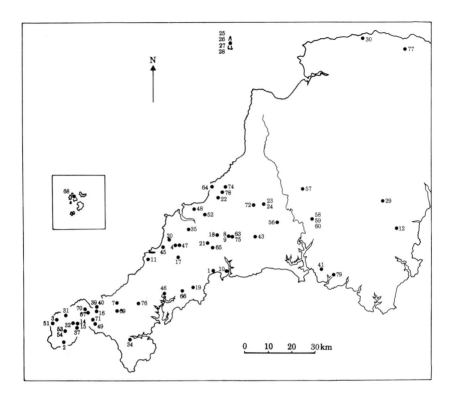

Figure I.1   Distribution map.
The distribution map identifies the inscribed stones by reference to their running numbers; thus '1' refers to 1 Biscovey, '2' to 2 Boskenna, and so on. All the inscribed stones still in existence appear on the map with three exceptions. These are: 13 Fardel, which is in the British Museum; 55 Sourton, which was temporarily stored in Okehampton Castle when the map was drawn and was only placed in its present position in 1993; and 6 Buckland Monachorum, whose exact location may not be made public. The ten stones which are now lost do not appear on the map. They are: 5 Bowden, 33 Madron III, 36 Parracombe, 38 Perranporth, 42 Porthgwarra, 44 Redruth, 50 St Just I, 61 Tavistock IV, 62 Tavistock V and 73 Tuckingmill. The map was prepared by Ann Preston-Jones.

The majority of the inscriptions are cut on pieces of undressed or roughly dressed stone, usually without any carved decoration. These stones are referred to as 'pillar-stones' and form Category 1. The inscriptions on cross-shafts and cross-bases form Category 2. A few stones fall into neither of these categories. A full discussion of the categories, including the classification criteria used in assigning stones to them, appears in Sections 3 and 4. Initially it was hoped to include in the corpus some account of the techniques used in the cutting of the inscriptions. Many of the texts are, however, in a poor condition. This has made it impossible to maintain with confidence even such a broad distinction as that between incision and pocking. Regrettably, therefore, information on the cutting technique has had to be omitted.

The texts of the stones show that many of the pillar-stones and also some of the crosses were commemorative. While the crosses stand in a clearly Christian tradition, it is not certain that the same is true of all the pillar-stones. Those containing a cross, a *chi-rho* symbol or a Christian formula, for example *hic iacet*, were presumably erected by or for Christians. We cannot be sure that the same was true of all those stones which lack explicit signs of Christianity.

There is not one certain instance of a stone found *in situ*. It is possible that some stones are, or were found, *in situ*, but that these are not now recognisable because of our lack of knowledge of the circumstances surrounding their original erection. Many stones are now in churches or churchyards. While some have been moved there in modern times for safe keeping, some have been there since they were first recorded.[4] These may include stones first erected as gravestones in an early Christian graveyard. A.C. Thomas suggested, for example, that the four Lundy stones were found in the cemetery where they had originally been erected.[5] It is indeed possible that one of them, Lundy IV, was associated with, presumably one of, 'two seemingly early graves'.[6] Yealmpton may have been found in association with a grave and just possibly Nanscow also.[7] Those stones, eight in number, containing a *hic iacet* formula are clearly gravestones.[8] Only one of these, however, was found in association with a grave (Hayle) and even in this case it is not certain that the stone and the grave belonged together.

Swanton and Pearce discussed in detail the relationship between the Lustleigh stone and its graveyard. They argued that the stone was originally erected in an early Christian graveyard and that the earliest church for which there is evidence (of Norman date) was later built inside this enclosed graveyard.[9] There is archaeological and place-name evidence for the existence of other early Christian graveyards in the south-west.[10] The problem of using such evidence in relation to the inscribed stones is that, all too often, the existence of an inscribed stone is in itself an integral part of the archaeological evidence.

Many of the stones were first recorded in clearly non-original contexts, in use as gateposts, for example, or re-used as building material. Details of the finding and subsequent history of each stone will be found in the

---

4. Details will be found in the individual Entries.
5. Thomas, A.C. *et al.* (1969) 139.
6. Thomas, A.C. *et al.* (1969) 142.
7. See the individual Entries.
8. See below, Section 4a.
9. Swanton & Pearce (1982) 139-43, esp. p. 140.
10. Pearce (1978) 67-75.

appropriate entry. A.G. Langdon was alarmed at this re-use of early Christian stones, describing it as 'deplorable desecration'.[11] On occasion, re-use has certainly resulted in loss of an inscription, as in the example Langdon gave of Treveneague.[12] On other occasions, however, it seems to me that re-use of inscribed stones as gateposts or as building material has aided their survival rather than the reverse. A few of the stones were first recorded some distance from a graveyard, a dwelling-place or even a gate, for example Madron I and Winsford Hill. Neither of these had any sign of a burial recorded in association with them. Pearce suggested that such stones may originally have been situated near early trackways.[13] This seems perfectly possible but is not susceptible to proof since most early trackways can no longer be traced with certainty.[14]

---

11. Langdon (1896) 20.
12. See Entry.
13. Pearce (1978) 29.
14. See, however, Entry 31, Madron I History.

Section 2: Previous Work on the Inscribed Stones

The inscribed stones of south-west Britain have attracted scholarly attention for the last four hundred years. The first works to mention the stones, in the sixteenth and seventeenth centuries, were the accounts of antiquaries surveying wide areas of Britain. These early references are of considerable interest for the light they shed both on the inscriptions and on contemporary historical method.

The earliest scholar was John Leland whose *Itinerary* was undertaken between about 1535 and 1543. Leland observed only one of the inscribed stones, Castledore.[1] John Norden, whose survey of Cornwall was probably made in 1584, mentioned the Castledore and Redgate stones and illustrated Redgate.[2] Editions of William Camden's *Britannia* published between 1594 and 1607 mention Redgate and, possibly, Winsford Hill.[3] Richard Carew, writing in 1602, noted the Castledore, Redgate and Worthyvale stones while Serenus (Hugh Paulin) Cressy knew of Redgate.[4] Thus by the year 1700 there were known three, possibly four, inscribed stones from the south-west.

In the eighteenth century, accounts of the stones by men living in the south-west become more common. These reflect interest and, perhaps, pride in the local history of the area. Walter Moyle collected material in the form of letters to and from his acquaintances; these letters are dated between 1700 and 1715. Moyle published some material collected by the scholar Edward Lhwyd who, in 1700, was the first to record Biscovey, Gulval I and Madron I.[5] Moyle himself was the first to record the Mawgan stone although Lhwyd had apparently seen it.[6] Like Moyle, the Rev. William Borlase lived in Cornwall. Writing in 1754, he described ten stones, including all the preceding ones except for Winsford Hill plus three new ones, Camborne, Indian Queens and St Clement.[7] In 1740 he had also noted Redruth.[8] The drawings and descriptions by these scholars are most

---

1. Leland (c. 1540), ed. Smith, L.T. (1907), I, 207.
2. Norden (1728) 58-9 & fig.; see Graham (1966) 6.
3. Camden (1594) 137: possible reference to Winsford Hill; Camden (1600) 155: Redgate noted; Camden (1607) 139 & fig.: Redgate described and illustrated.
4. Carew (1602) 136; 128-9 & fig.; 122, respectively; Cressy (1668) 746.
5. Lhwyd (1700b) (Biscovey, Gulval I) and Lhwyd (1700a) (Madron I). Neither of these works have page numbering.
6. Moyle (1726) 248-50 & fig.
7. Borlase, W. (1754) 365 & fig.; 364 & fig.; 356 & fig., respectively.
8. Borlase, W. (unpub. 1740) 52 & fig.

useful in establishing readings of the texts at this early date and in supplying information about the location of the stones.

In 1797 Richard Polwhele published his history of Devon which noted for the first time, although without illustration, four stones from that county: Lustleigh, Parracombe, Tavistock II and Yealmpton.[9] A probable reference to the Lanhadron cross-base occurs in Polwhele's history of Cornwall published in 1803.[10] In 1789 and again in 1806 Camden's *Britannia* was edited by Richard Gough. Both Polwhele's and Gough's works are useful in their accounts of the locations, conditions and readings of the inscribed stones then known. In addition, Gough was the first to describe and illustrate the Bowden stone.[11] The Porthgwarra stone was recorded in an eighteenth-century manuscript,[12] while St Endellion was probably first recorded in 1753.[13] By 1800 there were 19, possibly 20, inscribed stones known.

The first quarter of the nineteenth century saw the publication of four large historical works, two under the combined authorship of Daniel Lysons and Samuel Lysons, one by C.S. Gilbert and one by Fortescue Hitchins, edited by Samuel Drew. In 1814 Lysons and Lysons first noted and illustrated Lanherne, Rialton and Sancreed II, although they did not observe the inscription on Sancreed II;[14] in 1822 they recorded Tavistock I, a stone which Bray had known since 1804.[15] Neither Gilbert nor Hitchins published new stones, nor many drawings. Their work, especially Gilbert's, is useful for the accounts given of the locations, present and past, of the stones.[16] By 1830 there were 23, possibly 24 inscribed stones known from south-west Britain.

During the years from 1830 to 1850 the nature of the publications changed. Overall historical surveys became less common and notes and short articles on individual stones and groups of stones became more frequent. A.J. Kempe, for example, writing in 1830 and the Rev. E.A. Bray, in a letter dated 10 March 1834, both described the stones collected together by Bray into his vicarage garden at Tavistock.[17] By 1850 33, possibly 34, inscribed stones were known, the new ones being Hayle, Nanscow, Penzance, St Just I, St Just II, Stowford, Tavistock III, Tavistock IV, Tavistock V and Waterpit Down. From this time onwards, detailed and careful accounts by local amateurs are often of great value, especially when the stones were well known to them. Indeed such accounts are often of greater value than surveys of the material by scholars who examined the stones once or, sometimes, not at all. Such scholars from the mid-

9. Polwhele (1797) I, 151-2.
10. Polwhele (1803) II, 199n-200n.
11. Gough (1806) I, 50-1 & fig.
12. BL MS Stowe 1023 p. 39 & fig.; see Entry.
13. See Entry.
14. Lysons, D. & Lysons, S. (1814) ccxlv & fig.; ccxxiii & fig.; ccxlv & fig., respectively.
15. Lysons, D. & Lysons, S. (1822) cccviii & fig.; Bray (1836) 374.
16. Gilbert, C.S. (1817), vol. I, and Gilbert, C.S. (1820), vol. II; Hitchins (1824).
17. Kempe (1830) 116, 219, 495 & fig. opp. p. 489; Bray (1836) 360-82.

nineteenth century include D.H. Haigh and Ae. Huebner.[18]

The period from 1850 until the First World War was the most productive in the publication of works on the inscribed stones, both on newly discovered stones and on those known for some years. Some of the material is particularly useful in providing readings of texts which have since deteriorated badly. It would not be profitable to comment on all the vast output of material from this period, but certain people deserve to be mentioned. The earliest was J.T. Blight who between 1856 and 1872 examined a number of the Cornish stones. Blight's work is variable in its accuracy and must be treated with caution. The same is true of William Iago who published prolifically on the Cornish material between 1868 and 1895. Sir John Rhys, by contrast, was a sound and reliable scholar whose published material on the south-western inscriptions spanned the period 1873 to 1918 (a posthumous work). Not only did Rhys travel extensively to visit the stones, and record his observations with accuracy, but he brought to the task his considerable knowledge of Welsh inscriptions and of Primitive Welsh/Cornish.

A.G. Langdon and J. Romilly Allen are the two outstanding figures of this period. Langdon's particular interest was the carved crosses. His systematic discussion and excellent drawings of the carved interlace are still of value and his *Old Cornish Crosses* remains the standard published work on the subject.[19] Langdon's work on the inscriptions was, however, less accurate. Fortunately some of this work was published in conjunction with Allen, an epigraphist noted for his meticulous work. Their paper published in 1895, despite the poor quality of some of Langdon's drawings, remains of considerable value.[20]

In 1932 H.O'N. Hencken published his work on the archaeology of Cornwall and Scilly.[21] In this he gave detailed observations of the inscribed stones and attempted to classify and date them. In spite of the modest nature of Hencken's book, it is in many ways more useful than R.A.S. Macalister's *Corpus Inscriptionum Insularum Celticarum*, a work lacking in meticulousness.[22] Macalister's drawings, readings and interpretations of the inscriptions are often inaccurate and sometimes imaginative, which is not a term of praise in this context. These drawbacks to Macalister's *Corpus* are well-known.[23] Nevertheless it remains the only comprehensive collection of the Celtic inscriptions of the British Isles and has, therefore, been extensively used by scholars since its publication. Macalister's earlier paper on the south-western inscriptions, published in 1929, is rather more accurate than his *Corpus*.[24] Where possible I have quoted from this paper rather than from his later work.

---

18. Haigh (1858-9) 170-94; Huebner (1876).
19. Langdon (1896).
20. Langdon & Allen, J.R. (1895) 50-60.
21. Hencken (1932).
22. Macalister (1945), vol. I, and Macalister (1949), vol. II.
23. See, for example, Jackson's review of vol. I; Jackson (1946) 521-3.
24. Macalister (1929) 179-96.

Macalister's work on the Welsh inscriptions has been superseded by that of V.E. Nash-Williams.[25] In 1950 K.H. Jackson published a paper on the ogham inscriptions of southern Britain, followed, in 1953, by his *Language and History of Early Britain*.[26] This definitive work contains important material on the reading, interpretation and dating of many of the south-western inscriptions and much useful discussion on the etymology of the personal names. In recent years work on the archaeology and history of south-western Britain, including work on the inscribed stones, has been published by, among others, S.M. Pearce and A.C. Thomas. The work of both these scholars has made an important contribution to south-western studies.

Three pieces of relevant unpublished material from this century are preserved in the library of the Royal Institution of Cornwall in Truro. First are the diaries of C.G. Henderson (1900-1933) which were compiled between 1912 and 1917.[27] Despite Henderson's age at the time of writing, the diaries contain useful information on various stones, some not recorded elsewhere, for example Boskenna and Trencrom.[28] Second is a typescript, entitled *Cornish Crosses*, by R.D. Baird and his sister, Lady Adelaide White.[29] This brings together local information on the location and state of the crosses up to 1961. Third is a four-volume typescript by Mary Henderson, entitled *A Survey of Ancient Crosses of Cornwall 1952-1983*.[30] This is a comprehensive survey of the crosses and contains useful, up-to-date material on their present condition.

25. Nash-Williams (1950). Throughout the corpus I have followed Nash-Williams, not Macalister, in his account of the location of the Welsh stones and in his spelling of the Welsh place-names.
26. Jackson (1950) 197-213; Jackson (1953).
27. Henderson, C.G. (unpub. 1912-17).
28. Details will be found in the Entries.
29. Baird & White (unpub. 1961).
30. Henderson, M. (unpub. 1985).

Section 3: Classification of the Inscribed Stones

The inscribed stones are divided into categories primarily according to their form and function. Category 1 consists of pillar-stones, that is, pieces of undressed or roughly dressed stone usually without any carved decoration. Category 2 consists of carved crosses. Category 3 contains those stones which are neither pillar-stones nor crosses, for example, altar-slabs. Unclassifiable stones are listed after Category 3 stones.

Category 1

Category 1 stones are subdivided into 1a, 1b, and 1c. The sub-categories 1a and 1b are distinguished by the formulae of their texts.

Sub-category 1a contains stones whose text or texts consist(s) of a simple memorial formula:[1]

Boskenna	Boslow	Bosworgey	Bowden
Buckland Monachorum	Cardinham II	Cubert	East Ogwell
Fardel	Indian Queens	Lanivet	Lundy I
Lundy II	Lundy III	Lundy IV	Lustleigh
Lynton	Madron I	Madron II	Mawgan
Nanscow	Phillack I	Redruth	St Hilary
St Kew	Southill	Stowford	Tavistock I
Tavistock II	Tawna	Tresco	Treveneague
Welltown	Winsford Hill	Yealmpton	

Sub-category 1b contains stones whose text or texts consist(s) of a longer formula:[2]

Castledore	Gulval I	Hayle	Lancarffe
Lanteglos	Lewannick I	Lewannick II	Rialton
St Endellion	St Just II	Tavistock III	Tregony
Worthyvale			

Sub-category 1c contains those stones which were probably originally pillar-stones but which were subsequently re-cut to form crosses:

---

1. See Section 4a.
2. See Section 4a.

St Clement   Sourton   Whitestile

The St Clement stone was probably re-cut within the early Christian period; the Sourton and Whitestile stones may have been so too, or they may have been re-cut later. Two other Category 1 stones, Cardinham II and Lanteglos, had cross-heads attached to them in the last century, that on Cardinham II being still there.[3] Some Category 1 stones are now cemented into bases while others have had socket-holes observed on them. It is, however, most unlikely that any pillar-stone was intended to stand in a base or to have a cross-head attached to it.

Category 2

Category 2 stones are subdivided into 2a and 2b, depending on which part of the cross is inscribed.

Sub-category 2a contains those stones having inscribed cross-shafts, with or without cross-heads or cross-bases:

Biscovey	Cardinham I	Gulval II	Lanherne
Penzance	Plymstock	Redgate	Sancreed I
Sancreed II	Tintagel	Waterpit Down	

Sub-category 2b contains stones with inscribed cross-bases, none of which now has a cross-shaft:

Lanhadron   Trebyan   Trewint

Category 3

Category 3 stones are subdivided into:

3a, altar-slabs:
    Camborne   Treslothan

3b, undecorated slabs:
    Tavistock IV   Tavistock V   Trevarrack

3c, cross-slabs:
    St Columb Major

3d, stones containing only a *chi-rho* symbol:
    Phillack II   St Just I

---

3. Details of these stones will be found in the appropriate Entries.

Unclassifiable stones

Lost stones which were inadequately described or illustrated before their loss cannot be classified. These are:

Madron III	Parracombe	Perranporth
Porthgwarra	Tuckingmill	

One stone, Trencrom, although not lost is now too deteriorated to be classified.

Section 4: The Texts

Section 4a: Language and Formula

The language of almost all the texts is Latin. This is so even where the text consists of a name or names whose latinised character is indicated only by the inflexional ending -*i*, the inflexion described by Jackson as 'the convenient all-purposes Latin -*i*'.[1] There are four cases where the language used is not Latin. One is the stone from Lanteglos whose text is in English. The second is the Fardel stone some of whose texts might be in Primitive Irish, though this is by no means certain.[2] The third concerns the possibility that the inflexion -*i* on a Celtic name might on occasion be Celtic not Latin; Celtic *o*- stem nouns also had a genitive singular inflexion in -*i*. In texts containing no other Latin, the -*i* inflexion on a name of Celtic origin might be Celtic, the name belonging or assimilated to the *o*- stem class. The fourth is the group of stones with texts consisting of a single vernacular name in the nominative, without any inflexion. Certain examples of such texts on Category 1 stones are Stowford and Yealmpton and, on Category 2 stones, Cardinham I, Lanherne, text (ii) and Plymstock. Biscovey, text (i) (Category 2a) may be a further example, unless texts (i) and (ii) are to be read together.

The Latin used in the texts is often irregular in its orthography, grammar and syntax. *Hic*, for example, can appear as HIC or IC, while *filii*, genitive singular of *filius*, is usually spelt FILI. The verb *iacet* is almost invariably spelt IACIT and this is also the usual spelling on the Welsh stones.[3] Irregular spelling, grammar and syntax all occur on the Camborne stone whose text reads: LEUIUT IUSIT HEC ALTARE PRO ANIMA SUA, 'Leuiut ordered this altar for his own soul'. The verb IUSIT, a spelling of *iussit*, is here followed not by an infinitive but by a direct object, HEC ALTARE. The classical *altaria* commonly occurs in medieval Latin as *altare* and here HEC is presumably for HAEC or HOC. Unusual syntax can also be seen in the several instances of confusion between nominative and genitive, for example NONNITA, presumably for NONNITAE (Tregony), or CAVVDI FILIVS CIVI[L]I, '[the stone] of Cauudus son of Civil[l]us' (Lynton). Further discussion of these texts will be found in the appropriate Entries.

The most common formula used on the Category 1 stones is the simple memorial formula, that is, a text containing only one or more personal names, with or without a term of family relationship. The most usual form consists of two names in the genitive with *filius* also in the genitive, as on the Southill stone which reads, CVMREGNI FILI MAVCI. The genitive

---

1. Jackson (1953) 188.
2. See Entry.
3. Nash-Williams (1950) 8.

cases of FILI and of one of the names are presumably dependent on a noun to be supplied, perhaps 'stone'. The other genitive is dependent on FILI. The text can then be interpreted as, '[the stone] of Cumregnus, son of Maucus'. It is possible, though unlikely, that the names should be reversed giving, '[the stone] of Maucus, son of Cumregnus'. This point was also noted by Macalister in relation to the Irish ogham texts using a similar formula.[4] I have assumed throughout that the first name is that of the person commemorated, the second the patronymic. The Tregony stone provides evidence in favour of this. Its text is longer than the simple memorial formula, though clearly related to it, and reads, NONNITA ERCILI[V]I RICATI TRIS FILI ERCILINGI, probably, '[the stone] of Nonnita, of Ercili[v]us, [and] of Ricatus, three children of Ercilingus'. Here there is no question of ambiguity: the names of the commemorated come first with the father's name following.

Not all instances of the simple memorial formula occur in this form. The name or names may be in the nominative not genitive, as for example GOREVS on the Yealmpton stone. Texts with two personal names and no term of family relationship are difficult to interpret: it is not clear whether one person with two names or two people are referred to. An example of this is the Lustleigh stone which reads, DATUIDOC[-] CONHINO[.-], and may be interpreted, '[the stone of] Datuidoc Conhino[.]' or '[the stone of] Datuidoc, [son of] Conhino[.]'.

The simple memorial formula occurs on all stones of Category 1a and the use of this formula is the criterion for distinguishing the sub-categories 1a and 1b. It also occurs on St Clement (Category 1c). One stone from Category 1b, Lewannick II, is so classified on the evidence of its roman text which uses a longer formula containing *hic iacet* (*see* below). This clearly indicates that Lewannick II was a gravestone. Lewannick II does, however, also contain two ogham texts, both of which consist of simple memorial formulae. This suggests that, on at least some occasions, simple memorial formulae were used on gravestones. It is possible that the Worthyvale stone is a case similar to that of Lewannick II, but the ogham text on Worthyvale is now too deteriorated to be certain of its reading. Three stones containing simple memorial formulae, Lundy IV, Yealmpton and Nanscow, may possibly have been found in association with graves but there is no evidence to link any of the others with actual burials. The conclusion to be drawn is that the Category 1 stones containing simple memorial formulae are all commemorative, probably of the dead, and that at least some of them were actual gravestones. It seems reasonable to assume that those commemorated were important members of their society.

Texts similar to the simple memorial formula also occur on five crosses from Category 2a, Biscovey, Cardinham I, Lanherne, Plymstock and Sancreed I, as well as on the Treslothan altar-slab (Category 3a). The names on these stones are probably all in the nominative, not in the genitive, and there is only one example, on Biscovey, of a term of family relationship.

---

4. Macalister (1902) 28.

None of these Category 2 and 3 stones, with the possible exception of Biscovey, was found in association with a burial. The texts on these stones are probably also commemorative. In at least some cases, however, they are likely to commemorate the commissioner or carver of the cross or altar-slab; in others, the texts may commemorate the dead.

As mentioned above, stones containing a *hic iacet* formula must be gravestones. There are eight of these stones: Castledore, Gulval I, Hayle, Lancarffe, Lewannick II, St Endellion, St Just II and Worthyvale. An example of this formula is St Just II, text (ii) which can be read, SELVS IC IACIT, 'Selus lies here'. The name SELVS is here nominative but names in the genitive also occur, for example on Worthyvale, LATINI IC IACIT FILIUS MA[. . .]RI, perhaps to be interpreted, '[the stone] of Latinus; here lies the son of Ma[-]'.

Another group contains stones with texts which mention the soul of the deceased. Although clearly commemorative, such a formula does not necessarily indicate that the stone was erected as a gravestone, and indeed one of these stones, Camborne, is an altar-slab. The Redgate cross has an example of this formula: DONIERT ROGAVIT PRO A[N]IMA, probably, 'Doniert requested [this cross *or* prayers] for [his] soul'. The Tintagel cross probably had a similar text and the Lanhadron cross-base may also have done so, but it is now too deteriorated to be sure. The Lanteglos stone (Category 1b) has a related text, but in English not Latin. Other long texts, although unrelated in formula to this group, are Tintagel, text (ii), which probably contained the names of the four evangelists and the two lost stones from Tavistock (Tavistock IV and V, Category 3b).

Two stones probably used the 'Constantine' form of the *chi-rho* symbol (fig. I.2(a)), Phillack II and St Just I (Category 3d). The St Just stone has, however, been lost at least since 1891, and the genuine nature of the text on the Phillack stone has been doubted.[5] It is thus not absolutely certain that the 'Constantine' *chi-rho* was used in the south-west area. The later, monogram, *chi-rho* (fig. I.2(b)) does occur. It is used in addition to further text on St Endellion, St Just II and Sourton. Southill has also had a monogram *chi-rho* read on it but it is no longer possible to be certain whether this was a *chi-rho* or an ordinary cross.

Bu'lock made an analytical study of the early Christian memorial formulae used in those inscribed stones of Celtic Britain which he dated from the fifth to the seventh century.[6] In the case of the Welsh stones, he distinguished two main groups: those using a *hic iacet* formula and those using a *filius* formula. He found a significant difference in geographical distribution, the *hic iacet* formula predominating in north Wales, the *filius* formula in south Wales.[7] Bu'lock also identified a number of associations with these formulae found among the Welsh stones, for example that between the use of the *hic iacet* formula and the horizontal layout of the

5. See Entry 40, Phillack II.
6. Bu'lock (1956) 133-41.
7. Bu'lock (1956) 135-9 & maps.

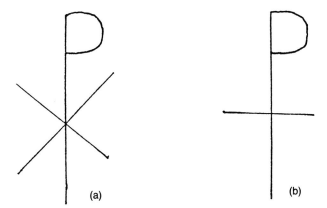

Figure I.2 The *chi-rho* symbol, (a) the 'Constantine' form and (b) the monogram form.

text. He also found associations between the use of a *filius* formula, the use of oghams (often using a MAQI formula) and the use of horizontal I.[8]

The position with the Category 1 stones of south-west Britain is not identical to that observed by Bu'lock in Wales. In the first place the *hic iacet* formula is less common and the two sorts of formula are less clearly distinguished. There are only eight south-western stones employing a *hic iacet* formula. Of these four, possibly five, also contain or contained the word *filius*: Castledore, Gulval I, Lancarffe, Worthyvale and possibly St Endellion. The remaining three (Hayle, Lewannick II and St Just II) do not, or did not, have the word *filius* although Lewannick II contains in addition two ogham texts using the simple memorial formula without a term of relationship. Moreover, these eight *hic iacet* stones show no significant pattern of geographical distribution.

The associations observed by Bu'lock are also difficult to distinguish in the south-western stones. Seven of the eight *hic iacet* stones are laid out vertically and the only one that was probably horizontal, Hayle, is now totally illegible. Six south-western stones contain an ogham text, or texts, in addition to their roman texts. In the case of two of these, Lewannick II and Worthyvale, the roman text uses a *hic iacet* not a *filius* formula. Only two actually contain the word *filius* (Lewannick I and Tavistock III), although Fardel may contain the Primitive Irish equivalent MAQVI and St Kew does use a simple memorial formula. The letter I occurs horizontally on 19 of the south-western stones, only one of which also contains an ogham text (Tavistock III). Nor can the use of horizontal I be associated with *filius* rather than *hic iacet* formulae since three of the seven legible *hic iacet* texts actually employ horizontal I.

8. Bu'lock (1956) 135-9.

The south-western inscriptions thus differ significantly from the Welsh ones in the formulaic associations observed by Bu'lock in Wales. One reason for this might be the difference in numbers: Bu'lock considered 134 Welsh stones while there are only 51 Category 1 stones from the south-west, several of which are lost or illegible. Bu'lock suggested that in Wales the use of oghams and the *filius* formula showed Irish influence, the use of the *hic iacet* formula and a horizontal layout showed continental influence. The less clear-cut situation in south-western Britain suggests that such a model is inappropriate here. It is argued in Section 5 below that various strands of influence might have combined to produce a localised south-western tradition.

Section 4b: Script

Two different scripts are used on the south-western stones, roman and ogham. Regardless of script, all the inscriptions are incised, none is in relief. The roman script appears in two broad varieties, capital and non-capital. The variety used is closely associated with the category to which the stones belong. The Category 1 stones, with only four exceptions (*see* Table 1b), employ a predominantly capital script which may contain an occasional non-capital form. The stones of Categories 2, 3a and 3b, with three exceptions, use a predominantly non-capital script with an occasional capital form.

The term 'insular' is used here to denote the non-capital script used. This script is similar to that used in insular manuscripts, that is, in Anglo-Saxon and Irish manuscripts of early Christian date. It is usually possible to distinguish texts employing a mainly insular script from those using a mainly capital one, although a few texts are in such poor condition that even this judgement is subjective. The presence or absence of a small incision or the exact curve of a line can make the difference between, for example, capital and insular T or capital and insular R (*see* Tables). Some texts certainly use an insular script. Even with these, however, it is not possible to distinguish with confidence between varieties of non-capital script such as minuscule, majuscule, uncial and half-uncial. These terms are therefore avoided.

The insular letter-forms used on the stones are clearly derived from manuscript letter-forms. There are, however, very few manuscripts from the south-west area and none dating from earlier than the ninth or tenth century.[1] Even if manuscripts existed in plenty it would still not be justifiable in my view to argue a direct chronological link between letter-forms used in dated manuscripts and letter-forms used on stones. A different medium requires different tools and different skills, no doubt often in the hands of different people. The letter-forms found on stones are usually considerably cruder than those in manuscripts; differences between

---

1. See Jackson (1953) 59–62.

forms of a letter, that may be crucial for dating purposes in a manuscript, are much harder to detect on stones.

The Tables showing the letter-forms used, and the discussion of the scripts, are based on my drawings of the texts. Lost and illegible inscriptions whose texts are known only from the drawings of others are therefore excluded. Also excluded are the Category 3d texts which contain only a *chi-rho* symbol. The tables do not include illegible letters or letters whose value is uncertain. Where two separate forms of one letter are used in one inscription, both forms are given. The letter Æ and the ligatures F/I and L/I are given respectively under A, F and L.

Ogham Script[2]

Six stones, all Category 1, contain an ogham text or texts in addition to a roman text or texts using capitals. They are Fardel, Lewannick I, Lewannick II, St Kew, Tavistock III and Worthyvale. Some of these ogham texts are now too deteriorated to be read at all, while others can only be partially made out. Two stones have legible ogham texts. In one, Lewannick II, the ogham texts are identical with part of the roman text; in the other, Fardel, the ogham texts are not the same as the roman texts. The three distinctive features of the roman script of Category 1 texts noted below (horizontal I and the ligatures F/I and L/I) are not particularly associated with those stones which in addition have an ogham text or texts. Ogham texts were also observed by Macalister on St Clement and St Endellion but it is unlikely that these stones ever contained ogham.[3]

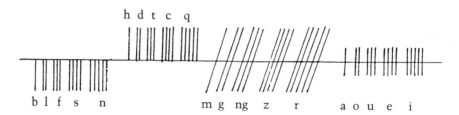

Figure I.3 The ogham alphabet.

Roman Script: Capital Letter-forms

Capital letter-forms occur in the predominantly capital texts of most Category 1 stones and also on Tintagel, Category 2a, and Trevarrack,

---

2. See fig. I.3.
3. Macalister (1945) no. 473, pp. 451-2 & fig. and no. 478, pp. 456-7 & fig. See the Entries for these two stones.

Table 1a Letter-forms of Category 1 texts using a predominantly capital script

	A	B	C	D	E	F	G	H	I	L	M	N	O	P	Q	R	S	T	U/V	Other
Boskenna	⋀		C		Ė								O						∪	
Bosworgey			C	D									O			ↄ			⊃	
Buckland Monachorum	⋀		C	Ρ						I		N		Ρ	∼					
Cardinham II									I				O		Դ					
Castledore	⋀		C			Ϝ			I	⌐	L	⋁N	O			R	S	⊤	X∨	
Cubert	⋈		C		E	F	ↄ		I⌐	⌐	L	⊏⋔Y	O			Ρ		⊤		
East Ogwell	⋀		E			F			I⌐	∼			O	Ρ						
Fardel	⋀					Ϝ	Ϩ		I	⌐		⋀⋁	O			9	RR		∨	
Gulval I	⋀		C	D	E	F			I⌐	H		HN				9	2	⊤	∨	
Indian Queens			C						I	⌐						∪			∨	
Lancarffe	⋀⋀		C	D	E	⋉	S	HI	⌐	L	⋀	⋁N	O					⊤	∨	
Lanivet	⋀		L			Ϝ			I	⌐	L	N							∨	
Lanteglos	Æ				E	Ϝ	Ϫ	H	⌐	L			O			R	S	⊤		⊔ ⋎Ρ⋈
Lewannick I					E				I			N							∨	
Lewannick II	⋀		C				S		I	L		N						⊤	∨	

Table 1a   continued

	A	B	C	D	E	F	G	H	I	L	M	N	O	P	Q	R	S	T	U/V
Lundy I					ƎƎ		2					HN			RR		Ɫ	⊤	V
Lundy II									ſ				OP					⊤	
Lundy III					ƎƎ		Ɫ									R	⊥	S	∪
Lundy IV																R	S	⊤	∪
Lynton	A		C	Ⴍ	Ⴗ				∣	Ⴗ	W							⊤	
Madron I	ᴙAB		C						∣—	Ⴋ		H	O		R	S		V
Madron II						F				∟			O		Z				
Mawgan					∈							m	O		q				∪
Nanscow	Ⴉ		C		E	F	ᔕ		∣—	∟		Z			R	S	∪		
Rialton		B			E				∣—	∟	M	Z	O		R			⊤	V
St Clement	A		C			F			∣—∣	∟		c	O		R	⊥	⊤	V	
St Endellion	Ⴉ	Ꮟ	ꓕ			f		H	∣—∣			S	O		Rᴊ	⊥	S	H	
St Hilary									∣—				O				⊤		
St Just II	A		C	E					∣—∣	∟		Z	O		R	ᔕ	⊤	V	
St Kew									∣	∟							Y	⊤	V

Table 1a continued

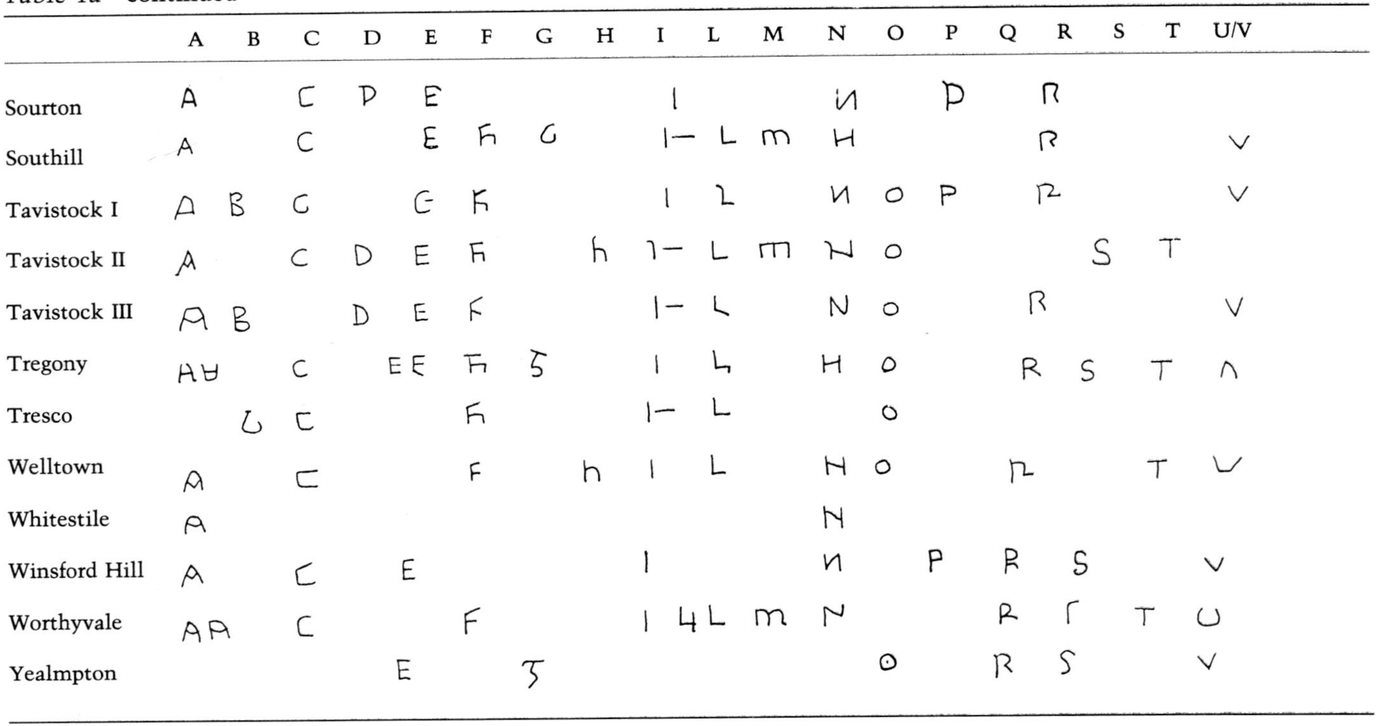

	A	B	C	D	E	F	G	H	I	L	M	N	O	P	Q	R	S	T	U/V
Sourton	A		C	Ρ	Ε							И		Ρ		R			
Southill	A		C		Ε	Ϝ	G		‖	L	Ε	Η				R			V
Tavistock I	Ꭰ	B				Ϝ				⅃		И	O	P		Ρ			V
Tavistock II	A		C	Ꭰ	Ε	Ϝ		ꜧ	⅃	⅃	Ε	⅃	O				S	T	
Tavistock III	Ꭰ	B		Ꭰ	Ε	Ϝ			∣	⅃		И	O			R			V
Tregony	ᴀ�序		C		ƐƐ	Ϝ	ᒉ		∣	⅃		Η	O			R	S	T	∧
Tresco	ᒐ		C			Ϝ			∣	⅃			O						
Welltown	A		C			ꓨ		ꜧ		⅃		Η	O		ᒉ			T	∪
Whitestile	A											И							
Winsford Hill	A		C		Ε				∣	ᒍ	Ɛ	Ⴈ		Ρ		R	S		V
Worthyvale	ᴀꓻ		C			Ϝ			∣	ꓶ	Ɛ	И				ꓒ	⅃	T	∪
Yealmpton					Ε	ꓵ							O			R	S		V

Table 1b Letter-forms of Category 1 texts using a predominantly insular script

	A	B	C	D	E	F	G	H	I	L	M	N	O	P	Q	R	S	T	U/V
Boslow					E													⊥	∪
Lustleigh	⋈		⊂	ⅾ				⊦	⌶			N	O					⊥	∪
Phillack I	⋀		∪	⊂					⌶	∟	⊏		O			⊓		⊥	
Stowford					⊖		⫞⋀			∟						↼			∟∪

Table 2a Letter-forms of Category 2 texts using a predominantly capital script

	A	B	C	D	E	F	G	H	I	L	M	N	O	P	Q	R	S	T	U/V
Plymstock					E					L				Þ					
Tintagel	҂ ⅄		C		E	F	ʒ		I		M		O			R	ʃ	T	

Table 2b Letter-forms of Category 2 texts using a predominantly insular script

	A	B	C	D	E	F	G	H	I	L	M	N	O	P	Q	R	S	T	U/V
Biscovey			c			f			i	l		n	o			r			
Cardinham I	ᴈ							h								r			
Lanhadron			c		ϵ			h								r			ᴠ
Lanherne	҂	B		ᗞ	E			h	i	l	m		o			r			ᴝ
Penzance		b	c	ᗞ	E	F			i		m	ᖾ	o	ρ	ᑫ	ᑫ		ᙠ	ᑌ
Redgate	ᴈ		c		ᗞ	ϵ	ʒ		i		m	ᖾ	o	ρ		ᖯ		ᙠ	ᑌ
Sancreed I								h		l		m	o			r			
Waterpit Down			c																ᴠ

Table 3a Letter-forms of Category 3 texts using a predominantly capital script

A	B	C	D	E	F	G	H	I	L	M	N	O	P	Q	R	S	T	U/V

Trevarrack Λ Β D E I L Ν S

Table 3b Letter-forms of Category 3 texts using a predominantly insular script

A	B	C	D	E	F	G	H	I	L	M	N	O	P	Q	R	S	T	U/V

Camborne Ѫ C G ɦ | L ɱ ɳ O p ſ ſ ⊥ ⊔

Treslothan E ƿ Ч

Category 3b (Tables 1a, 2a, 3a). There are also occasional capitals used in the predominantly insular texts of stones of all categories (Tables 1b, 2b, 3b). The forms used in all these cases are similar to each other. The chief variations are noted below; in addition there are occasional inverted letters.

A: A can have a straight or pointed top (A or A); the cross-bar can be horizontal, curved or in a v-shape (A, A, A).

F: F can have the top bar horizontal or sloping upwards (F or F). F can be ligatured with a following I; see below.

G: G is less often capital than insular (3) or the so-called 'sickle-shape' (G); on occasion these two forms are hard to distinguish from each other.

I: I can be vertical or horizontal and can occur in ligature with a preceding F or L (F or L); see below.

L: L can be ligatured with a following I; see below.

M: insular M (m) is as common as capital M.

N: forms of N vary both in the angle of the cross-bar and in the point at which the cross-bar meets the verticals (for example N or H).

Q: all instances are of the insular form (q).

R: R varies in whether or not the cross-bar touches the vertical (R or R); in some cases the latter variety approaches the insular form (r) which also occurs.

T: T can have the cross-bar horizontal or curved upwards (T or T).

U/V: V is more common than U and a bucket-shaped form also occurs (U).

As noted above, there are distinctive features concerning the letter I which, with one exception, occur only on Category 1 stones. These are the use of horizontal I, the ligature F/I and the ligature L/I.

There are 20 stones using horizontal I, 10 of which contain more than one example. The Category 1 instances are: Bosworgey, Buckland Monachorum, Cardinham II, Cubert (2 examples), East Ogwell (2 examples), Gulval I, Lancarffe (2 examples), Lundy I (2 examples), Lynton (4 examples), Madron I (2 examples, possibly 3[4]), Nanscow, Rialton (2 examples), St Clement, St Just II, Sourton, Southill (2 examples), Tavistock II (3 examples), Tavistock III and Tresco (1 doubtful example). Trevarrack (Category 3b) has two examples. That is, there are 34 occurrences of horizontal I (two of which are doubtful) as opposed to hundreds of occurrences of vertical I. Horizontal I is usually, but not invariably, used at the end of a word or name to render the Latin genitive singular inflexion; more commonly, this ending is represented by vertical I. Two inscriptions where horizontal I occurs in the middle of a word are St Just II, in IACIT, and Lynton where all three instances in CIVI[L]I are horizontal.

According to Nash-Williams, horizontal I is found on 'upwards of 36' Welsh inscriptions, mainly from south Wales and all belonging to his

---

4. See Entry 31, Madron I.

Group I, that is, simple inscribed stones.[5] He also noted one instance on a stone from Santon, Isle of Man.[6] Nash-Williams said that on the Welsh stones 'horizontal final -I, [is] limited to the I-ending of the 2nd Declension Genitive Singular'.[7] This is thus comparable with, but not identical to, the usage of horizontal I in south-western inscriptions.

There are eight Category 1 stones employing the distinctive ligature of F and I; Lancarffe, Lanivet, Lynton, Southill, Tavistock I, Tavistock II, Tregony and Tresco. The use of this ligature is confined to the word *filius*. Five of these eight stones also use horizontal I. Four Category 1 stones employ the distinctive ligature of L and I: Gulval I, Lynton, Tregony (3 examples) and Worthyvale. Two of the Tregony examples occur in personal names while the other instances are all in the word *filius*. Two of these stones, Gulval I and Lynton, also use horizontal I and two of them, Lynton and Tregony, also use the ligature F/I. There is thus an apparent association between the use of two or more of these distinctive forms involving the letter I.

The ligatures F/I and L/I are both found in Welsh inscriptions of Nash-Williams' Group I.[8] There is also one example of the ligature L/I in a stone of Group II, cross-decorated stones.[9] While F/I is confined to the word *filius*, L/I occurs both in this word and in others.[10] There is also an observable association between these ligatures and the use of horizontal I. The Welsh stones thus appear comparable in their use of these distinctive forms to the south-western Category 1 stones.

Eleven of the 20 stones using horizontal I are dated, on grounds unrelated to script, to the period of the fifth or sixth century to the eighth century.[11] It may tentatively be suggested that the use of horizontal I is itself an indication of a sixth- to eighth-century date for a stone. Six of the eight stones using the ligature F/I and three of the four using the ligature L/I are dated, on grounds other than script, to this same period. It may be that the use of these ligatures is a criterion for an early date but in my view the numbers involved are too small to make this certain.

Roman Script: Insular Letter-forms

Insular letter-forms occur in the predominantly insular texts of most stones in Categories 2 and 3 and in four texts of Category 1 stones (*see* Tables 1b, 2b, 3b). There are occasional insular forms used in the predominantly capital scripts of stones of all categories (*see* Tables 1a, 2a, 3a). The insular

---

5. Nash-Williams (1950) 11; quotation is from footnote 5. See also his Appendix I.
6. Nash-Williams (1950) 11; Macalister (1945) no. 505, pp. 482-3 & fig.; Kermode (1907) 74-5, 114-15 & figs.
7. Nash-Williams (1950) 226; see also p. 11.
8. Nash-Williams (1950) 11, 228 & fig. 257.
9. Nash-Williams (1950) no. 184, p. 126 & fig.
10. As, for example, in Nash-Williams (1950) no. 92, pp. 88-90 & fig.
11. See Section 7.

forms which occur in capital texts are similar to those used in the predominantly insular texts. The chief variations in letter-form that occur are as follows.

A: variants of the form CC are usual.
B,D,P: these letters can all occur either closed or open (c̣).
E: E occurs in rounded (ϵ) or angular form. The rounded form can have the cross-bar either touching or not touching the curved portion (ϵ or ϲ).
L: capital L is more common than the insular form.
T: T can have the top-bar horizontal or curved up at one end (T or Ṭ).
U/V: U is usual and is often bucket-shaped (⨆).

Section 4c: Layout of the Texts

The texts of Category 1 stones are generally laid out in an irregular manner. The letters very often vary in size and are frequently not set in straight lines. Most of the texts lack panels and incised framing-lines are also rare.[1] Those containing a panel or incised line of some sort are: Lanivet, Lundy III, Lundy IV, Lustleigh, Madron II, St Endellion, St Just II, St Kew and probably Tavistock III. These stones do not form a homogeneous group and their use of panels or incised lines cannot be linked to any other feature common to them all. By contrast, the majority of the stones of Categories 2 and 3a are carefully set out. The letters are more regular in size; the texts are integrated into the design of the carving and are usually set within panels, although rarely with framing-lines.

The majority of the texts of Category 1 are set vertically downwards with the bottoms of the letters towards the left hand of the viewer. This is described as 'downwards facing left'. There are, however, a few Category 1 stones where the text is set horizontally: Lewannick I, Lundy III, Lundy IV and probably Hayle, though this text is now illegible. The two *chi-rho* texts from Category 1 stones, as well as the *chi-rho* stones Category 3d, are or were also set horizontally: St Endellion, text (i); St Just II, text (i); Phillack II; St Just I. The text of the Tawna stone, Category 1, is set vertically but it is now too deteriorated to be sure which way the letters faced. It is often stated that vertical layout is derived from the layout of ogham texts.[2] This may be so, although an association between vertical layout and the use of oghams is not obvious among the south-western stones; Lewannick I, one of only six stones containing an ogham text, is one of only four Category 1 stones having a horizontal, not a vertical, roman text.

---

1. 'Panels' refer to the lines surrounding a text, 'framing-lines' to those separating one line of a text from the next.
2. See, for example, Jackson (1953) 168.

There are nine stones from Category 1 which are now ·in a horizontal position, either recumbent or imbedded in walls. From their size and shape these stones were no doubt originally erect pillar-stones. The stones in question are: Boskenna, Cubert, East Ogwell, Lancarffe, Rialton, Tregony, Tresco, Whitestile and Worthyvale. Both Bowden and Redruth, though now lost, seem also to have belonged to this group. The texts of these 11 stones could have read downwards facing left, or upwards facing right, depending on which way up the stones were set. Of the other 40 pillar-stones of Category 1, 35 are set with the text reading downwards facing left; four are set horizontally; and one, Tawna, is too deteriorated to tell whether it reads vertically upwards or vertically downwards. Even in Categories 2 and 3 there is no text which is unequivocally set upwards facing right, although Sancreed II, text (i), might have been. It is, therefore, reasonable to assume that these 11 Category 1 stones, when erect, had their texts reading downwards facing left.

The majority of the texts of Categories 2 and 3 are set horizontally, although there are some exceptions and some cases where the position is now unclear. Sancreed II is very deteriorated; text (i) is set vertically, although it is unclear which way the letters face, while text (ii) could have been set horizontally or vertically. Penzance has both texts set downwards facing left. Tintagel has text (ii) set in an idiosyncratic manner.[3] Lanhadron and Camborne are both set around the four sides of the face of the stone. Lanhadron is set anti-clockwise with the letters facing outwards, Camborne clockwise with the letters facing inwards. Tavistock IV probably had text (ii) set downwards on the thickness of the slab, with the letters facing the back of the stone.

Of the 11 cross-shafts of Category 2a, six have the text or texts set low down on the shaft: Gulval II, Lanherne, Penzance, Plymstock, Sancreed I, Sancreed II. The text of Redgate may also have been placed low on the shaft but it is impossible to be sure since the shaft is now incomplete. There is also one cross-base that is certainly inscribed (Lanhadron) and two that may have been: Trebyan and Trewint. The remaining south-western cross texts are not set low on the shafts; Cardinham I has its text towards the top of the shaft, Biscovey and Waterpit Down were probably set in the middle of the shafts, while the texts of Tintagel start at the top and take up the remainder of the existing shaft. Higgitt described the placing of a text low on the cross-shaft or on the cross-base as being 'in the Irish manner'.[4] Although common in Ireland, this placing of the text is rare on crosses from Wales and Anglo-Saxon England.[5] The way in which the south-western crosses do not seem to fit precisely into either of these patterns may suggest that they developed their own tradition, perhaps as much dependent on Ireland as on Wales.

---

3. See fig. II.64 (ii).
4. Higgitt (1986) 141.
5. Higgitt (1986) 125-32, esp. p. 143.

Section 4d: Summary of Differences Between Categories 1 and 2

The stones of Category 2 are dressed and often contain decorative carving. Frequently their texts form an integral part of the whole design of the stone. In contrast, the stones of Category 1 are undressed or only roughly dressed. In the case of those few Category 1 stones that contain decorative carving, the text and decoration are often not integrated into a single design.

The scripts used in the texts of the stones show significant differences. The majority of Category 1 texts use a predominantly capital script while the majority of Category 2 texts use a predominantly insular script. Ogham texts are confined to Category 1 stones. Similarly, differences are observable in the layout of the texts. Category 2 texts are set out in an orderly manner, mostly inside panels, while Category 1 texts are set out in a less orderly way and are rarely inside panels. The majority of Category 1 texts are laid out vertically while the majority of Category 2 texts are laid out horizontally.

The formulae used in the texts show less striking differences. The simple memorial formula is used in both categories although the *hic iacet* formula is confined to Category 1 stones. In the Category 1 texts the simple memorial formula is likely always to have commemorated the dead. In the Category 2 texts it may have commemorated either the dead, or the carver or commissioner of the cross.

Section 5: Sources of Influence

There are several possible sources of influence on the inscribed stones of the south-west: Romano-British, Gaulish, Irish and Welsh.

Romano-British

One source of influence could have been the inscribed stones of the Romano-British period. The majority of these stones were public inscriptions, religious or official, thus differing in purpose from the early Christian inscriptions which are largely personal. There are also, however, some Romano-British personal stones, the funerary monuments. The practice of erecting Romano-British inscribed stones was known in the south-west. Five 'milestones' exist in Cornwall.[1] There are also some 50 Romano-British inscriptions from Somerset, mostly from Bath, including about 10 tombstones.[2] There are, however, no Romano-British tombstones from south-west of Bath.

Not only do the majority of Romano-British inscriptions differ in purpose from the early Christian inscriptions, but they also differ in execution. Typically, Romano-British inscriptions are incised on dressed stone, are carefully set out in horizontal lines and use capital letter-forms of a uniform size with frequent abbreviation. By contrast, the majority of the early Christian inscriptions are cut on undressed or roughly dressed stone and are generally set vertically, often in irregular lines; they use letters of differing sizes with a mixture of capital and insular letter forms and abbreviation is rare.

The majority of Romano-British inscribed stones thus differ quite markedly from the majority of early Christian inscriptions and their influence is likely to have been general not specific. There are three cases in which more particular influence might perhaps be seen.

First, some Romano-British inscribed stones are less carefully executed than the majority and use letters of differing sizes. Examples of these include some of the tombstones from Chester.[3] Most of the existing Romano-British stones from Cornwall are, however, reasonably carefully

---

1. These are listed in Appendix B. I have not personally examined all the Romano-British stones, on which see Collingwood, R.G. and Wright, R.P. (1965). See also Sedgley (1975) and Todd (1987) 217-19.
2. Collingwood, R.G. & Wright, R.P. (1965) nos. 138-87, pp. 42-61 & figs and no. 2229, pp. 693-4 & fig.
3. Collingwood, R.G. & Wright, R.P. (1965) nos. 475-568, pp. 156-89 & figs. Cf. in particular nos. 483, 488, 494, 508.

executed. Moreover, Irish and Welsh stones furnish numerous examples of inscribed stones carelessly executed with letters of differing sizes. Romano-British influence is no more than possible here.

Second, some south-western inscriptions use Latin personal names, many of which are also recorded on Romano-British inscribed stones. These Latin names could suggest a fifth- or sixth-century sub-Roman population likely to have been still influenced by other aspects of Romano-British culture, such as the erection of inscribed stones. Latin names could have remained traditional for several generations and might have been particularly favoured by Christians. On the other hand, Latin names also occur in both the Welsh and Gaulish stones and could have spread to the south-west from these areas. It cannot be argued that Latin names necessarily indicate Romano-British influence, although they may do so.

Third, although the Romano-British tombstones differ from the early Christian stones in the formulae used, in length, complexity and vocabulary, there is an instance of similarity in the use of the word *filius* on Romano-British tombstones, for example, F for FILIUS on a now lost tombstone from Bath.[4] However, the use of the word *filius* is not confined to Romano-British and early Christian south-western inscriptions, but also occurs on early Christian stones from Ireland and, very commonly, on those from Wales.

Were it certain that the Romano-British practice of erecting inscribed tombstones was known to the south-west of Bath, then it could be argued that these might have influenced the south-western stones in one or more of the ways indicated above. We have, however, direct evidence only of the erection of Romano-British official 'milestones' in the south-west. Moreover, in each of the possible instances of influence cited above, there is an alternative explanation. It seems to me most likely that Romano-British influence, in so far as it existed, was general not specific, confined to the idea of inscribing and erecting a piece of stone, rather than to providing a model of how this should be undertaken.

Gaulish[5]

There is some evidence, linguistic, literary and archaeological, demonstrating a degree of cultural affinity between Gaul and south-west Britain in the early Christian period.[6] One part of the evidence is the large number of Gaulish inscriptions dating from the fourth to the seventh century which resemble the south-western Category 1 stones in script and

---

4. Collingwood, R.G. & Wright, R.P. (1965) no. 158, p. 52 & fig.
5. I have not personally examined the Gaulish stones. The information in this section is derived largely from the illustrations in Le Blant (1856) and Le Blant (1865). Figs I.4, I.5 and I.6 are taken from Le Blant (1856), plates 4, 26 and 40, and are included to illustrate the points made. See also Rhys (1905-6), Rhys (1911-12) and Rhys (1913-14).
6. Pearce (1978) 90, 140-4, 157; Jackson (1953) 25-8.

in formulae. Despite the clear linguistic links between south-west Britain and Brittany, there are very few inscribed stones from the period in Brittany.[7]

The script used on the Gaulish stones is generally a capital one with the letters less regular in size and shape than those used on most Romano-British monuments. Some Gaulish inscriptions have an occasional cursive form in a predominantly capital text. These features can be seen in Le Blant's plates.[8] In formulae there are also resemblances.[9] The *hic iacet* formula, which occurs or occurred on eight south-western stones, is fairly common in Gaul. One of these eight, Hayle, is now illegible but may also have contained the common Gaulish formula *in tumulo*. The *chi-rho* symbol occurs occasionally in the south-west but more frequently in Gaul. The *bone memoriae* formula, very common among Gaulish inscriptions, may occur on one south-western stone, Rialton. Names of both Celtic and Latin origin occur on both the Gaulish and the south-western stones.

There are, however, some striking differences between Gaulish and south-western stones. First, although the script used is somewhat similar, the layout of the texts is not. Unlike the south-western ones, the Gaulish texts are often carefully set out and spaced, sometimes with margins, and they are invariably set horizontally, not vertically. Second, while carved decoration is rare on the south-western Category 1 stones, it is quite common on stones from Gaul. Third, although the Gaulish and south-western texts employ some of the same formulae, there are other commonly used Gaulish formulae not found in the south-west, for example *hic pausat, hic requiescit, in hoc loco.* The most common south-western formula, the simple memorial formula, does not occur in Gaul. Fourth, several of the Gaulish stones include an actual date, usually consular, in their text. No south-western stone contains a date of any sort.

In addition to these differences between the Gaulish and south-western stones, it should be noted that the resemblances listed above are not confined to these two groups of stones. The formulae *hic iacet* and *in tumulo* are also found among Welsh inscriptions, as are names of both Celtic and Latin origin and the use of cursive letter-forms in a predominantly capital script. The *chi-rho* symbol in its monogram form occurs also in Ireland and Wales.[10] There are no instances of the *bone memoriae* formula in Wales but *memoria* does occur once.[11]

It thus seems to me possible that there was some Gaulish influence on

---

7. I have not personally examined the Breton stones but have relied on the information and photographs in Bernier (1982). Bernier notes only 18 contemporary inscribed stones from Brittany, several of which are now lost; Bernier (1982) 155 ff.
8. See figs I.4, I.5 & I.6. The use of occasional cursive letters in a capital script can be seen in drawing numbered 13, corresponding to Le Blant's stone no. 13, p. 37.
9. All the following features can be observed in figs I.4, I.5 & I.6.
10. Hamlin (1972) 22–8.
11. Macalister (1945) no. 358, pp. 342–3 & fig.; Nash-Williams (1950) no. 138, p. 107 & fig.

Figure I.4 Gaulish stones (1) (from Le Blant (1856) plate 4).

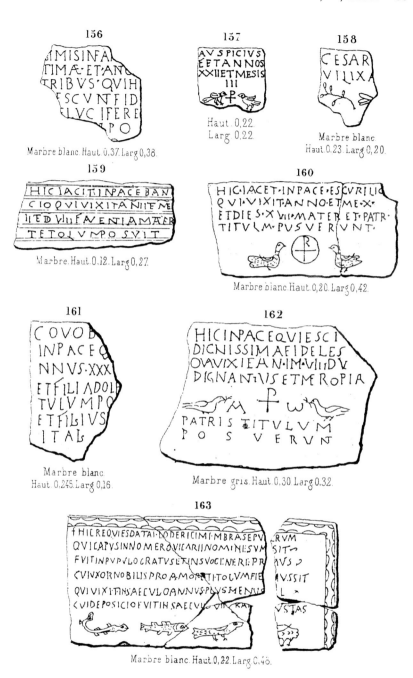

Figure I.5   Gaulish stones (2) (from Le Blant (1856) plate 26).

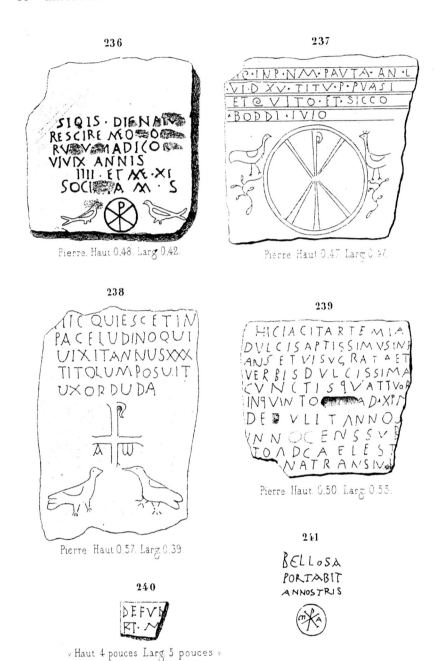

236

237

SIQIS · DIGNAI
RESCIRE MO
RVGV MADICO
VIVIX ANNIS
IIII · ET ME · XI
SOCIGA M · S

Pierre. Haut 0.48. Larg 0.42.

P · INP · NM · PAVTA · AN · L
VI · D XV · TITV · P · PVASI
ET G VITO · ET · SICCO
· BODDI · IVIO

Pierre Haut 0.47. Larg 0.37.

238

IIC QUIESCET IN
PACE LUDINO QUI
VIXIT ANNUS XXX
TITOLUM POSUIT
UXOR DUDA

Pierre Haut 0.57. Larg 0.39.

239

HIC IACIT ARTEMIA
DVLCIS APTISSIMVS INF
ANS ET VISVG RAT A ET
VERBIS D VL CISSIMA
CVNCTIS SQVATTVOR
IN9VIN TO D · XPI
DEO VLIT ANNO
NNOCENSSVR
TOADCAELES T
NATRANSIVI

Pierre Haut. 0.50. Larg. 0.55.

240

DEFVI
RT · N

« Haut 4 pouces Larg 5 pouces »

241

BELLOSA
PORTABIT
ANNOSTRIS

Figure I.6   Gaulish stones (3) (from Le Blant (1856) plate 40).

the inscribed stones both of south-west Britain and of Wales, in particular in the script used and in the use of certain formulae.

Some of the Breton stones fit into the general description of Gaulish stones outlined above. A few of them, however, resemble the south-western Category 1 stones in having a vertical layout, little carved decoration and in using the simple memorial formula, for example the stone from Louan-nec.[12] The ninth- and tenth-century Breton stones are rather different from the south-western Category 2 stones. It seems likely that the custom of erecting pillar-stones in Brittany came, along with the language, from south-west Britain, and that subsequently the two traditions diverged.

Irish[13]

The Irish tradition of erecting inscribed memorial stones to individuals seems likely to have influenced the erection of the south-western stones. This is particularly obvious in the case of those south-western stones which contain ogham texts. The ogham script is Irish in origin and there exists a large number of Irish ogham stones dating mainly from the fifth to the seventh century.[14] The Irish ogham texts are usually incised on undressed or roughly-dressed pillar-stones, usually with no carving. As is common with ogham stones, the texts are set vertically. The Irish ogham texts frequently use a simple memorial formula, often consisting of a single name in the genitive, or of two or more names joined by a term of family relationship, often MAQI 'son of'.[15]

The texts of the six south-western ogham stones are not all legible. Those that can be read are similar to the Irish ogham stones and on one, Fardel, the Primitive Irish word MAQI might be used in one of the ogham texts and possibly also in one of the roman ones.[16] The south-western ogham texts differ from the Irish ones in one particular. The south-western ogham stones all contain both ogham and roman texts, while this is comparatively rare in Ireland. In Wales, however, 26 out of 35 ogham stones also contain a roman text.[17]

In Ireland there are not only ogham stones but also a large group of stones inscribed in insular script. A few of the Irish texts in insular script are incised on roughly-dressed pillar-stones, often with little or no carving except perhaps an incised cross; these texts tend to be short and can be set

---

12. Bernier (1982) 164–5 & figs.
13. I have not personally examined all the Irish stones. For those that I have not seen I have relied on the descriptions and drawings in Macalister (1945) and Macalister (1949).
14. There may be some fourth-century examples and probably a few eighth-century ones; see Jackson (1953) 152–3.
15. McManus (1991) 44–54.
16. See Entry 13, Fardel.
17. Nash-Williams (1950) 3.

horizontally or vertically. Examples of these are some of the large number of inscribed stones from Clonmacnois.[18] These stones, except in their use of insular script, resemble quite closely the south-western Category 1 stones. The majority of the Irish insular texts, however, are incised on decorated cross-slabs with the lettering laid out horizontally around the carving. The Irish insular texts on these slabs resemble some of the Category 2 stones in script but not in the sort of monument inscribed, cross-slabs being rare in south-west Britain. They also differ in the formulae used; the common Irish OROIT formula, for example, is entirely absent from south-western stones.

Another instance of Irish influence on the south-western stones is the use of Primitive Irish personal names.[19] These occur both on south-western stones with ogham texts and also on those with texts only in roman script. As noted above, Fardel may use the Primitive Irish noun MAQI, but alternatively this may be part of a Primitive Irish personal name.

It has been suggested that Irish influence is to be seen in the vertical layout of most of the Category 1 stones. Ogham texts are usually set vertically, often utilising the edge of the stone against which and through which are incised the grooves that form the letters. Jackson suggested that non-ogham texts laid out vertically showed Irish ogham influence.[20] This may be so although, as noted above, Lewannick I has both a vertical ogham text and a horizontal roman one. Vertical layout is not confined to ogham texts; Norse runic texts, for example, are usually set vertically.[21] Vertical layout does not, in my view, necessarily indicate Irish influence. Finally, it has recently been suggested that the placing of a text on the base, or low on the shaft, of a cross is an Irish feature.[22]

In summary, Irish influence on Category 1 stones can clearly be seen in the use of ogham script and of Irish personal names and may be seen in the use of the simple memorial formula. Similarities with the Category 2 stones, such as the use of insular script, have to be set against differences in the types of monument inscribed and of formulae employed. Irish influence on Category 2 stones is probably to be seen in the positioning of the text on the cross.

Some of these features are also found on Welsh stones. The use of a simple memorial formula in Ireland, Wales and the south-west may be due not to influence but to a shared heritage. As Jackson said, '. . . to define a man's name by adding his father's is a formula absolutely typical of all the Celtic languages at all periods'.[23] Others, like ogham script and Primitive Irish personal names, suggest Irish influence both on Wales and on the south-west. Some Irish features, for example the positioning of texts on crosses or the use of Primitive Irish personal names, may be relatively less

---

18. For example, Macalister (1949) nos. 606, 614, 616 and 618, pp. 44-5 & figs.
19. See Section 6.
20. Jackson (1953) 168.
21. I am indebted to Professor R.I. Page for this information.
22. Higgitt (1986) 125-32; see also Section 4c.
23. Jackson (1953) 168.

common in Wales than in the south-west; others are certainly more common, for example the use of ogham script. In some instances Irish influence may have entered the south-west directly; in others it may have come indirectly from Wales. The extent of Irish immigration into Wales and the south-west is the subject of debate but that there was some Irish immigration is not disputed.[24]

Welsh[25]

The inscribed stones of Wales are in many ways similar to the south-western stones. The possibility that the south-western inscribed stones are directly derived from those of Wales therefore deserves serious consideration.

Nash-Williams' Group I, simple inscribed stones, and some of his Group II, cross-decorated stones, resemble the south-western Category 1 stones. The first similarity is in the undressed or roughly dressed nature of the stone. The second lies in the scripts used. In Wales, a large number of stones contain both ogham and roman texts. As in the south-west, many of the Welsh roman texts use a predominantly capital script with an occasional insular form. The ligatures F/I and L/I and the use of horizontal I also occur in both Welsh and south-western texts.[26] Horizontal I is indeed confined to Wales and the south-west except for one example from the Isle of Man.[27] Other Welsh stones, as in the south-west, use a predominantly insular script.

The third similarity is in the layout of the texts. Most of the Welsh Group I and the south-western Category 1 stones have their texts set out vertically not horizontally. Fourth, the inscriptions are similar in language. In both cases the usual language employed is Latin with Celtic, though occasionally other vernacular, or Latin, personal names. The fifth similarity lies in the formulae used. Some, though not all, of the formulae used are similar, especially in the case of the simple memorial formula.[28]

There are some differences between the Welsh Group I and the south-western Category 1 stones. There is, for example, a higher proportion of stones containing both roman and ogham texts in Wales than in the south-west. There are also nine stones with only an ogham text; such stones are not found in the south-western area. The *hic iacet* formula, although found in the south-west, is much more common in Wales. In Wales there are

---

24. Pearce (1978) 159-68; Davies (1982) 87-8.
25. I have not personally examined the Welsh stones. I have largely relied on the descriptions and drawings in Nash-Williams (1950) although I have also used those in Macalister (1945) and Macalister (1949).
26. See Section 4b.
27. Nash-Williams (1950) 11; Macalister (1945) no. 505, pp. 482-3 & fig.; Kermode (1907) 74-5, 114-15 & figs.
28. For a full discussion of formulae used, see Section 4a. See also Nash-Williams (1950) 4-10.

differences in distribution between on the one hand ogham texts and a *filius* formula and on the other hand the use of the *hic iacet* formula.[29] Such differences of distribution are not discernible in the south-west.

Nash-Williams suggested two main sources of influence, Irish and Gaulish, for the Welsh Group I stones:

> The Ogam inscriptions are thus of Irish origin, and, as their distribution shows, clearly represent an infiltration of colonists into south Wales from southern Ireland in the fifth and following century. . . . The Latin inscriptions, on the other hand, both in language and in lettering, are akin to the Early Christian inscriptions of the western Roman Empire, especially Gaul, and thus indicate direct and continuing intercourse between Wales and Gaul in the sub-Roman period.[30]

He discounted direct Romano-British influence on the grounds of 'general absence of monuments from the earlier Roman centres of settlement' implying 'a cultural break between the two periods'.[31] Davies, however, argued cogently in favour of 'some continuous relationship' between Roman and early medieval Christianity in Wales.[32]

The Welsh Group I stones were thus seen by Nash-Williams to have been inspired by two of the three sources of influence discussed above for the south-western stones. It could be argued that the Welsh Group I stones were themselves the major source of influence on the south-western Category 1 stones. The Irish and Gaulish influences would then be indirect, having entered by way of Wales. The alternative argument is that in both Wales and in south-western Britain similar influences were at work, that Gauls and Irish travelled directly to both Celtic areas. This model seems to me inherently more probable. It also fits the facts rather better. It was argued above that Irish influence on the south-west was likely, at least in some instances, to have been direct. There are also the various differences between the Welsh and south-western stones noted above. These suggest that both groups of stones, Welsh and south-western, are likely to have been inspired by the same Irish and Gaulish influences. This is not, of course, to deny that the Welsh stones could also have influenced the south-western stones. The similarities between the two groups of stones might indeed argue in favour of some direct influence from Wales.[33] It may be that the Welsh stones formed one of several influences on the erection of the south-western Category 1 stones.

The position is a little different with south-western Category 2 stones. Nash-Williams' Group III stones, sculptured crosses and cross-slabs, share

---

29. See Section 4a and also Bu'lock (1956) 135-9.
30. Nash-Williams (1950) 4.
31. Nash-Williams (1950) 1.
32. Davies (1982) 169-71, quotation from p. 171.
33. This is accepted by Preston-Jones & Rose (1986) 155 & references.

some features with the Category 2 stones but there are also considerable differences. Both groups contain carved and sculptured crosses. In both groups the texts are usually laid out horizontally not vertically. Both sets of texts use a predominantly insular script. The script of the Welsh texts is, however, akin to manuscript hands: 'The lettering of the inscriptions is round half-uncials in the full calligraphic style'.[34] Such a fine description of the script of the south-western texts is impossible; even a broad distinction between 'capital' and 'insular' is at times hard to maintain. Again, the two groups differ in formulae used. The Welsh Group III stones contain formulae 'more formal and doctrinal' than those of Groups I and II.[35] The south-western texts are neither formal nor doctrinal; the formulae used are simpler and more personal than those on the Welsh stones.

The Welsh Group III stones may have been one source of influence on the south-western Category 2 stones. Such Welsh influence is, however, less likely than in the case of the Category 1 stones. Nash-Williams argued that in the ninth century foreign craftsmen may have come to Wales: 'The immediate impulse behind the development [of the crosses] may have been the arrival in Wales at this time of foreign – Northumbrian, Irish, and Scottish (or Manx) – or foreign-trained craftsmen'.[36] While such craftsmen may well have provided an impulse for the erection of crosses in Wales, it is less certain that large numbers of them had reached the south-west by the ninth century. However, foreign influence can be observed. The placing of texts on cross-bases or low on cross-shafts may show Irish influence.[37] From the ninth century onwards there was increasing contact between the south-west and Anglo-Saxon England. Anglo-Saxon influence can be observed in some of the carved interlace of the crosses and in the use of names of English origin. It seems likely that the Welsh Group III stones provided one of various sorts of influence on the erection of the south-western Category 2 stones.

Conclusion

The conclusion suggested by the foregoing discussion is that several strands of influence can be observed in the south-western Category 1 stones. Romano-British public inscriptions may have provided inspiration, although probably in a general rather than a specific manner. Romano-British tombstones might have been a particular source of influence were it certain that the custom of erecting them was known in the south-west. Gaulish stones, which are somewhat similar in script and in formulae, may suggest direct Gaulish influence brought about by contacts between the two areas. Irish influence seems likely to have been direct. It is seen in the use of ogham script and Primitive Irish personal names. The similar Welsh

---

34. Nash-Williams (1950) 42.
35. Nash-Williams (1950) 42.
36. Nash-Williams (1950) 29.
37. See Section 4c and also Higgitt (1986) 125–32.

Group I stones may also have directly influenced the Category 1 stones in script, layout, language and formulae used. In my view, the most likely hypothesis is that some or all of these possible sources of influence combined to form a south-western tradition of inscribing Category 1 stones, akin but not identical to that of Wales.

In the case of the inscribed crosses of Category 2, similarities with the Welsh stones (Group III) are less striking than is the case with the Category 1 stones. This may suggest that the traditions of erecting inscribed stones in Wales and in south-west Britain began under the same sorts of influences but that the traditions subsequently diverged. The Category 2 stones show Irish and Anglo-Saxon influence and seem to represent a south-western tradition inspired by several sources of influence.

Section 6: Personal Names

The majority of inscriptions contain or contained at least one personal name and many of them more than one. In the lists that follow the names are given in the forms in which they appear on the stones. In some cases names have been reconstructed from early drawings or readings; where this is so attention is drawn to it and the reconstructed part appears within brackets. Names whose forms are entirely irrecoverable are excluded.

The majority of the names are of Celtic origin. Some of these are Q-Celtic, that is Primitive Irish, others are P-Celtic, that is, Primitive Welsh/Cornish. Others could be either; it is of course likely, unless there is evidence to the contrary, that Celtic names on south-western stones are Primitive Welsh/Cornish. The etymology of each name is discussed more fully in the appropriate Entry below. Hypocoristic names are not noted as such in the following lists but are discussed in the appropriate Entries.

The names, of whatever origin, are frequently latinised and usually appear in the genitive singular in *-i*. This assimilation to the Latin second declension was probably aided by the fact that Celtic masculine *o*-stem names would also regularly appear in *-i* in the genitive singular.[1] In the translation of each text in its Entry, the names are given a normalised nominative inflexion, usually in *-us*.

The majority of the names, about 53 per cent, are Celtic. Latin names account for about 20 per cent of the total, followed by English with about 8 per cent. The origin of the remaining 19 per cent of the names is uncertain.

Celtic Names

Certainly Celtic, Either P-Celtic or Q-Celtic

[BROCAGNI], St Endellion[2]
CARAACI, probably for CARATACI, Winsford Hill
CLO[TUALI], Phillack I[3]
CONBEVI, Tavistock I

---

1. See Jackson (1953) 187-8.
2. The name is reconstructed from what is legible today and from early drawings and readings.
3. The name is reconstructed from what is legible today and from early drawings and readings.

CONET[O]CI, Cubert
CONHINO[C], Lustleigh
CV[N]OMORI, Castledore
CVNOVALI, Madron I
DATUIDOC, Lustleigh
DINVI, Gulval I
DOBVNNI, Tavistock III
DVNO[C]ATI, Lancarffe
ERCILINGI, Tregony
ERCILI[V]I or ERCILI, Tregony
FANONI, Fardel
GOREVS, Yealmpton
[G]U[RG]LE[S], Stowford
[NADOTTI], St Endellion[4]
RIALOBRANI, Madron I
RICATI, Tregony[5]
TEGE[R]NOMALI, Cubert
[T]I[G]ERNI, Lundy I
TORRICI, St Clement

Specifically P-Celtic

DONIERT, Redgate

Specifically Q-Celtic

[E]NABARRI, Tavistock III
MACCODECHETI, Tavistock II
ME[S]CAGNI, Lancarffe
QVENATAVCI, Gulval I
[VA]ILAT[H]I, Welltown
VLC[A]GNI, U[L]CAG[.I] and [.L]CAG[.]I, Lewannick II[6]
VLCAGNI, Nanscow
VROCH[ANI], Welltown

Probably or Possibly Celtic, Either P-Celtic or Q-Celtic

CAVVDI, Lynton
CA[-]OCI, East Ogwell

---

4. The name is reconstructed from early drawings and readings.
5. The reading could alternatively be [V]IRICATI, a name of unknown origin.
6. These three names are likely to refer to one person.

[CI]LRORON, Biscovey
[CVNATDO] or [CVNAIDE], Hayle[7]
[GENAIVS], Mawgan[8]
IGNIOC, St Clement
IVGDOCI, [R]IVGDOCI, IVSDOCI or [R]IVSDOCI, Bosworgey
LEUIUT, Camborne[9]
MAVCI, Southill
NONNITA, Tregony
RESGEVT[A], Lundy III
RŪHOL, probably for RUNHOL, Lanherne[10]
QICI, Fardel[11]
SAFAQQUCI, Fardel
[VALCI], Bowden[12]

Probably Q-Celtic

MAQVIRINI, Fardel[13]
MAQIQICI, Fardel[14]
MO[BRA]TTI, Phillack I

Celtic names, other than specifically Primitive Irish names, occur on stones from each of Categories 1, 2 and 3. They also occur on stones dated both early and late. The St Endellion stone, for example, is dated from the sixth to the eighth century on the evidence of its monogram *chi-rho*; although the names on this stone are reconstructed from the remaining traces and from early drawings and readings, they are clearly Celtic. The Lanherne cross, on the other hand, which probably contains a Celtic name, is dated on artistic evidence to the tenth or eleventh century. In a similar way, Celtic names on Welsh stones occur on stones in Nash-Williams' Groups I, II, III and IV which cover the period from the fifth to the thirteenth century. The use of a Celtic name (other than a Primitive Irish one) does not therefore in itself give any indication of the date of the stone.

The Q-Celtic or Primitive Irish names all occur on Category 1 stones. Three of the stones which contain a Primitive Irish name, Fardel,

---

7. This name is reconstructed from early drawings and readings.
8. The name is reconstructed from early drawings and readings; GEN- could be Celtic or Latin.
9. Alternatively this name could be English.
10. RUN- could just possibly be an English name element, although this is unlikely; see Entry.
11. Alternatively QICI could be part of a Primitive Irish name MAQIQICI.
12. The reading is taken from an early drawing.
13. A name MAQVIRINI would be Primitive Irish. Alternatively, the reading could be MAQVI, that is, 'son of' and RINI; the name RINI would be of unknown origin.
14. A name MAQIQICI would be Primitive Irish. Alternatively, the reading could be MAQI, that is, 'son of' and QICI, probably a Celtic name.

Lewannick II and Tavistock III, contain also an ogham text. On the evidence of their ogham texts, it is argued below that these three stones probably date from the fifth or sixth to the eighth century.[15] Primitive Irish names and the Irish ogham script are likely to have entered the south-west during the same period and the use of a Primitive Irish name can itself be taken as evidence indicating a date from the fifth or sixth to the eighth century for a stone.

Latin Names

The names of the evangelists on Tintagel are excluded from this list since these are Biblical not personal.

Certainly Latin

CIVI[L]I, Lynton
CVMREGNI, Southill
IV[S]TI, St Kew
LATINI, Worthyvale
NOTI and NOTI, St Hilary
SA[B]INI, Tavistock II
SEVERI, Nanscow

Certainly Latin but not Certainly a Personal Name

BO[N]EMIMORI, Rialton[16]
FABRI, Tavistock III
NEPVS, Winsford Hill
TRIBVNI, Rialton

Probably Latin

ANNICV, Lanivet
NEPRANI, Tavistock I
[PO]TIT, Lundy II
SELVS, St Just II[17]
TIMI, Lundy IV
VITALI, St Clement[18]

---

15. See Section 7.
16. This might be a name BO[N]EMIMORI, or a name BO[N]E with a common noun MIMORI, or two common nouns; see Entry.
17. Other readings of the name are possible, for example SENILVS, which might also be Latin, or SELNIVS, of unknown origin.
18. This name is likely to be Latin though it could possibly be Celtic; see Entry.

Possibly Latin

[E]VOCA[.], Boskenna[19]
[I]N[.EN.]VI, Lewannick I

In addition the following names, listed above as probably or possibly Celtic, could alternatively be of Latin origin.

[GENAIVS], Mawgan
NONNITA, Tregony

These Latin names all occur on Category 1 stones. Similarly, Latin personal names on Welsh stones all occur on Nash-Williams' Group I stones, which he dated from the fifth to the seventh century. Eight out of the 17 south-western stones bearing a certain or possible Latin name contain dating evidence. Lewannick I, St Kew, Tavistock III and Worthyvale all have ogham texts. It is argued below that an ogham text suggests a fifth- or sixth- to eighth-century date for the stone.[20] The *chi-rho* symbol on St Just II and the possible *chi-rho* symbol on Southill, also suggest a sixth- to eighth-century date.[21] Nanscow and Tavistock II contain Irish personal names; it is argued above that Irish names are also evidence for a date from the fifth or sixth to the eighth century. In view of this dating evidence, and that provided by the comparable Welsh material, it may be suggested that the use of a Latin name is itself an indication of a sixth- to eighth-century date for a stone.

English Names

Certainly English

ÆLSEL[Ð], Lanteglos
ÆLWYNEYS, Lanteglos

Probably English

[ÆLNA]T, Tintagel
GENE[REÐ], Lanteglos
[-FRIDVS], Tavistock V[22]

---

19. The lost letter may have been T; see Entry.
20. See Section 7.
21. See Section 7.
22. This reading is taken from an early drawing.

Possibly English

[ELEW], Plymstock
HEY[SEL], Lanteglos[23]

In addition the following names, listed above as probably or possibly Celtic, could alternatively be of English origin.

LEUIUT, Camborne
RŪHOL, Lanherne

The English names occur on stones from Categories 1, 2 and possibly 3. There is dating evidence for each of these stones, although it is not always independent of the evidence of the names. Lanherne and Camborne are both dated to the tenth or eleventh century on artistic grounds. Plymstock and Tintagel are dated to the ninth to eleventh century by virtue of being Category 2 stones. Lanteglos is dated to the eleventh century on linguistic evidence which includes, but is not confined to, the spelling of these names. Tavistock V is now lost but was presumably late, although the evidence for this dating is based in part on the text. On historical grounds, English names on south-western stones are likely to date from the ninth century onwards, with the absorption of the south-west peninsula into the Anglo-Saxon kingdom. This dating is entirely compatible with the other dating evidence for the stones with English names.

Names of Unknown Origin

Included here are names where at least part of the reading is reasonably certain.

BREID, Lanherne
[CNEGVMI], Mawgan[24]
[-CO]BI, Tresco
[D]AP[-], Buckland Monachorum
G[A]G[R]A[NV]I or G[A]G[R]A[SN]I, Fardel
[I]MAH, Lanherne[25]
[NEMIAVS], Treveneague[26]
[NICI]N[..] SC[I], Buckland Monachorum
[.]R[A]H, Cardinham I
T[..T]UEN[T], Boslow[27]

---

23. This word could be a name or perhaps a pronoun; see Entry.
24. This name is reconstructed from early drawings and readings.
25. This name could be connected with the Irish name *Imchadh*; see Entry.
26. The reading is taken from an early drawing.
27. Alternatively the reading could be T[..T]UER[T].

In addition there are two names already noted which could be of unknown origin, *see* footnotes 13 and 5.

RINI, Fardel
[V]IRICATI, Tregony

These names are all on Category 1 stones except for Lanherne, which belongs to Category 2.

Section 7: Dating of the Inscribed Stones

Evidence for Dating the South-west Inscribed Stones

There is no direct evidence for dating any inscribed stone from south-west Britain. No stone contains a date of any kind nor can any individual named in an inscription be identified with certainty. The series of stones thus lacks any fixed dating points. The dating evidence that there is (historical, artistic, linguistic, epigraphic and comparative) can do no more for each individual stone than suggest a date-range within the early Christian period, defined here as *c*. AD 400 to *c*. AD 1100.

The 16 stones of Categories 2 and 3a are more easily datable than the rest. The cross-shafts of Category 2a are dated, on the evidence of their carved decoration, to the ninth to the eleventh century. The three uncarved cross-bases of Category 2b, if genuine, can reasonably be assigned to the same period as the cross-shafts. Some of the cross-shafts can be dated a little more closely: Cardinham I, Lanherne, Penzance and Sancreed I are generally agreed on artistic evidence to date to the tenth or eleventh centuries.[1] The two altar-slabs of Category 3a are also dated to the tenth to eleventh centuries, on the evidence of their carving, especially their use of the T-fret.[2]

With only two exceptions, the texts of the stones in Categories 2 and 3a use a predominantly insular script. This script is perfectly compatible with the ninth- to eleventh-century date assigned to these stones on artistic grounds. The script does not, however, offer any closer dating of the stones within this period. The two exceptions are Tintagel and Plymstock, both of which use a predominantly capital script. These are the only two cross-shafts that contain personal names that are probably of English origin. I am not sure whether this is a suggestive association or merely a coincidence.

The remainder of the stones of Category 3 can be briefly mentioned. Two of the three stones of Category 3b are lost and one, Trevarrack, cannot be closely dated. From the existing drawings the two lost stones, Tavistock IV and V, appear to be late, perhaps even after AD 1100. The one cross-slab of Category 3c, St Columb Major, cannot be dated. Category 3d contains two stones with only a *chi-rho* symbol and with no other text. One of these, St Just I, is lost and the genuine nature of the other, Phillack II, has been questioned. Both stones use, or used, the 'Constantine' form of the

---

1. See, for example, Thomas, A.C. (1967) 97, 104–6; Pool (1974) 7; Pearce (1981) 216.
2. Cf. Thomas, A.C. (1967) 104–6; Thomas dated one slab, Camborne, to the tenth century and the other, Treslothan, to possibly the eleventh century.

chi-rho symbol. Hamlin pointed out that on the continent this form of *chi-rho* dates from the fourth or fifth century, while in Britain all the instances, apart from these two and the Anglo-Saxon Jarrow dedication stone, are Romano-British.[3] The Jarrow stone is dated to AD 685 but, since it is Anglo-Saxon, Hamlin considered it to be in a tradition different from the other examples.[4] If St Just I and Phillack II are or were genuine, they are likely to be dated within the context of the continental examples, perhaps to the fifth century. Finally, the unclassifiable stones are unclassifiable either because they are highly deteriorated or because they are lost with no adequate drawing or description surviving. In both cases they are undatable.

The majority of the inscribed stones are from Category 1 and these are harder to date than the stones of Categories 2 and 3a. They have been dated to the fifth century or even to as early as the fourth century.[5] The evidence suggests to me that Category 1 stones have a date-range from the fifth or sixth century to the eleventh century. This dating evidence is of various sorts but excludes artistic evidence; only nine Category 1 stones contain any carved decoration and in each case the amount is so small that no artistic dating is possible.

The Chi-rho *Symbol*[6]

The *chi-rho* symbol that is found on Category 1 stones is the monogram form. It certainly occurred on St Endellion, St Just II and Sourton and may also have occurred on Southill. Hamlin dated the examples of the monogram *chi-rho* symbol from Britain and Ireland to the sixth, seventh and possibly eighth centuries.[7]

Ogham Texts

Six Category 1 stones contain both ogham and roman texts: Fardel, Lewannick I and II, St Kew, Tavistock III and Worthyvale. The ogham script was introduced from Ireland; in Ireland ogham inscriptions are found from the fifth, or even the late fourth century, to the seventh century and probably also into the eighth century.[8] Irish raids into Wales may have begun in the fourth century and Irish settlement probably dates from the fifth century.[9] Links between the Irish colonists and Ireland probably continued for some

---

3. Hamlin (1972) 24.
4. The Jarrow stone is Okasha (1971) no. 61, pp. 85-6 & fig.; cf. Hamlin (1972) 27.
5. Thomas, A.C. (1978) 75: '[They] mostly fall in the period c. 450 to 700'. Pearce dated the earliest stones 'from the late fourth century to the earlier part of the sixth'; Pearce (1978) 24.
6. See Section 4a.
7. Hamlin (1972) 24.
8. Jackson (1953) 153.
9. Davies (1982) 87-8.

time, perhaps even until the eighth century.[10] The introduction of oghams into Wales thus seems likely to date from the fifth or sixth century to the eighth century. Although direct evidence is lacking, it seems probable that the introduction of oghams into south-west Britain took place during the same period.

Linguistic Evidence

The language of the texts is usually Latin and vernacular personal names are frequently latinised. The Latin element is not uncommonly confined to a latinised inflexion and the word *filius*. Such texts cannot offer sufficient linguistic evidence for dating purposes. One stone, Fardel, has a text that may be in Latin or in Primitive Irish;[11] even if the latter is the case, uncertainty makes any linguistic dating evidence doubtful. One stone, Lanteglos, has a longer text than is common and the language used is English. On linguistic grounds this text is likely to date from the eleventh century.

The spelling of the Celtic personal names might be expected to yield linguistic dating evidence. The standard authority on this subject, K.H. Jackson, proposed a chronology of P-Celtic sound changes where much of the evidence for the fifth to the seventh century was based on the early Christian inscriptions of Wales and the south-west.[12] He first dated the inscriptions on epigraphic grounds, stating that, apart from 'the memorials of known people . . . the only way to date the rest of the British inscriptions is through the forms of their letters'.[13] He then used these dates as part of the evidence for the dates he assigned to the various sound-changes. I do not accept Jackson's dating by letter-form, as I argue below.[14] Moreover, Jackson admitted the unreliability of some of the spelling evidence.[15] For these reasons, and in particular to avoid circular argument, I have not made use of Jackson's dating of the Celtic sound-changes in dating the inscriptions.

Personal Names

The personal names used on the stones are usually Celtic, sometimes specifically Primitive Irish, although some Latin and English names also occur. On historical grounds, names of English origin are likely to date from the ninth century onwards. It was argued in Section 6 that Latin

---

10. Jackson (1953) 155.
11. Details of the language of this stone and of the following one (Lanteglos) will be found in the appropriate Entries.
12. Jackson (1953).
13. Jackson (1953) 159.
14. See below, pp. 54-5.
15. Jackson (1953) esp. pp. 176-9.

names may date their texts to the sixth to eighth century, and Primitive Irish names to the fifth or sixth century to the eighth century. The use of those Celtic names which may be either P-Celtic or Q-Celtic does not offer any dating evidence for these stones.

Layout of the Texts

It has often been suggested that Category 1 stones with texts set horizontally are older than stones with texts set vertically;[16] the reason given is usually that Romano-British and/or Gaulish inscribed stones almost always contain horizontal texts. I have argued in Section 5 that Romano-British and Gaulish inscriptions may have been two sorts of influence on the south-western inscribed stones. There are, however, other possible sources of influence, notably Irish and Welsh. In both these traditions, texts set vertically are common. The use of layout as a dating criterion must be rejected. As Jackson said: 'It is not a question of different dates but of different strands of epigraphic tradition'.[17]

Script

It has frequently been suggested that the inscriptions can be dated on the evidence of their capital letter-forms. This argument usually takes the form of assuming that the more 'Roman' the letter-forms are, the earlier the text is. This would only be valid if the origin of the capital letter-forms were Romano-British capitals or Gaulish capitals. In fact, the capitals of the south-western stones resemble those of the Welsh stones more than they resemble those of either Romano-British or Gaulish stones.

An extension of this argument suggests that the fewer insular letter-forms that occur, the older is the text; as the centuries wore on, more manuscript letter-forms were introduced into the capital texts. This would be valid if the earliest inscribers knew only capital script and as time went on learnt manuscript scripts. This hypothesis seems, however, most improbable.

There are only four Category 1 stones using insular script, Boslow, Lustleigh, Phillack I and Stowford. These texts do not differ in any way, except script, from the rest of the Category 1 stones. They resemble the other Category 1 stones in the nature of the pillar-stones, in layout, in language, in personal names used and in formulae. On the other hand, the stones of Categories 2 and 3a, datable on artistic grounds to the ninth to eleventh centuries, with only two exceptions, use a predominantly insular script.

Clearly then insular script had chronological significance, but other factors must have been involved as well as those of date. It is difficult to

---

16. Cf., for example, Pearce (1981) 168-9.
17. Jackson (1953) 168, fn. 1.

imagine that any literate person could have been literate only in capital letters, to have had no access to any form of manuscript hand. It must be that the choice of script was, to some extent at least, a deliberate one. Capital letter-forms may traditionally have been considered more suitable for pillar-stones, insular script for crosses and altar-slabs. This could explain why the eleventh-century Category 1 stone, Lanteglos, still uses a predominantly capital script. Then again, the inscribers of pillar-stones could have favoured the more angular capital letter-forms which were easier to cut; sculptors of crosses could perhaps have cut with greater facility the more rounded insular letter-forms.

It seems to me that the date of the inscribing of the stone is one factor involved in the choice of script but not the only one. The four Category 1 stones using insular script are perhaps to be dated to around the time of the earliest stones of Categories 2 and 3a, perhaps to around the eighth or ninth century; the Primitive Irish name on Phillack I makes it, at least, unlikely to be later than this date. The actual form of insular letters used on the Category 1 stones, as on those of Categories 2 and 3a, do not afford any clear evidence of date. I have argued in Section 4b that it is unjustifiable to date insular letter-forms in inscriptions from similar letter-forms in dated manuscripts.

There is one piece of dating evidence based on an individual letter-form. This is the use of horizontal I, which occurs only in texts using a capital script. It was argued in Section 4b that the use of horizontal I might suggest a sixth- to eighth-century date for a stone.

Comparable Welsh Inscribed Stones

The Category 1 stones are comparable to Nash-Williams' Group I stones which he dated from the fifth to the seventh century.[18] The Category 1 stones resemble the Welsh stones in layout, script, language and formula used. There are some differences, as in the numbers of ogham stones (*see* Section 4b), in the use of the English language on Lanteglos and in the occasional use of insular script on pillar-stones. Even if Nash-Williams' dating is correct, it is not essential that the south-western stones should be of exactly the same date. Indeed, if the Welsh stones constitute one source of influence on the south-western stones, some at least of the Welsh stones would necessarily be earlier in date than the south-western ones.

Jackson put forward a reasoned case for the dating of the Welsh and south-western inscriptions as a group, based on the form of roman script used. He suggested four dating bands. In the first, from the fifth to early sixth century, the script used was 'more or less pure, if often rough and debased, Roman monumental capitals, with some vulgar and cursive forms'.[19] In the second band, during the sixth century, he saw an increasing use of vulgar forms and 'the appearance of certain uncial and half-uncial

---

18. Nash-Williams (1950) 2.
19. Jackson (1953) 159.

letters derived from Gallic epigraphy, becoming commoner as the century went on'.[20] The third band, from the late sixth century to perhaps the late seventh century, was characterised by the use of fewer capitals, more uncials and half-uncials and, in particular, by 'half-uncial letter forms evidently taken from manuscript writing'.[21] In the fourth band, from the eighth to the twelfth or thirteenth century, the use of manuscript uncials and half-uncials evolved into 'the full Hiberno-Saxon half-uncials'.[22]

However valid this chronology may be for the Welsh inscriptions, it does not accord with the evidence of the south-western stones. First, as argued above, a theory based even in part on the idea that the more 'Roman' the letters look the earlier must be the text, must be rejected. Second, the letter-forms of south-western texts cannot be differentiated so precisely as Jackson's argument supposes. Many of the texts are in a poor condition. It is usually possible to maintain the difference between 'predominantly capital' and 'predominantly insular' scripts. It is not possible to make precise distinctions between, for example, uncials and half-uncials, still less between half-uncials of Gallic origin, half-uncials of manuscript origin, and Hiberno-Saxon half-uncials. Third, Jackson held that capital script had died out by the eighth century; Lanteglos, however, is dated on linguistic grounds to the eleventh century and uses a predominantly capital script. Fourth, as Jackson himself recognised, his theory was open to the criticism that it assumed the sixth century to be overcrowded with stones using different letter-forms. Jackson attempted to answer this criticism by dating some of the stones to the first half of the seventh century,[23] but some overcrowding remains.

Jackson's arguments, along with Nash-Williams', have formed the basis of most chronological work on the Welsh inscriptions. Jackson's chronology may be applicable to the Welsh stones. There are more inscribed stones in Wales than in the south-west and some at least of them are in good condition. Nevertheless I suspect that some of Jackson's more precise distinctions, for example between different sorts of half-uncials, may be hard to maintain even among Welsh stones. In so far as it refers to the stones of south-west Britain, Jackson's chronology has to be rejected.

Proposed Chronology for the South-western Inscribed Stones

In my view the Category 1 stones range in date from the fifth or sixth century to the eleventh century. Many of these stones can be dated a little more precisely, as has been argued above. In summary, those containing an ogham text or a Primitive Irish personal name probably date from the fifth

---

20. Jackson (1953) 159.
21. Jackson (1953) 159.
22. Jackson (1953) 160.
23. Jackson (1953) 160-2.

or sixth century to the eighth century; those with a Latin name or a monogram *chi-rho* are likely to be sixth- to eighth-century in date; those using a horizontal I may also date from the sixth to the eighth century; those using insular script probably date from the eighth or ninth century onwards; the one stone with an English text dates from the eleventh century. Those Category 1 stones that lack any of these dating features cannot be dated precisely within the date-range. Common sense suggests that those stones which, although lacking dating features, closely resemble pillar-stones dated from the fifth or sixth to the eighth century, are likely themselves to date from earlier rather than later in the date-range.

The stones of Categories 2 and 3a date from the ninth to the eleventh century. They thus overlap chronologically with the later of the Category 1 stones. This helps to explain some of the similarities, for example in script and formula employed, between stones of these categories. Some stones from Categories 2 and 3a can be dated more precisely within their date-range, for example those with carving datable on artistic grounds to the tenth to eleventh centuries.

The two stones of Category 3d, if genuine, may date from the fifth century. The remaining stones of Categories 3b and 3c, as well as the unclassifiable stones, cannot be dated.

This dating model is shown diagrammatically in fig. I.7.

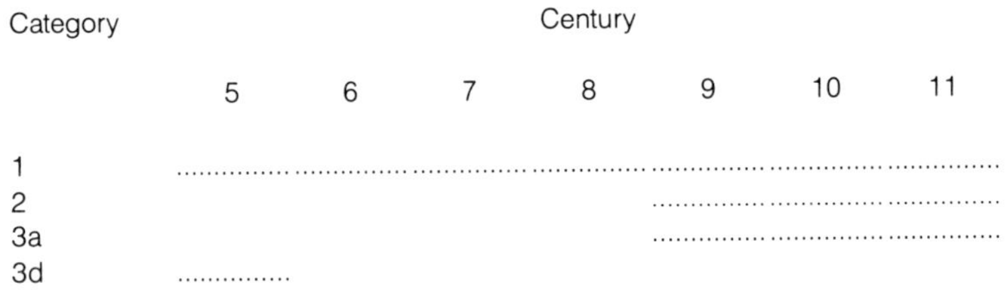

Category	Century						
	5	6	7	8	9	10	11
1	....						
2					....		
3a					....		
3d	....						

Figure I.7   Dating model for the south-western inscribed stones.

Some conclusions may be drawn from this discussion of dating. First, one real objection to my dating model is that the *terminus ante quem* of the Category 1 stones is based largely on one stone, Lanteglos. Were that stone to prove to be a later medieval forgery, or a copy of an earlier pillar-stone, then the whole series of Category 1 stones could terminate two hundred years earlier. Lanteglos seems to me to be a genuine early Christian inscription. However, a theory based in part on only one stone cannot be taken as more than a working hypothesis.

Second, it is clear that the sub-categories 1a and 1b, which are distinguished by the sorts of formula used on the stones, do not carry chronological significance. The stones of Category 1c may be datable to a period before the ninth to the eleventh century, the date-range of Category 2 stones, since the cutting of the pillar-stones to form crosses may date from then.

Third, it is clear that no stone can be dated more precisely than to within one or two centuries. In my opinion no inscription can be dated with the exactitude that has sometimes been suggested. The Lustleigh stone, for example, has been dated on the evidence of its formula, layout and letter-forms to 'fairly late in the sequence', having been 'probably erected somewhere between AD 550 and 600, or even a decade or so later'.[24] Such a precise dating must be rejected.

Finally, the use of predominantly capital versus predominantly insular letter-forms does seem to me to be of chronological significance but not to be a dating criterion which should take precedence over all other sorts of evidence. Capital letters were used most often in the early period, the fifth or sixth to the eighth century, although they continued sporadically until the eleventh century. Inscriptions using predominantly insular script appeared from the eighth or ninth century and became increasingly common. The choice of script may have significance beyond the mere chronological. Insular script was the script of manuscripts, of liturgical and devotional works. Crosses and altar-slabs, being public and visible signs of organised Christianity, might have been considered more suitably inscribed in an insular script rather than a capital one. Indeed, the use of a manuscript script could even have enhanced their value as ecclesiastical objects of veneration within the community.

---

24. Swanton & Pearce (1982) 140.

Section 8: Guide to the Entries

Each Entry begins by describing the present location of the stone. To facilitate the finding of the stones, both a verbal description and an eight figure National Grid Reference are given.[1] The National Grid References are taken from the county Registers of Sites and Monuments.[2] The date or dates on which the stone was examined are also given here.

History

The history of the stone since it was first observed or discovered is given in this section. Where possible the exact words of earlier scholars are quoted.

Description

In this section the stone and the text as they are today are described. The terms 'left-hand side' and 'right-hand side' refer to the left and right of a person facing the stone. The measurements of the stone include the height from the topmost point to the ground unless some different lower point (for example, the base of a cross) is specified. Since many stones are irregular in shape, maximum and minimum measurements of width and thickness are often given. Similarly, the height of the letters is frequently given with maximum and minimum values. The term 'incised' is used to refer to the cutting of a text; it does not imply that the technique of incision was used as opposed to any other possible technique, for example pocking. Where a text is described as 'primary', this means that the stone was always intended to contain the text; the text may refer to the stone (as, 'this altar') or it may form an integral part of the design of the stone. Where

---

1. In the cases of the groups of stones on Lundy Island and in Tavistock vicarage garden, a six figure National Grid Reference is given to the location, not to the individual stones.
2. I am most grateful to Ann Preston-Jones, Sites and Monuments Register, Cornwall County Council, and to Frances Griffith, Sites and Monuments Register, Devon County Council, for supplying me with the National Grid References.

there is no evidence, as is the case with most Category 1 texts, the phrase 'appears to be primary', is used. A distinction is made between 'framing-lines' and 'panels'. A panel, often but not invariably consisting of four lines, surrounds a text, while a framing-line separates one line of text from the next. The phrase 'downwards facing left' is used to describe texts which are set vertically downwards, with the bottoms of the letters towards the left-hand side of the viewer.

The legibility of the texts is described in one of five ways. The term 'legible' means that the reading of the text is certain; 'slightly deteriorated' means that the text is a little damaged but that the reading is reasonably certain; 'rather deteriorated' means that the text is somewhat damaged but that a reading can be attempted; 'highly deteriorated' means that the text consists largely of editorial reconstruction; 'illegible' means that no meaningful text can be read.

Text

The text is transliterated in lines, and with the letters spaced, as on the stone. The following system of transliteration is used. This system differs slightly from the one which I have used elsewhere, in particular in the indication of damaged letters.[3] It is hoped that the present system will make the texts more easily accessible to the reader.

A   indicates a legible letter A.
A   indicates a letter damaged but legible.
[A]   indicates a damaged letter where the reading is reasonably certain.
[A]   indicates a legible and undamaged letter of unusual form, probably A.
A/B   indicates a ligature of A and B.
A̅   indicates A with a suprascript line, usually an abbreviation mark.
:   indicates one or more non-accidental dots in the text.
[.]   indicates one letter lost in the text, [..] two letters lost, etc.
[-]   indicates several letters lost in the text or complete loss of text at beginning or end.

In the case of stones now lost, the Description and Text are given together, with the information taken from earlier works.

Discussion

This section contains interpretation of the text, as opposed to the factual information of the preceding sections. The text as it reads today is

---

3. See Okasha (1971) 45.

translated; where relevant, earlier readings and translations are also given. In the case of a text which is now wholly or partially illegible, earlier drawings and readings are used to reconstruct what the text is likely to have read. Where a text is given from an earlier authority, the text is transliterated according to the system outlined above; when the text is printed in one line, | is used to indicate the end of a line of text. Personal names appearing with a genitive in *-i* are given in the translation with a normalised nominative, usually in *-us*. The origin of each personal name, the category to which each stone is assigned and a date-range are also given.

Bibliography

The bibliography is arranged in chronological order. Illustrations of any sort are described as 'figs'. The Bibliography includes almost all works known to me which mention the stone. Reviews, newspaper articles and unpublished works are, however, excluded unless they contain a substantial discussion of the stone. Also excluded are works which merely list the stone, unless they contain an illustration or date from soon after the discovery of the stone.

ENTRIES

1 Biscovey

The stone is now in the churchyard of St Mary's Church, Biscovey, Par. It stands outside the priest's door, on the south side of the church. National Grid Reference SX 0582 5358. Examined 9 July 1984 and 8 July 1985.

History

The stone was first mentioned in two letters from Lhwyd, one to T. Tonkin, dated 29 November 1700, and one to F. Paynter, dated 30 November 1700.[1] Lhwyd described the stone as 'a Cross by the Alms-House at *St. Blasey*'.[2] In 1754 W. Borlase recorded that the stone was in 'the parish of St. Blasey',[3] and that, 'In a little meadow adjoining to the place where this stone now stands, many human bones have been found, and I suspect that this Cross may have been remov'd from thence'.[4] The stone was still there in 1838, at 'the eastern end of the almhouse, close by the turnpike gate'.[5] In 1851 it was again described as, 'Near the turnpike'.[6] It was first noted in use as a gatepost by Polsue in 1867, 'Near S. Blazey turnpike gate is an ancient inscribed monumental stone, now used as a gate post'.[7] It is not clear how far it had been moved to be utilised as a gatepost, but presumably not far. It remained there until September 1896 when the Rev. D.R. Vaughan had it moved to its present position.[8]

Description

The stone is a cross-shaft, carved and probably complete but with no base. Modern holes testify to its use as a gatepost. It measures 222 cm. in height, 38 to 45 cm. in width and 15 to 20 cm. in thickness. Text (i) is incised in three lines on one face of the stone (fig. II.1(i)). It is set without framing-lines but inside a panel 53 cm. high by 31 cm. The letters, 6 to 7 cm. in height, are slightly deteriorated and read horizontally. The text is primary

---

1. See Lhwyd (1700b) and Moyle (1726) 237.
2. Moyle (1726) 237, in a letter dated 10 March 1714/15 quoting Lhwyd's letter.
3. Borlase, W. (1754) 363.
4. Borlase, W. (1754) 364.
5. Penaluna (1838) I, 57.
6. (-) (1851b) 197.
7. Polsue (1867) 62.
8. Langdon (1906) 419. Langdon said that Vaughan 'bought' the stone.

Figure II.1(i)   Biscovey, text (i) (photograph Woolf/
Greenham Collection).

and is in a predominantly insular script. Text (i) is probably complete,
although it is possible that the space above the first line once contained
further lettering. Text (ii) is incised in two lines on the opposite face of the
stone (fig. II.1(ii)). It is set without framing-lines but inside a panel 25 cm.
high by 36 cm. The letters are 5 to 6 cm. in height and read horizontally.
The text is probably complete, unless more letters are lost from a higher

Figure II.1(ii) Biscovey, text (ii) (photograph Woolf/
Greenham Collection).

panel, and was probably primary. It is highly deteriorated and its script is
uncertain.

Texts

(i)   + [CI]L
       RO
       RON

(ii)   [-]
       [+ F/ILI-]

Discussion

That both texts have been difficult to read for some time is suggested by Polwhele's comment: 'The characters are defaced, but were legible not many years ago',[9] and by Penaluna's: 'too much effaced to be decyphered'.[10]

Text (i) probably reads, + [CI]LRORON, perhaps a personal name. W. Borlase read ALRORON, a reading supported by his drawing.[11] Gough's drawing suggests a similar reading although he gave three alternatives: ALSOSON, ALRORON and ALDROEN.[12] Similar readings were recorded by most commentators although Langdon and Allen once read CILORON, a reading they later abandoned,[13] and Rhys read CILRORON.[14] The first element [CI]L-, if this is the reading, could be Celtic.[15]

Text (ii) now reads, [-+FILI-] that is, 'son of —'. The first line is completely illegible and two or three letters may be lost from the end of the second line. This text has always been less clear than text (i). W. Borlase said, 'The characters are much worn' but nevertheless read, 'VILICI, or ULLICI' followed by 'a cross, and, most certainly, *filius*', a reading substantiated by his drawing.[16] Gough's drawing suggests a similar reading, UILI[..] [.]ILIUS,[17] while Rhys read, + GU ... VILIR + CUS.[18] There was presumably a personal name preceding [+ FILI-] but it is not now recoverable. The texts may have read together or separately.

This stone belongs to Category 2a, inscribed cross-shafts. Category 2 stones date from the ninth to the eleventh century but this stone cannot be more closely dated.

---

9. Polwhele (1803) II, 198.
10. Penaluna (1838) I, 57.
11. Borlase, W. (1754) 364 & fig.
12. Gough (1789) I, 16 & fig.
13. Langdon & Allen, J.R. (1888) 307; cf. Langdon & Allen, J.R. (1895) 56 & fig.
14. Rhys (1875) 368.
15. Cf. Jackson (1953) 302-3.
16. Borlase, W. (1754) 364 & fig.
17. Gough (1789) I, 16 & fig.
18. Rhys (1875) 368.

Bibliography

Lhwyd (1700*b*).[19]
Moyle (1726) 237 & figs (letter of 10 March 1714/15, quoting letter of 30 November 1700).
Borlase, W. (1754) 363-4 & figs.
Gough (1789) I, 16 & figs.
Britton & Brayley (1801) 418.
Polwhele (1803) II, 198-9, 203.
Lysons, D. & Lysons, S. (1814) ccxxiii.
Gilbert, C.S. (1817) 202-3.
Hitchins (1824) I, 444-6.
Penaluna (1838) I, 57-8.
Redding (1842) 57n.
(-) (1851*b*) 197.
(-) (1856) 214.
Polsue (1867) 62.
Iago (1871-3) 67.
Rhys (1875) 368.
Huebner (1876) no. 19, p. 7 & figs.
Iago (1878-81) 401.
Langdon & Allen, J.R. (1888) 307, 318.
Langdon (1889*a*) 319.
Langdon (1890-1) 36, 91 & *passim*.
Langdon (1894*b*) 308-15 & figs.
Langdon & Allen, J.R. (1895) 50, 56, 59 & figs.
Langdon (1896) 6, 22, 24, 368-72, *passim* & figs.
Hammond (1897) 310.
Daniell (1906) 244.
Langdon (1906) 419, *passim* & figs.
Holder (1907-13) cols. 24-5, 576.
Henderson, C.G. (1925) 154.
Macalister (1929) 180.
Hencken (1932) 271, 305.
Macalister (1949) no. 1053, p. 183 & figs (figs numbered 1054).
Henderson, C.G. (1953-6*a*) 33.
Adams, J.H. (1968-70) 215.
Pevsner (1970) 131.
Beagrie (1972) 71.
Pool (1977) 140.
Pearce (1978) 181.

---

19. There is no page numbering in this part of the work.

2 Boskenna

The stone lies in the garden of Boskenna, St Buryan. National Grid Reference SW 4225 2366. Examined 2 July 1984 and 3 July 1985.

History

C.G. Henderson, writing probably between 1912 and 1914, reported that the stone was then, 'On the lawn at Boskenna'.[1] It has been in Boskenna garden since then. Henderson added that it had been 'accidently [sic] found by the Late Canon Martyn of Buryan';[2] Canon Martyn was rector of St Buryan from 1882 to 1913. When found, the stone was 'doing duty as a gatepost at Vellansajer'.[3]

Description

The stone is a pillar-stone, probably complete (fig. II.2). Originally it was probably erect, measuring 153 cm. in height, 39 to 42 cm. in width and 24 to 28 cm. in thickness. At one end of the visible face are traces of either carving or now illegible text. There are three, presumably modern, holes gouged out of the face. The text is incised without framing-lines or panels in two lines on the visible face of the stone, the letters varying between 6 and 14 cm. in height. The text is rather deteriorated and is unlikely to be complete; further text may have been lost from one end or both ends of the face. The letters probably read downwards facing left, *see* Introduction, Section 4c. The text appears to be primary and is in a predominantly capital script.

Text

[E]VOCA[.]
[C]A[.-]

---

1. Henderson, C.G. (unpub. 1912-17) I, 54. Judging by the handwriting and the place of this entry, it is likely to date from the earlier part of the diary, that is, from 1912 to 1914.
2. Henderson, C.G. (unpub. 1912-17) I, 54.
3. Henderson, C.G. (unpub. 1912-17) I, 54.

Figure II.2   Boskenna (photograph Woolf/Greenham Collection).

Discussion

The text probably reads, [E]VOCA[.] and [C]A[-], and may have contained two personal names. The first could perhaps be read as [E]VOCA[T], possibly a Latin name. A.C. Thomas 'tentatively' read two names, EVOCALI or EVOCATI and CAT-.[4] In addition Thomas read α and ω at the top of the stone.[5] There are traces of carving and lettering at the top of the stone but nothing, in my view, to justify a reading of α and ω.

This stone belongs to Category 1a, pillar-stones with a simple memorial text. Category 1 stones date from the fifth or sixth centuries to the eleventh century but this stone cannot be more closely dated.

Bibliography

Henderson, C.G. (1953-6a) 61-2.
Russell (1959-60) 142.
Russell (1971) 81.
Radford (1975) 10.
Maxwell (1976) 10.
Pearce (1978) 29.
Thomas, A.C. (1980) 107-9 & figs.
Thomas, A.C. (1981) 165 & fig.
Henderson, C.G. (unpub. 1912-17) I, 52-4 & fig.

---

4. Thomas, A.C. (1980) 107-8.
5. Thomas, A.C. (1980) 108 & fig.

3 Boslow

The stone stands near Carnyorth Farm, St Just. It is close to the junction of several lanes leading to the farm from the B 3318, Pendeen to Penzance road. National Grid Reference SW 3924 3303. Examined 5 July 1984.

History

The stone was found in the summer of 1877 by G.B. Millett on the moor 'under Carn Kenidjack'.[1] It has remained in the place where it was found. Langdon said, 'It appears to be *in situ*',[2] but gave no reasons for this assertion.

Description

The stone is a pillar-stone and is probably complete (fig. II.3). It measures 111 cm. in height, 34 to 38 cm. in width and 27 to 40 cm. in thickness. The only carvings on the stone are two incised crosses. The text is incised on one face of the stone; if it is taken to be on the face of the stone, then one cross is incised on the right-hand side. The text is incised without framing-lines or panels in two lines with the other cross incised alongside. The letters are 6 to 10 cm. in height. The text, which is probably complete but highly deteriorated, reads downwards facing left. The text appears to be primary and is in a predominantly insular script.

Text

T[..T]
UE[.T]
+

Discussion

The text appears to read, T[..T]UEN[T] + or T[..T]UER[T] + . The letter

---

1. (-) (1880-4a) 20.
2. Langdon (1906) 420.

Figure II.3   Boslow (photograph Woolf/Greenham Collection).

preceding the last T is undamaged but it could read N or R. Earlier drawings of the stone suggest that the text has always been hard to read and in 1888 it was said to contain 'scarcely-distinguishable letters'.[3] Langdon and

3. (·) (1888–92) 29.

Allen read, UAETUENA +,[4] and Macalister, TAETUERA +.[5] The text is likely to be a personal name, but the form of the name is uncertain and its origin unknown.

The stone belongs to Category 1a, pillar-stones with a simple memorial text. Category 1 stones date from the fifth or sixth centuries to the eleventh century. The insular script used in this text suggests a date from the eighth century onwards for this stone.

Bibliography

(-) (1880-4a) 20.
(-) (1888-92) 29.
Borlase, W.C. (1893) 183.
Langdon & Allen, J.R. (1895) 50, 56, 59 & figs.
Langdon (1896) 6.
Langdon (1906) 420, *passim* & figs.
Macalister (1929) 180 & figs.
Hencken (1932) 265, 300.
Macalister (1949) no. 1055, p. 185 & figs (figs numbered 1056).
Russell (1958-9) 101.
Russell (1962) 111.
Nicholas (1968) 25 & fig.
Russell (1971) 81-2.
Rowe, L. (1973) & fig.[6]
Radford (1975) 6, 13.
Maxwell (1976) 10.
Weatherhill (1981) 66, 78 & fig.

---

4. Langdon & Allen, J.R. (1895) 56 & fig.
5. Macalister (1929) 180 & fig.
6. There is no page numbering in this book.

4 Bosworgey

The stone is now set upright into the wall of a barn on Bosworgey Farm, St Columb Major. National Grid Reference SW 9012 6343. Examined 8 July 1986.

History

The stone was first seen by M. Henderson in its present position around 1960,[1] but nothing is known of it before that. It seems to have been used at some time as a gatepost since the remains of two hooks are visible on the inscribed face. C.G. Henderson did not mention the stone but he quoted Hals who, in the late seventeenth century, saw the ruins of a chapel 'upon Bodeworgy lands'.[2] C.G. Henderson said that the chapel had disappeared but that, around 1916, a tenant of Bosworgey dug up 'a portion of a paved floor' in the orchard in front of the house.[3]

Description

The stone is a complete pillar-stone containing no carving on the visible surfaces (fig. II.4). It measures 185 cm. in height and 40 to 52 cm. in width; that part of the stone's thickness protruding from the wall measures 14 cm. The text is incised without framing-lines or panels in two lines on the visible face of the stone. The text is probably complete but rather deteriorated. The letters, which measure 9 to 12 cm. in height, read downwards facing left. The text appears to be primary and uses a predominantly capital script.

Text

[.O̲..]I[.]N̲I
[.R̲]IVG̲DOCI

---

1. Mary Henderson, in a personal communication in December 1985: 'about 25 years ago'.
2. Henderson, C.G. (1953-6a) 87.
3. Henderson, C.G. (1953-6a) 89.

Figure II.4   Bosworgey (photograph Woolf/Greenham Collection).

Discussion

The first line of text probably reads, [.O..]I[.]NI, although the N could be a H. The second line is more legible and reads, [.R]IVGDOCI, unless the G is to be read as S. There are traces of what may have been further text at the end of the second line. The text is likely to consist of two personal names in the genitive, perhaps '[the stone] of [-] [and] of [R]iugdocus'. The first name is now irrecoverable but the second could be either IVGDOCI, IVSDOCI or [R]IVGDOCI, [R]IVSDOCI. Such a name, especially on the evidence of -OCI, is likely to be Celtic. Jackson discussed the Celtic names *Iuscar* and R(I)UALLAUN;[4] either of these might contain a first element comparable to the present name. A comparable name IVODACCA occurs on an Irish ogham stone from Grange.[5]

The Bosworgey stone probably belongs to Category 1a, pillar-stones with a simple memorial text. Category 1 stones date from the fifth or sixth centuries to the eleventh century; the use of horizontal I might suggest a sixth- to eighth-century date for this stone.

Bibliography

Unpublished

---

4. Jackson (1953) 425, 393n.
5. Macalister (1945) no. 269, p. 265 & fig.

5 Bowden

The stone is now lost.

History

The stone was first recorded in a letter of 1774 from Mr Browse Trist of Bowden to Mr Swinton, paraphrased by Gough in 1806. The stone was found at Bowden; it 'had been thrown into a watery ditch near a public high road, which ditch was cleansed that the water might more readily be drained from a new turnpike road there making'.[1] All subsequent references to the stone derive directly or indirectly from Gough.

Description and Text

The description and text are taken from the drawing and description given by Gough (fig. II.5). The stone was 'about three feet long, and two wide at the bottom',[2] that is, about 80 by 60 cm. From the drawing it appears to have been an uncarved pillar-stone, though whether complete or incomplete is uncertain. The text was set in three lines, probably without framing-lines or panels, on the one face of the stone that is shown. Originally the text probably read downwards facing left, *see* Introduction, Section 4c. The text used a predominantly capital script. It is unclear whether or not the text was complete or primary. The text appears to have been legible and to have read:

VALCI
FILIV[...]
AIVS

Discussion

The text may have read, VALCI FILI V[-]AIVS, '[the stone] of Valcus, son of V[-]aivs'. The intervening letters of V[-]AIVS appear to be undamaged but are difficult to interpret; this name is not now recoverable. The name VALCI could be Celtic: Rhys suggested that it might be 'identical with our

---

1. Gough (1806) I, 50-1.
2. Gough (1806) I, 50; see also fig.

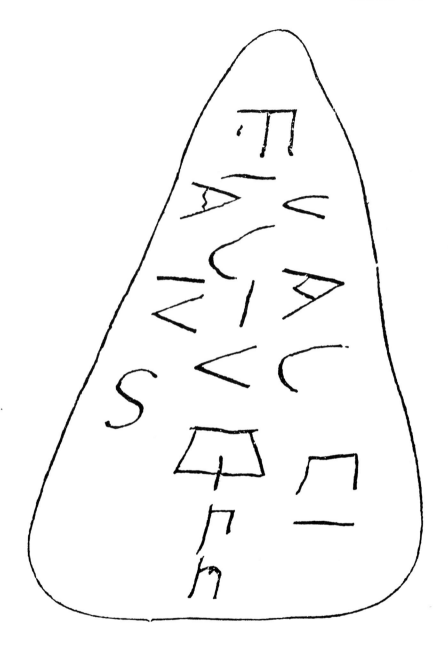

Figure II.5 Bowden (from Gough (1806) 51).

[i.e. Welsh] *gwalch* in *Gwalchmai'*.[3]

The stone probably belongs to Category 1a, pillar-stones with a simple memorial text. Category 1 stones date from the fifth or sixth centuries to the eleventh century but this stone cannot be more closely dated.

Bibliography

Gough (1806) I, 50-1 & fig.
Huebner (1876) no. 30, p. 11 & fig.
Rhys (1879) 359, 401-2.
Iago (1883-5a) 281.
Loth (1890) 47-8.
Holder (1907-13) col. 86.
Chanter (1910) 482.
Macalister (1929) 192.
Alexander (1937) 153-4.
(-) (1966) 51.

---

3. Rhys (1879) 402; see also p. 359.

6 Buckland Monachorum

The stone now stands in a field in the parish of Buckland Monachorum. The owner of the land is not willing to allow publication of any further details of the location of the stone.[1] Examined 4 July 1986.

History

The existence of the stone was notified by the owner of the land to Pearce in 1982.[2] It may have been used at one time to prop up a linhay, now largely destroyed, in the corner of the field where the stone stands.[3] The stone remains where it was in 1982.

Description

The stone is an uncarved pillar-stone, probably complete except for some crumbling at the sides (fig. II.6). It measures 173 cm. in height, 26 to 31 cm. in width and 34 to 37 cm. in thickness. The text is incised in one line without framing-lines or panels on one face of the stone. The text is complete but rather deteriorated. Due to the text's having been set close to the left-hand edge of the face of the stone, the lower parts of many of the letters are lost where the stone has crumbled. The letters measure 6 to 8 cm. in height and read downwards facing left. The text appears to be primary and uses a predominantly capital script.

Text

[D]AP[...NICI]N[..]SC[I]

Discussion

The second lost letter might perhaps have been the ligature [F/I]. This gives a possible, though highly tentative, reading, [D]AP[.] [F/I.] [NICI]N[..]SC[I],

---

1. Requests to examine the stone should be addressed to Messrs Wolferstans, Solicitors, 4 Plymouth Road, Tavistock, Devon PL19 8AY.
2. Pearce (1982) 16.
3. Information kindly supplied to me from the owner of the land.

Figure II.6 Buckland Monachorum (photograph Exeter City Museums).

'[the stone] of [D]ap[-], [? son of] [Nici]n[-]sc[us]'. Even if this tentative reconstruction is correct, the origin of the names is unknown.

The stone probably belongs to Category 1a, pillar-stones with a simple memorial text. Category 1 stones date from the fifth or sixth centuries to the eleventh century; the use of horizontal I might suggest a sixth- to eighth-century date for this stone.

Bibliography

Pearce (1982) 5-6, 16-17 & fig.

7 Camborne

The stone is now in the church of St Martin and St Meriadoc, Camborne. It is set on a modern pedestal and is in use as an altar at the east end of the south aisle. National Grid Reference SW 6452 4003. Examined 14 July 1964 and 4 July 1984.

History

The stone was first noted by W. Borlase in 1754: 'It lies at present a little without the church yard of Camborn'.[1] It remained there until some time before 1819 when it was described as 'placed against the wall of the church'.[2] It was still there in 1867, 'Against the outside of the wall of the Tehidy transept'.[3] By 1889 it had been moved inside the church to 'beneath the Communion-Table'.[4] Thomas stated: 'By 1900, the slab had been again set upright to form a kind of frontal panel under a communion table' and around 1920, 'it was finally elevated to its present position'.[5] Langdon stated that the stone was 'said to have come from a little church at Newton, near Treslothan, demolished about 120 years since'.[6] Thomas concluded that this must refer to the chapel of St Ia, Newton, Troon.[7]

Description

The stone is a slab, complete and measuring 106 cm. in length, 83 cm. in width and 17 cm. in thickness (fig. II.7). The face is decorated with a T-fret in a margin round the edge and an incised cross, 18.5 cm. by 19 cm., in the centre. Apparently there are also five crosses incised on the under side of the slab; this cannot now be verified since the stone is set on a pedestal. The text is complete and legible. It is incised without framing-lines inside the panel formed by the margins on the face of the slab. It is set clockwise around the face in five lines with the letters facing inwards. The letters vary in height between 4 and 8 cm. and the panel measures 82 by 59 cm. The text is primary and uses a predominantly insular script.

---

1. Borlase, W. (1754) 365.
2. Penaluna (1819) 27.
3. Polsue (1867) 186.
4. Langdon (1889b) 356; Thomas, quoting this reference, gave the date as 1879, presumably in error: Thomas, A.C. (1967) 101.
5. Thomas, A.C. (1967) 101.
6. Langdon (1906) 415.
7. Thomas, A.C. (1967) 102.

Figure II.7 Camborne (photograph E.N. Masson Phillips).

Text

LEUIUTIUSIT:
HECALT
ARE:PROA
N̲IMA +
SUA:

Discussion

The text reads, LEUIUT IUSIT : HEC ALTARE : PRO ANIMA + SUA :, that is, 'Leuiut ordered this altar for his own soul'. The spelling IUSIT is for IUSSIT; HEC is presumably for HAEC, neuter accusative plural, or for HOC, neuter accusative singular. ALTARE is the usual medieval Latin form of classical *altaria* (neuter plural). The name LEUIUT may contain the Celtic element *leu-*.[8] Alternatively it could be of English origin since in Domesday Book the Old English element *leof-* occurs with such spellings as *leuu-*, *leue-*, *leui-*, and *leuiet* is recorded as a spelling of *leofgeat*.[9]

The stone belongs to Category 3a, altar-slabs. It is dated to the tenth or eleventh century on artistic grounds, especially on the evidence of the T-fret, and Thomas suggested it was tenth-century work.[10]

8. Jackson (1953) 384.
9. Feilitzen (1937) 310-11.
10. Thomas, A.C. (1967) 104-6.

Bibliography

Borlase, W. (1754) 365 & fig.
Gough (1789) I, 14 & fig.
Polwhele (1803) II, 203.
Penaluna (1819) 27.
Hitchins (1824) I, 447-8; II, 142-3.
Penaluna (1838) I, 101-2.
Redding (1842) 57n.
(-) (1851*b*) 148.
(-) (1856) 161.
Blight (1865) 102-3.
Paull (1866-7*a*) xii.
Polsue (1867) 186.
Iago (1871-3) 63n, 67.
Rhys (1875) 366.
Huebner (1876) no. 8, p. 3 & fig.
Iago (1878-81) 399.
Langdon & Allen, J.R. (1888) 311-13, 316.
Adams, A. (1888-92) 206-7.
Allen, J.R. (1889) 129, 217, 220, 222.
Langdon (1889*a*) 319, 327.
Langdon (1889*b*) 356-7 & fig.
Iago (1890-1) 262.
Langdon (1890-1) 36 & *passim*.
Borlase, W.C. (1893) 184.
Langdon & Allen, J.R. (1895) 50, 56, 59 & fig.
Langdon (1896) 30.
Rhys (1905) 29.
Daniell (1906) 255.
Langdon (1906) 415, *passim* & fig.
Sedding (1909) 163-4.
Henderson, C.G. (1925) 39.
Macalister (1929) 180.
Hencken (1932) 280, 294.
Macalister (1949) no. 1044, p. 177 & fig.
Henderson, C.G. (1953-6*a*) 67.
Thomas, A.C. (1963) 78.
Wilson (1964) 231.
Thomas, A.C. (1967) 71-2, 81-5, 90, 101-10 & figs.
Pevsner (1970) 50.
Thomas, A.C. (1970) 138.
Laing (1975) 141.
Radford (1975) 14.
Pearce (1978) 179.
Thomas, A.C. (1978) 77.
Todd (1987) 293, 299.
Henderson, C.G. (unpub. 1912-17) I, 256-7.

8 Cardinham I

The stone stands in Cardinham churchyard, near the porch on the south side of the church. National Grid Reference SX 1230 6868. Examined 8 July 1984 and 5 July 1985.

History

Until 1872 the cross was imbedded in two pieces in the fifteenth-century chancel wall of the church. During restoration of the church in that year, the pieces of cross were removed and the cross re-erected in its present position. Iago recorded that the work had been completed by 1877: 'Head and shaft are now re-united, and the cross stands opposite to the south porch'.[1] In 1896 Langdon reproduced a drawing, supplied by Iago, showing the two portions of the cross still in the exterior east wall of the chancel, the inscribed face being built inwards.[2]

Description

The stone is a cross, complete and containing carving (fig. II.8); it has no base. The shaft measures 173 cm. in height, 46 to 61 cm. in width and 27 to 40 cm. in thickness. Comparison with Langdon's measurements suggests that some 82 cm. of the shaft is now beneath the ground.[3] The text is incised without framing-lines inside a panel at the top of one face of the shaft. The panel measures 36 cm. in height by 33 cm. and the letters 4 to 8 cm. in height. The text is probably complete but rather deteriorated; it is set in three lines reading horizontally. The text is primary and uses a predominantly insular script.

Text

[.]R
[A]H
+

---

1. Iago (1874–8) 363.
2. Langdon (1896) 354 & fig.
3. Langdon (1896) 354–5.

Figure II.8 Cardinham I (photograph Royal Commission on the Historical Monuments of England).

Discussion

The text probably reads, [.]R[A]H + and may be a personal name of unknown origin. Iago's drawing, made when the stone was found, suggests a text, t $\overset{+}{_+}$ h.[4] In 1889 Langdon recorded that, 'only the letter "R" is distinct; the other markings look like a "G" and +'.[5] Iago's drawing and Langdon's description suggest that the text was then in a similar condition to today. Subsequently Langdon and Allen read, ARTHI+, a reading they attributed to Iago and which their drawing to some extent substantiates;[6] Macalister read, ARAHI+.[7]

The stone belongs to Category 2a, inscribed cross-shafts. Category 2 stones date from the ninth to the eleventh century; this stone is dated to the tenth or eleventh century on artistic grounds.

Bibliography

Iago (1874-8) 363-4 & figs.
Langdon & Allen, J.R. (1888) 312, 316.
Langdon (1889a) 318-19, 323-5.
Langdon (1889c) 239 & figs.
Langdon (1890-1) 35 & *passim*.
Borlase, W.C. (1893) 183-4.
Langdon & Allen, J.R. (1895) 50, 57, 59 & fig.
Langdon (1896) 354-7, *passim* & figs.
Daniell (1906) 245.
Langdon (1906) 415, *passim* & fig.
Henderson, C.G. (1925) 40.
Collingwood, W.G. (1927) 149.
Macalister (1929) 181.
Hencken (1932) 270, 274-6, 294 & figs.
Jenkin (1934) 31.
Dexter, T.F.G. & Dexter, H. (1938) 161-2, 165 & figs.
Macalister (1949) no. 1046, p. 178 & fig.
Ellis, G.E. (1952-3a) 57-9 & figs.
Chadwick (1963) 121, 226 & fig.
Pevsner (1970) 51.
Laing (1975) 140 & figs.
Pearce (1978) 178.
Thomas, A.C. (1978) 78.
Pearce (1981) 216 & fig.
Todd (1987) 296 & figs.

4. Iago (1874-8) 364 & fig.
5. Langdon (1889a) 324.
6. Langdon & Allen, J.R. (1895) 57 & fig.
7. Macalister (1949) 178 & fig.

9 Cardinham II

The stone stands in Cardinham churchyard, beside the gate. National Grid Reference SX 1232 6871. Examined 8 July 1984.

History

The inscribed stone now has a cross-head cemented on to it, but originally it was probably a pillar-stone (fig. II.9). The cross-head was removed from the east end of the chancel wall in 1872, along with Cardinham I, and placed on the ground by the south porch.[1] The inscribed stone is presumably the one described in 1877 by Iago as 'a huge granite monolith, smoothed on its four sides like a gigantic cross shaft'.[2] In 1896 Langdon described Iago's stone as 'now leaning against the churchyard-wall, near the south-east corner'.[3] In 1902 Langdon identified this stone as the 'shaft' of the cross which had been formed by the cementing on of the cross-head in November 1896.[4] According to Langdon, both the shaft and the cross-head were trimmed before being joined.[5] The inscription was first observed by Langdon in 1901.[6] The stone remains where it was placed in November 1896.

Description

The stone was originally a pillar-stone. It is probably complete, uncarved and now measures 195 cm. in height, 24 to 42 cm. in width and 34 to 40 cm. in thickness. Langdon gave its height as 10 feet 7 inches (that is, c. 317 cm.) saying that some 4 feet (that is, c. 120 cm.) were beneath the ground.[7] The text is incised without framing-lines or panels on one face of the stone. The text is highly deteriorated; it may be complete although traces of further lettering could remain beneath. It is not certain what script

---

1. See Entry 8, Cardinham I: History; see also Ellis, G.E. (1952-3a) 60.
2. Iago (1874-8) 364.
3. Langdon (1896) 226.
4. Langdon (1902) 51-2.
5. Langdon (1902) 52; see also his figure.
6. Langdon (1902) 50-2: 'While in Cornwall last September . . . On examination I at once noticed that it was an inscribed stone.'
7. Langdon (1902) 51-2; see also his figure.

Figure II.9 Cardinham II (photograph Woolf/Greenham Collection).

was used. The letters measure 8 to 9 cm. in height and are set in one line reading downwards and facing left. The text appears to be primary.

Text

[-N.] ORI

Discussion

The text reads, [-N.]ORI with about two letters lost before the [N]. It is likely to have been a personal name in the genitive. Langdon read the text as, ORI, a reading substantiated by his drawing, adding that there was also 'perhaps the remains of an "A"'.[8] Less moderately, Macalister read, RANOCORI FILI MESGI, describing the first line, that is RANOCORI, as 'certain', but the second as 'a little more doubtful'.[9] Jackson suggested NANOCORI.[10] There may once have been a second line of text but, in view of Langdon's reading and drawing, this does not seem very likely. The text as it is today is not inconsistent with a reading of RANOCORI or NANOCORI but Langdon's evidence suggests that the name cannot now be reconstructed with any certainty.

The stone belongs to Category 1a, pillar-stones with a simple memorial text. Category 1 stones date from the fifth or sixth centuries to the eleventh century; the use of horizontal I might suggest a sixth- to eighth-century date for this stone.

Bibliography[11]

Iago (1874-8) 364.[12]
Langdon (1896) 226.
Langdon (1902) 50-3 & figs.
Langdon (1906) 415, *passim* & fig.
Jenner (1922-5) 58.
Macalister (1929) 181 & fig.
Hencken (1932) 264, 294.
Macalister (1945) no. 458, pp. 435-7 & fig.
Jackson (1946) 523.
Nash-Williams (1950) 11n.
Ellis, G.E. (1952-3a) 60-1 & figs.
(-) (1966) 50.
Pevsner (1970) 51.
Pearce (1978) 71, 178.
Weatherhill (1985) 69.

---

8. Langdon (1902) 52 & fig.
9. Macalister (1929) 181 & fig.
10. Jackson (1946) 523.
11. References to the uninscribed cross-head before it was cemented on to the inscribed shaft are omitted.
12. It is likely but not certain that Iago was describing the inscribed stone.

10 Castledore

The stone is now on the left-hand side of the A 3082, Par to Fowey road, about 1.5 km. short of Fowey. National Grid Reference SX 1112 5224. Examined 9 July 1984 and 8 July 1985.

History

The stone was first mentioned by Leland *c.* 1540. He described it as 'a broken crosse' and said it was 'A mile of' from 'Casteldour'.[1] If the stone was one mile from Castledore in the direction of Fowey, it would have been about 2.5 miles (4 km.) from Fowey; otherwise it would presumably have been further. In 1602 Carew recorded the stone: 'In a high way neere this towne [that is, Fowey], there lieth a big and long moore stone'.[2] In a letter dated 22 August 1711 Moyle recorded: "tis not many Years since 'twas again set upright', adding that it was then 'about a Mile' from Fowey, 'in the high Road which leads to *Lestwithiel*'.[3] In 1754 W. Borlase recorded that the stone had been 'remov'd, about twelve years since from the four Cross-ways a mile and half North of Fowey, and lies now in a ditch, about two bow-shots farther to the North, in the way from Fowey to Castledôr'.[4] The history of the stone up to 1754 can be summarised thus: in 1540 it was 2.5 miles (4 km.) or more from Fowey. At some time between 1540 and 1711, probably before 1602, the stone was moved to the roadside about 1 mile (1.6 km.) from Fowey. This may or may not have been the crossroads 1.5 miles (2.4 km.) north of Fowey mentioned by Borlase. Around 1742 the stone was moved to a ditch a short distance from this crossroads along the road to Castledore.

In 1803 the stone was still lying in the ditch.[5] In 1817, however, C.S. Gilbert recorded that 'many years since it was again set upright',[6] presumably in the same location. Redding was almost certainly out of date when in 1842 he described the stone as 'flung into a ditch'.[7] In 1875 Rhys gave a detailed description of how he reached the stone. He walked from Par 'about four miles on the way to Fowey, but when we reached the eastern entrance to Menabilly, we walked a short distance along a cross

---

1. Leland (*c.* 1540) part III, fol. 18, ed. Smith, L.T. (1907) I, 207.
2. Carew (1602) 136r.
3. Moyle (1726) 179.
4. Borlase, W. (1754) 357.
5. Polwhele (1803) II, 198.
6. Gilbert, C.S. (1817) 188.
7. Redding (1842) 57n.

road towards Newton, and found the stone we were looking for on the road-side near some cottages'.[8] This is almost certainly the place in which the stone had been re-erected before 1817. J.H. Rowe published a drawing made around 1870 by J.J.G. Fuller showing the stone, presumably at Newton.[9] A short while before September 1894 the stone was moved to 'the centre of the highway outside Menabilly Lodge gates'.[10] This is the road junction where the B 3369 Fowey to Lostwithiel road meets the A 3082 Fowey to Par road, about 1 mile (1.5 km.) from Fowey. This may or may not be the same crossroads as that mentioned by Borlase. Rowe recorded that at this junction the stone was placed on a 'pedestal of lofty steps'.[11] In 1971 the stone was moved a few metres to its present position.[12]

Description

The stone is a pillar-stone, partially broken and uncarved except for a T shape in relief on one face. The stone stands some 250 to 300 cm. high and is cemented into a modern base. It measures 32 to 54 cm. in width and 25 to 45 cm. in thickness. The earliest measurements of the stone were given by Moyle. On one occasion Moyle said that the stone was about nine feet high (that is, *c.* 270 cm.) and on another that it was about eight feet high (that is, *c.* 240 cm.);[13] *pace* Mandach, this confirms that the stone has always been approximately the same height.[14] The text is incised without framing-lines or panels on one face of the stone, the back, if the T is taken as being on the face of the stone (fig. II.10). The text is rather deteriorated but probably complete, unless there was originally further lettering above the present first line. The text is in two lines with the letters, 6 to 7 cm. in height, reading downwards and facing left. The text appears to be primary and uses a predominantly capital script. The Ordnance Survey symbol has been incised on the back of the stone at the end of the second line of text.

Text

[CIRV-V-NCIACIT]
CV[N]O[M]ORIFILIVS

---

8. Rhys (1875) 368-9.
9. Rowe, J.H. (1926-8) 446-9 & fig.
10. (-) (1893-5) 142.
11. Rowe, J.H. (1926-8) 447.
12. Mildren (1977) 3.
13. Moyle (1726) 176 (letter dated 19 September 1709) and 179 (letter dated 22 August 1711).
14. Mandach (1978) 227-42.

Figure II.10 Castledore (photograph O.G.S. Crawford).

Discussion

The first lacuna probably contained three letters, the second probably four. A further letter might be lost at the end of the first line and possibly a further one or two at the end of the second line. The [M] in the second line is upside down. The text probably reads [CIRV-V-NC] [IACIT] CV[N]OMORI FILIVS, perhaps for, '[here lies Cirv-], son of Cu[n]omorus'. The second name is Celtic and is well-attested in Cornwall.[15]

For a long time the first line of text has been less legible than the second. The earliest drawing, in a letter dated 22 August 1711, suggests a reading of the first line of, CERVSIVS HIC IACET.[16] In 1814 Lysons and Lysons noted, 'the first two words are now obliterated',[17] and in 1824 Hitchins, or perhaps his editor Drew, recorded that he would not have believed that there had ever been a first line of text were it not for the 'combined authority of . . . celebrated antiquarians'.[18] The first name has been read in various ways including CIRUSIUS,[19] SIRVSIVS,[20] DRVSTAGNI[21] and CIRVSINIVS.[22] In view of this past uncertainty, and of the present deteriorated state of this part of the text, the first name must be considered irrecoverable. *Pace* Mandach, it is in my view highly improbable that there was ever a third line of text.[23]

Much has been written on the supposed identity of CV[N]OMORI on the stone with: (a) *Kynwawar*, that is *Cynfor*, a name appearing twice in a fourteenth-century Welsh genealogical tract,[24] (b) Chonomor, a sixth-century Breton prince mentioned in his *History* by Gregory of Tours,[25] and (c) Quonomorius, a name given to King Mark by Wrmonoc in the ninth century.[26] This whole question was discussed by Bromwich, by Pearce and by Padel.[27] In my view, there is insufficient evidence to identify CV[N]OMORI on the stone with any other person.

The stone probably belongs to Category 1b, pillar-stones with a longer text. Category 1 stones date from the fifth or sixth centuries to the eleventh

15. Jackson (1953) 291; Padel (1981) 77.
16. Moyle (1726) 176, 180 & fig.
17. Lysons, D. & Lysons, S. (1814) ccxxii.
18. Hitchins (1824) I, 436.
19. Lhwyd, quoted in Moyle (1726) 238.
20. Haslam (1846b) 389 & fig. The reading is suggested by the figure.
21. Rhys (1875) 369.
22. Macalister (1945) 466 & fig. The reading is suggested by the figure.
23. Mandach (1978) 227–42.
24. Bodleian Library, Oxford, Jesus College MS 20, fols 33v and 36r, published in Bartrum (1966) 43–6. A photograph of fol. 36r is printed in Pearce (1978) pl. 31.
25. In IV, 4: 'nomen Chonomorem'; Buchner (1955) 196, lines 29–30.
26. The reference is at the beginning of chapter 8: '. . . fama ejus regis Marci pervolat ad aures quem alio nomine Quonomorium vocant'. This is edited from the Fleury MS; according to Cuissard, the Paris MS reads 'Quonomonum': Cuissard (1881–3) 431; see also p. 416.
27. Bromwich (1961) 444–6; Pearce (1978) 141, 154–5; Padel (1981) 55, 77–9.

century but this stone cannot be more closely dated. The T cross need not be contemporary with the text.

Bibliography

Leland (*c.* 1540) part III, fol. 18, ed. Smith, L.T. (1907) I, 207.
Carew (1602) 136r-136v.
Lhwyd (1700*b*).[28]
Moyle (1726) 176 (letter of 19 September 1709); 178-89 & fig. (letter of 22 August 1711); 238-9 (letter of 10 March 1714/15, quoting letter of 30 November 1700); 240-1 (letter of 10 March 1714/15).
Norden (1728) 59.
Borlase, W. (1754) 356-7 & figs.
Gough (1789) I, 16 & figs.
Polwhele (1803) II, 196-8; fig. in vol. I.
Lysons, D. & Lysons, S. (1814) ccxxi-ccxxii & fig.
Gilbert, C.S. (1817) 188-9.
Hitchins (1824) I, 435-8.
Kempe (1830) 219.
Penaluna (1838) II, 264.
Redding (1842) 57n.
Haslam (1845) 30 & figs.
Haslam (1846*b*) 388-9 & figs.
Haslam (1847) 307-8 & figs.
Spence (1849) 212.
Coppard (1851) 205.
(-) (1851*b*) 220.
Wright, T. (1852) 456.
(-) (1856) 238-9.
Blight (1858*a*) 127 & fig.
Haigh (1858-9) 184-5.
Wilkinson (1862) 52.
Harding (1867) 21.
Polsue (1868) 27-8.
Haddan & Stubbs (1869) 163.
Iago (1871-3) 63n.
Polsue (1872) appendix p. 83.
(-) (1874-8) 141.
Rhys (1875) 368-9.
Huebner (1876) no. 20, p. 7 & fig.
Brash (1879) 403.
Rhys (1879) 403.
Allen, J.R. (1887) 97.
Rashleigh (1887) 10, 22.
Langdon & Allen, J.R. (1888) 306-9, 316.
Loth (1890) 44.
Borlase, W.C. (1893) 182-3.
(-) (1893-5) 142-3.
Langdon & Allen, J.R. (1895) 50, 53, 59 & figs.
Holder (1896) cols 1195, 1335.
Langdon (1896) 6, 24 & *passim.*
Lot (1896) 20-1.
Rhys (1901) II, 480n.

---

28. There is no page numbering in this part of this work.

Rhys (1905) 65.
Daniell (1906) 241.
Langdon (1906) 416, *passim* & figs.
Loth (1912) 16-17.
Jenner (1919) 125.
Jenner (1922-5) 59.
Henderson, C.G. (1925) 175.
Rowe, J.H. (1926-8) 446-9 & fig.
Macalister (1929) 181.
Hencken (1932) 222, 227-31, 243, 297.
Jenkin (1934) 29.
Henderson, C.G. (1935) 27-8.
Vendryes (1937) 255.
Dexter, T.F.G. & Dexter, H. (1938) 161, 165-6 & fig.
Macalister (1945) no. 487, pp. 465-7 & fig.
Radford (1946-52) 7, 96, 117-19 & fig. (= plate II).
Keast (1950) 3-4 & fig.
Jackson (1953) 291.
Henderson, C.G. (1953-6*b*) 180-1.
Bromwich (1954) 122-3.
Bromwich (1955) 47-8, 59-60.
Thomas, A.C. (1957-8) 62.
Best (1959) 439.
Bromwich (1961) 329-30, 444-6.
(-) (1961) 35-8 & fig.
Chadwick (1963) 120-1, 226 & fig.
Fox (1964) 160, 162.
Chadwick (1965) 279-80.
Morris, J. (1966) 381-2.
(-) (1966) 51.
Evans (1967) 226.
Radford (1968) 82 (illus. no. 59), 96 & fig.
Pevsner (1970) 116-17.
Alcock (1971) 161, 212.
Rahtz (1971) 49.
Thomas, A.C. (1971*a*) 116.
Mandach (1972) 389-425.
Ellis, P.B. (1974) 24-5.
Mandach (1975) 3-35.
Radford (1975) 4, 7, 12-13.
Mildren (1977) 3.
Pool (1977) 140.
Mandach (1978) 227-42 & figs.
Pearce (1978) 21-30, 141, 154-5, 162 & fig.
Padel (1981) 55, 77-9.
Weatherhill (1981) 63.
Brewer & Frankl (1985) 46 & fig.
Quinnell & Harris (1985) 130-1.
Weatherhill (1985) 25-6, 116, 122 & figs.
Thomas, A.C. (1986) 67, 70-1 & fig.
Todd (1987) 237, 249-50 & fig.
Courts (unpub. 1785) & figs.[29]

---

29. This work is a single sheet map and hence has no page numbering.

11 Cubert

The stone is built into the west exterior wall of the tower of Cubert church. National Grid Reference SW 7859 5775. Examined 6 July 1984.

History

The stone was discovered by Jones, probably in 1861. He stated: '. . . the inscribed stone, as yet unedited, but which we deciphered and delineated last summer, has been built with due care into the west wall of the church tower'.[1] In 1863 Jones stated that the stone 'was found when some repairs and reconstructions were lately carried on there'.[2] C.G. Henderson assumed that the stone had been re-used by the fifteenth-century masons of the church tower;[3] however, Jones' statements seem to imply that the stone was placed in its present position in the nineteenth century.

Description

The stone is set into a wall and it is not certain whether or not it is complete (fig. II.11). Presumably it was originally an erect pillar-stone; its visible face is uncarved. When erect, its height would be 128 cm. and its width 26 to 47 cm. The text is incised without framing-lines or panels on the visible face of the stone. The text may be complete, although if the stone were incomplete further text could have been lost. The text is in three lines and originally it probably read downwards facing left, *see* Introduction, Section 4c. The letters measure 4 to 13 cm. in height and are slightly deteriorated. The text appears to be primary and is in a predominantly capital script.

Text

CONET[O]CI
[F]ILITEGE[R]NO
MALI

---

1. Jones (1862) 136.
2. Jones (1863) 289.
3. Henderson, C.G. (1953-6*b*) 136.

Figure II.11   Cubert (photograph Woolf/Greenham Collection).

Discussion

The text reads, CONET[O]CI [F]ILI TEGE[R]NOMALI, that is, '[the stone] of Conet[o]cus, son of Tege[r]nomalus' with [F]ILI for FILII. The names are both Celtic.[4]

The stone belongs to Category 1a, pillar-stones with a simple memorial text. Category 1 stones date from the fifth or sixth centuries to the eleventh century; the use of horizontal I might suggest a sixth- to eighth-century date for this stone.

Bibliography

Jones (1862) 136, 139.
Jones (1863) 289-90 & fig.
Barham (1866) 426-8.
Barham (1866-7) 47, 55-8 & fig.
Paull (1866-7a) xi.
Polsue (1867) 276.
Haddan & Stubbs (1869) 163.
Iago (1871-3) 61n, 63n.
Iago *et al.* (1871-3) xlvi-xlvii.
(-) (1871-3a) xxx-xxxi.
Huebner (1876) no. 12, p. 4 & fig.
Brash (1879) 403.

---

4. Jackson (1953) 274n, 291, 645; 447, 463-6. See also Rhys (1879) 358, 403-4.

Rhys (1879) 33, 209, 211, 358, 403-4.
Langdon & Allen, J.R. (1888) 307-8, 318.
Loth (1890) 44, 47.
Borlase, W.C. (1893) 182-3.
Iago (1893) 192.
Sharrock (1893) 166.
Langdon (1894*b*) 315.
Langdon & Allen, J.R. (1895) 50, 54, 59 & fig.
Holder (1896) col. 1098.
Langdon (1896) 23.
Holder (1904) col. 1841.
Rhys (1905) 85.
Daniell (1906) 240.
Langdon (1906) 420, *passim* & fig.
Rhys (1918) 193.
Jenner (1922-5) 58.
Henderson, C.G. (1925) 51.
Macalister (1929) 179.
Hencken (1932) 264, 296.
Macalister (1945) no. 477, p. 455 & fig.
Nash-Williams (1950) 11n.
Jackson (1953) 274, 291, 447, 463-4, 645.
Henderson, C.G. (1953-6*b*) 136.
(-) (1966) 50.
Pevsner (1970) 61.
Thomas, A.C. (1971*a*) 25 & fig.
Thomas, A.C. (1971*b*) 110-11.
Pearce (1978) 71, 178.
Thomas, A.C. (1985*a*) 178.
Weatherhill (1985) 46 & fig.

12 East Ogwell

The stone is now in two pieces, both built into the exterior of East Ogwell church. Both are placed some 4m. from the ground, above the buttresses. Stone (i) is at the junction of the east wall and the north aisle wall (fig. II.12(i)), stone (ii) at the junction of the west wall and the north aisle wall (fig. II.12(ii)). National Grid Reference SX 8382 7005. Examined 7 July 1985 and 25 September 1987.[1]

History

The stones were first observed, in their present positions, in 1964 by S. Taylor and D.J. Seymour.[2] Radford suggested that the stones were placed in these positions during the rebuilding of the buttresses and quoins in 1884-5.[3]

Description

The two pieces of stone are both uncarved and both probably incomplete. Originally they probably formed part of an erect pillar-stone. Stone (i) measures 30 to 35 cm. in height, 103 cm. in width and 25 to 27 cm. in thickness. Stone (ii) measures 34 cm. in height, 117 cm. in width and 25 cm. in thickness. If the stone originally stood erect it would therefore have measured at least 220 cm. in height. Both texts are incised without framing-lines or panels and both are probably primary. Both use a predominantly capital script with the letters measuring 6 to 9 cm. in height. Both texts are in two lines and originally they probably read downwards facing left, *see* Introduction, Section 4c. Text (i) is set on the east face of stone (i). It is slightly deteriorated and is probably incomplete. Text (ii) is set on the west face of stone (ii). It is legible and may be complete. The texts read together with probably a small portion lost where stone (i), and possibly also stone (ii), was trimmed for re-building.

---

1. I am most grateful to Ernest Dickson, East Ogwell, for his help which enabled me to examine this stone.
2. Radford (1969) 79.
3. Radford (1969) 79.

Figure II.12(i) East Ogwell, stone (i) (photograph Totnes Community Archive).

Figure II.12(ii) East Ogwell, stone (ii) (photograph Totnes Community Archive).

Text

CA[-]OCIFILI
[..-]PLICI

Discussion

The text reads, CA[-]OCI FILI [-]PLICI, that is, '[the stone] of Ca[-], son of [-]plicus', with FILI for FILII. The two letters missing at the beginning of the second line might be E, or possibly P or R, followed perhaps by S, but it is uncertain how many letters are lost from each lacuna and the names are not therefore recoverable. Radford read the second name, with no letters missing, as POPLICI which Jackson took to be a Latin name.[4] The remaining traces do not seem to me to support this reading. The -OCI of the first name suggests that it was Celtic.[5]

This stone belongs to Category 1a, pillar-stones with a simple memorial text. Category 1 stones date from the fifth or sixth centuries to the eleventh century; the use of horizontal I might suggest a sixth- to eighth-century date for this stone.

Bibliography

Radford (1969) 79-81 & fig.
Radford (1975) 13.
Pearce (1978) 71, 182 & fig.
Pearce (1981) 188.
Pearce (1982) 7.
Swanton & Pearce (1982) 143.

---

4. Radford (1969) 80, quoting Jackson.
5. See, for example, Jackson (1953) 290-2.

13 Fardel

The stone is now in the British Museum, no. 61, 2-9, 1. Examined 15 March 1984, 17 July 1986 and 24 September 1987.

History

The stone was first recorded by Smirke in 1861. It had been lying across a stream 'called Fardel brook, on the road passing within a short distance, perhaps a quarter of a mile, from the farmhouse of Fardel'.[1] Crossing recorded that the stone was 'at the lower end' of the bridge, which position had contributed to its preservation from damage.[2] Mr Pearse of Cadleigh had it placed in the farmyard at Fardel;[3] Brash stated that it was 'set up as a ring-post of a shed in the yard of Fardel Manor-house'.[4] Later in 1861, Captain Pode, the owner of the farm, presented the stone to the British Museum. In 1862 Jones noted that 'some ill-advised person has taken the liberty of applying, very awkwardly, some black pigment or other to the letters. The effect is most disastrous'.[5]

Description

The stone is a pillar-stone, complete and uncarved, standing in a modern base. It measures 168 cm. in height, 80 to 87 cm. in width and 19 to 25 cm. in thickness. Comparison with Smirke's measurements seems to suggest that the stone was then some 20 cm. taller than it is today.[6] Text (i) is incised in two lines on the face of the stone (fig. II.13(i)). This text is complete and is set without panels or framing-lines. The letters, reading downwards and facing left, are 8 to 11 cm. in height. This text appears to be primary and is in a predominantly capital script. Text (ii) is incised in one line on the back of the stone (fig. II.13(ii)). Text (ii) is complete and is set without panels or framing-lines. The letters, reading downwards and facing left, are 12 to 15 cm. in height and are in a predominantly capital script. Text (ii) also appears to be primary.

---

1. Smirke *et al.* (1861) 175-6, quotation from p. 176.
2. Crossing (1902) 32.
3. Smirke (1861a) 22.
4. Brash (1879) 349.
5. Jones (1862) 136.
6. Smirke *et al.* (1861) 179.

Figure II.13(i) Fardel, texts (i), (iii), (iv) (photograph British Museum).

Figure II.13(ii) Fardel, text (ii) (photograph British Museum).

There are two ogham texts, texts (iii) and (iv) (fig. II.13(i)). Text (iii) is incised on the upper part of the edge between the face and the right-hand side of the stone. Text (iv) is incised on the upper part of the edge between the face and the left-hand side of the stone, and extends on to the edge between the face and the top of the stone. Both ogham texts read vertically upwards and are legible and complete; they both appear to be primary. The letters of all the texts were covered in black paint in 1861 or 1862.[7] The painted texts are clearly legible but the original texts are probably rather deteriorated. Examination of the texts suggest that the paint was applied rather inaccurately.

Texts

(i)   FANONI
        MAQVIRINI
(ii)   G[.]G[R]A[..]I
(iii)   [ogham] MAQIQICI
(iv)   [ogham] SAFAQQUCI

Discussion

Text (i) can be read, FANONI MAQVI RINI, that is, '[the stone] of Fanonus, son of Rinus' with Primitive Irish MAQVI 'son of'. Alternatively, it could be read, FANONI MAQVIRINI, that is, '[the stone] of Fanonus, [son] of Maqvirinus'. The name MAQVIRINI would be Primitive Irish,[8] but the name RINI would be of unknown origin. FANONI is Celtic; a similar name, FANNVCI, occurs on a stone from Stackpole Elidyr, Wales.[9]

Text (ii) may read, G[A]G[R]A[NV]I, that is '[the stone] of G[a]gra[nv]us'. The letters read here as [NV] are clear but uncertain in value. Readings of [HV] or of [HN] are possible but seem contextually unlikely. A reading [SN] with insular S is possible, giving G[A]G[R]A[SN]I. The exact form of this name remains uncertain. The name has generally been read with an initial S, usually as SAGRANVI, although the first and third letters seem to be identical in form. This problem was noted by Jones who tentatively suggested a reading of SASRAMNI.[10] Jackson listed this stone as one of those containing names 'too obscure or corrupt to make discussion profitable'.[11] Since elsewhere Jackson discussed SAGRANI on a stone from

---

7. See above; Jones (1862) 136.
8. See Jackson (1953) 140-1 and Rhys (1879) 18, 265, 401.
9. Macalister (1945) no. 455, pp. 431-2 & fig.; Nash-Williams (1950) no. 403, p. 217. Cf. Rhys (1879) 359, 401.
10. Jones (1862) 139.
11. Jackson (1953) 187.

St Dogmaels, Wales, he presumably rejected such a reading on the Fardel stone.[12]

Text (iii) reads, MAQIQICI or perhaps MAQI QICI. As with text (i), MAQI could either be part of a name or be the Primitive Irish for 'son of'. The text can be translated as, '[the stone] of Maqiqicus' or as, '[the stone] of the son of Qicus'. If the name were MAQIQICI, the MAQ- would indicate a Primitive Irish name, if QICI, the name would be Celtic; the phrase MAQI QIC- occurs on an Irish ogham stone from Ballyvooney.[13] The word MACVS and the name MAQVICOLINE both probably occur on a stone from Wroxeter.[14] Text (iv) reads, SAFAQQUCI, probably a Celtic name.[15] It is possible that texts (iii) and (iv) were intended to be read together as, for example, '[the stone] of Safaqqucus, son of Qicus'. The names of the ogham texts (iii) and (iv) are not the same as those of the non-ogham texts. If one or more of these texts do use the Irish language, this is unique among south-western inscribed stones.

The stone belongs to Category 1a, pillar-stones with simple memorial texts. Category 1 stones date from the fifth or sixth centuries to the eleventh century. On the evidence both of the ogham texts and of the Irish nature of texts (i) and (iii), this stone is likely to date from the fifth or sixth century to the eighth century.

Bibliography

Pettigrew (1861) 293-310 & fig.
Smirke (1861*a*) 20-33 & figs.
Smirke (1861*b*) 5-16 & figs.
Smirke *et al.* (1861) 175-82 & figs.
Jones (1862) 134-42 & figs.
Pedler (1864-5) 12-13.
Barham (1866) 427-8n.
Barham (1866-7) 57n.
Brash (1869) 164-7 & figs.
Haddan & Stubbs (1869) 162.
Iago (1871-3) 61n, 65n.
Rhys (1873*a*) 75-6.
Bate (1873-6) 392.
Huebner (1876) no. 24, p. 9 & figs.
Brash (1879) 348-50, 396 & figs.
Ferguson (1879*c*) 184.
Rhys (1879) 18-19, 207-9, 216, 265-6, 268, 283-4, 359, 397, 401.
Stephens, G. (1884) 8.
Worth, R.N. (1886) 179-80.

---

12. Jackson (1953) 180. The St Dogmaels stone is Macalister (1945) no. 449, pp. 425-6 & fig. and Nash-Williams (1950) no. 384, pp. 211-13 & figs. See also MacNeill (1929-31) 40.
13. Macalister (1945) no. 271, p. 267 & fig. (fig. numbered 270); see also Jackson (1953) 140-1; Rhys (1879) 18-19, 265-6, 359, 401; Holder (1904) col. 1063.
14. Wright, R.P. & Jackson (1968) 296-300 & fig.
15. Rhys (1879) 19, 266.

Ferguson (1887) 117-18.
Langdon & Allen, J.R. (1888) 304.
Alford (1890) 233.
Loth (1890) 45.
Page (1890*b*) 309.
Langdon (1892*a*) 336.
Langdon (1892*b*) 251.
Langdon (1892-3) 285.
Borlase, W.C. (1893) 106-7.
Burnard (1895) 228-9.
Holder (1896) col. 1492.
Crossing (1902) 32-3.
Holder (1904) cols 414, 1063, 1191, 1295-6, 1649-50.
Macalister (1907) 128.
Chanter (1910) 481.
Thurneyson (1918) 411-12.
Smith, R.A. (1923) 121.
Macalister (1929) 192.
MacNeill (1932) 133-4.
Alexander (1937) 153-4.
Macalister (1945) no. 489, pp. 468-9 & figs.
Jackson (1950) 199, 205.
Jackson (1953) 171n, 187.
Fox (1964) 160, 245 & figs.
(-) (1966) 50.
Evans (1967) 210n.
Thomas, A.C. (1971*a*) 63 & figs.
Laing (1975) 125.
Pearce (1978) 21-30, 161 & figs.
Pearce (1981) 172.
Pearce (1982) 1.
Todd (1987) 251.
McManus (1991) 8, 61-2, 98, 114, 126, 176n.

14 Gulval I

The stone now stands by the hedge near one end of a footbridge called 'Bleu Bridge' at Barlowena Bottom, about 1.5 km. from Gulval. The bridge is approached by a path leading off to the right from the unclassified Gulval to Zennor road which leads off the B 3311 St Ives to Penzance road. National Grid Reference SW 4767 3179. Examined 11 July 1984.

History

The stone was first mentioned in two letters from Lhwyd, one to T. Tonkin, dated 29 November 1700, and the other to F. Paynter, dated 30 November 1700. In the latter the stone was described as 'a Foot-bridge at *Gulval*, . . . call'd the Blue-Bridge'.[1] The text was on the underneath of the bridge.[2] The stone remained in use as a footbridge at least until 1841.[3] In 1845 the stone was described as having been 'lately' raised from forming part of the bridge 'and is now placed upright by the road side'.[4] Blight's drawing, published in 1861, shows the stone in this position.[5] In the autumn of 1894 the stone fell into the stream during a storm. On 28 November 1894 it was lifted out and placed 'about 20 feet S.W. of its former position, by the side of the pathway leading to the Bridge, and against the hedge'.[6] This is its present position.

Description

The stone is a pillar-stone, uncarved and probably complete (fig. II.14). It measures 150 cm. in height, 48 to 56 cm. in width and 25 to 32 cm. in thickness. Comparison with the length of the stone when it was a bridge suggests that some 80 cm. are now below ground level.[7] The text is complete and legible. It is incised without framing-lines or panels on one face of the stone. The letters are set downwards in two lines facing left and

---

1. Moyle (1726) 238, in a letter dated 10 March 1714/15 which quoted Lhwyd's letter of 30 November 1700.
2. Paris (1824) 126n.
3. Cornish *et al.* (1892-8) 84.
4. Courtney (1845) 98.
5. Blight (1861) 204 & fig.
6. Iago (1893-5*a*) 112-14, quotation from p. 114, from a letter to Iago from the Rev. W.W. Wingfield, dated 29 November 1894.
7. Polsue (1868) 123: length given as seven feet, nine inches.

Figure II.14   Gulval I (photograph Woolf/Greenham Collection).

measure 6 to 13 cm. in height. The text appears to be primary and is in a predominantly capital script.

Text

QVENAṮAVCIIC
DINVI[F]I[L/I]VS

Discussion

The first I is set above the preceding C and the text reads, QVENATAVCI IC DINVI [F]I[LI]VS, that is, '[the stone] of Quenataucus here, son of Dinvus'. IC is for HIC and [F]I[LI]VS is nominative instead of genitive. The text may show confusion between the simple memorial formula with genitive *filii*, and a *hic iacet* formula with nominative *filius*. QVENATAVCI is a Primitive Irish name discussed by Jackson,[8] while DINVI is Celtic.[9]

The stone belongs to Category 1b, pillar-stones with a longer text. Category 1 stones date from the fifth or sixth centuries to the eleventh century. The Primitive Irish name suggests a date between the fifth or sixth century and the eighth century for this stone, a date which the use of horizontal I probably corroborates.

Bibliography

Lhwyd (1700*b*).[10]
Moyle (1726) 238 & fig. (letter of 10 March 1714/15, quoting letter of 30 November 1700).
Borlase, W. (1754) 359 & fig.
Gough (1789) I, 13 & fig.
Polwhele (1803) II, 200-1.
Lysons, D. & Lysons, S. (1814) ccxxii.
Gilbert, C.S. (1817) 188.
Penaluna (1819) 84.
Hitchins (1824) I, 438-9.
Paris (1824) 126n.
Penaluna (1838) I, 231.
Courtney (1845) 98.
(-) (1851*b*) 156.
Blight (1856) 67, page opp. p. 61 & figs.
(-) (1856) 169.
Edmonds (1858*a*) 183 & fig.
Haigh (1858-9) 184.

8. Jackson (1953) 140-1, 171-2, 296n.
9. Holder (1896) col. 1284.
10. There is no page numbering in this part of this work.

Blight (1861) 204 & fig.
Halliwell (1861) 57-8.
Edmonds (1862) 65, 213 & fig.
Jones (1862) 135-6, 139.
Jones (1863) 288-9 & fig.
Dodd (1864) 100-1.
Paull (1866-7*a*) xi.
Polsue (1868) 123.
Haddan & Stubbs (1869) 163.
Rhys (1873*b*) 198.
(-) (1873) 46.
Huebner (1876) no. 3, p. 2 & fig.
Brash (1879) 402-3.
Rhys (1879) 18, 207-8, 216-18, 265, 397, 405-6.
Iago (1883-5*c*) 366 & fig.
Birch (1885) 407.
Langdon & Allen, J.R. (1888) 308, 316.
Loth (1890) 46.
Langdon (1890-1) 92.
Cornish *et al.* (1892-8) 81-4 & figs.
Borlase, W.C. (1893) 182-3.
Langdon (1893) 107-8.
Iago (1893-5*a*) 112-14.
Langdon & Allen, J.R. (1895) 50, 53, 59 & fig.
(-) (1895) 58.
Holder (1896) col. 1284.
Langdon (1896) 24 & *passim*.
(-) (1903-5) 329-30.
Holder (1904) col. 1062.
Rhys (1905) 70.
Daniell (1906) 239.
Langdon (1906) 416, *passim* & fig.
Macalister (1929) 180.
Hencken (1932) 242, 244, 297-8.
Macalister (1945) no. 462, pp. 439-40 & figs.
Nash-Williams (1950) 11n.
Jackson (1953) 140-1, 171-2, 295-6.
Thomas, A.C. (1958) 33.
Russell (1965) 73.
(-) (1966) 50.
Thomas, A.C. (1969-72) 258 & fig.
Pevsner (1970) 76-7.
Russell (1971) 81.
Thomas, A.C. (1971*a*) 61 & fig.
Thomas, A.C. (1971*b*) 111 & fig.
Laing (1975) 125.
Maxwell (1976) 10 & fig.
Pool (1977) 140.
Pearce (1978) 27, 161-2.
Pearce (1981) 172.
Weatherhill (1981) 64, 81 & fig.
Thomas, A.C. (1985*b*) 174.
Weatherhill (1985) 90 & fig.
Thomas, A.C. (1986) 143.
McManus (1991) 62, 126.
Pool (undated) 13 & fig.

15 Gulval II

The stone is now in Gulval churchyard, near the porch on the south side of the church. It is cemented upside down into the ground. National Grid Reference SW 4847 3177. Examined 5 July 1984 and 2 July 1985.

History

The stone was found on 18 September 1885 'in taking down a portion of the east wall of the chancel of Gulval Church, preparatory to the insertion of an enlarged east window'.[1] Langdon added the information, supplied by the vicar, the Rev. W.W. Wingfield, that the stone had been used as a quoin in the east end of the chancel.[2] In 1889 Langdon recorded the stone in the churchyard,[3] and in 1890-1 he said it had been 'lately erected upside down'.[4] In 1896 Langdon recorded that the stone 'stands near the south-west angle of the church, but ... mounted upside down'.[5] This is its present position and probably the same place as that described by Langdon in 1890-1.

Description

The stone is carved and is a cross-shaft, probably complete but with no cross-head or base (fig. II.15). It measures 135 cm. to where it is cemented into the ground, 44 to 47 cm. in width and 27 to 31 cm. in thickness. The text is incised on one face of the stone, at the bottom of the shaft, inside a panel 46 cm. in height by 30 cm.; the two lines of text are separated by a framing-line. The text may be complete but is now illegible. It is uncertain what script was used; the letters are *c.* 8 cm. in height and read horizontally. Since the text is incised in a panel it is likely to have been primary.

Text

The text is now illegible.

---

1. Millett (1884-8) 145.
2. Langdon (1896) 372.
3. Langdon (1889*a*) 319.
4. Langdon (1890-1) 39n.
5. Langdon (1896) 372.

Figure II.15   Gulval II (photograph Woolf/Greenham Collection).

Discussion

Langdon and Allen read two lines of text, as shown in their accompanying drawing, VN VI.[6] Macalister, however, read the text as, VRI VI, a reading supported by his drawing.[7] In view of these differences and of the state of the text today, the original reading cannot be recovered.

The stone belongs to Category 2a, inscribed cross-shafts. Category 2 stones date from the ninth to the eleventh century but this stone cannot be more closely dated.

Bibliography

Lach-Szyrma (1883-5) 374.
(-) (1883-5) 320.
Cornish (1884-8) 314.
Millett (1884-8) 145-6, 202.
Lach-Szyrma (1886-9) 56.
Langdon (1889a) 319.
Langdon (1890-1) 36, 39n & *passim.*
Langdon & Allen, J.R. (1895) 51, 58, 59 & fig.
Langdon (1896) 372-4, *passim* & figs.
Baring-Gould (1899-1900) 130.
Daniell (1906) 245.
Langdon (1906) 416, *passim* & fig.
Macalister (1929) 183.
Hencken (1932) 271, 278-9, 297.
Macalister (1945) no. 463, p. 440 & fig.
Ellis, G.E. (1952-3a) 58.
Russell (1965) 73.
Pevsner (1970) 76.
Russell (1971) 81, 84.
Rowe, L. (1973) & fig.[8]
Maxwell (1976) 10.
Pearce (1978) 71, 179.
Baird & White (unpub. 1961) vol. IV, D-G.[9]

6. Langdon & Allen, J.R. (1895) 58 & fig. There is a better drawing in Langdon (1896) 373.
7. Macalister (1945) 440 & fig.
8. There is no page numbering in this book.
9. There is no page numbering in this typescript.

16 Hayle

The stone is now set into a bank in a public park, King George VI Memorial Plantation, in Hayle. National Grid Reference SW 5565 3717. Examined 11 and 12 July 1984 and 1 July 1986.

History

The stone was discovered in December 1843 by workmen engaged in building a road in the grounds of Carnsew, belonging to a Mr Harvey. The stone was 'lying in a horizontal position at the depth of about four feet from the surface'.[1] To the north of it was a grave made of 'unshapen and uncemented stones, some placed on their edges to serve as a wall, and the rest laid over them as a covering. This grave was filled with a mixture of sand, charcoal, and ashes'.[2] It is possible, but by no means certain, that the stone and the grave belonged together. When the stone was moved it broke into three parts. Mr Harvey had it fixed into 'the wall of his new road on Carnsew Cliff, within a few feet of the spot where it was discovered'.[3] The stone has remained there since. Beckerlegge recorded that at some date between September 1948 and 1953, 'well-meant but clumsy efforts to preserve the stone in its setting have been made by somebody quite unqualified for specialist work'.[4] This seems to have contributed to the deterioration of the text. A modern plaque has been set into the bank immediately adjacent to the stone.

Description

The stone is now in four pieces; it is probably incomplete and its visible face contains no carving (fig. II.16(i)). The stone measures 132 cm. in height and 27 to 31 cm. in width. When found the stone was said to be 6 feet (c. 180 cm.) long;[5] this suggests that some 48 cm. is now in the ground, or was broken off or cut away when the stone broke. The text is set on the visible face and is now illegible, with only occasional traces of lettering visible. No further description of the text is possible.

---

1. Edmonds (1844) 69.
2. Edmonds (1844) 69.
3. Edmonds (1844) 70.
4. Beckerlegge (1953) 173.
5. Edmonds (1844) 69.

Figure II.16(i) Hayle (photograph Herbert Hughes).

Figure II.16(ii) Hayle (from Langdon & Allen (1895) fig. 9).

Text

The text is now illegible.

Discussion

To some extent the text can be reconstructed from earlier drawings and readings. Three early drawings survive. The first was made by Willis shortly after the stone was found and was published by Edmonds.[6] Willis' drawing suggests that, although some letters were legible, the text was even then difficult to decipher. The second drawing was made around 1847 and is kept in Penzance Library.[7] The third drawing was made by Edmonds and published by him in 1862;[8] it shows a text closely similar to Willis'. Taken together these three drawings suggest a reconstructed text in ten horizontal lines reading, [HI]C CEM[.] REQVIEVIT CVNATDO HIC [IN] TVMVL[O] IACIT VIXIT ANNOS XXXIII.

Subsequently, around 1891-2, Iago drew the text.[9] This drawing suggests a reading, HIC PACE NVP REQVIEVIT SILVANVS CONIVX CVNAIDE HIC [IN] TVMVLO IACIT VIXIT ANNOS XXXIII. In 1895, Langdon and Allen published a drawing showing a text very similar to Edmonds' (fig. II.16(ii)); their reading, however, differed in various respects from his.[10] They read, HIC [IN PA]CEM REQVIEVIT [-] CVNAIDE HIC [IN] TVMVLO IACIT VIXIT ANNOS XXXIII.

By 1948, when Beckerlegge examined the stone, the text had deteriorated considerably.[11] Beckerlegge's drawing and comments suggest a reading, HIC P[A]CE [-] REQVIEVIT [.]VNAID HIC TVMVL[.] IACIT VIXIT [.]NO XXXIII.

The text has now disappeared altogether. Since earlier drawings and readings are not totally consistent, any reconstruction of the text must be approached with caution. I tentatively suggest a reconstructed text, [HI]C [PA]CE [-] REQVIEVIT CVNATDO HIC [IN] TVMVLO IACIT VIXIT ANNOS XXXIII, perhaps, 'Here in peace has rested Cunatdo. Here he lies in the tomb. He lived for 33 years'. Although the three earliest drawings all show CVNATDO, the name has been read at least since 1879 as CVNAIDE; Jackson took CVNAIDE as a Celtic feminine name, perhaps Irish.[12]

---

6. Edmonds (1844) 69-71 & fig.
7. MS *Miscellaneous Extracts, Drawings and Prints*, no. 14, p. 45. I am most grateful to the Librarian, The Penzance Library, Morrab Gardens, Penzance for supplying me with a copy of this drawing. See also Beckerlegge (1953) 174.
8. Edmonds (1862) 60-2 & fig.
9. The drawing is dated both 7 December 1891 and 22 August 1892, and is written into his own copy of Edmonds (1862), plate opp. p. 60. This annotated copy is in the possession of Professor A.C. Thomas and I am most grateful to him for supplying me with a photocopy of the relevant pages.
10. Langdon & Allen, J.R. (1895) 54 & fig.
11. Beckerlegge (1953) 173-7 & fig.
12. Jackson (1953) 188, 329n; see also Rhys (1879) 216, 405.

The stone belongs to Category 1b, pillar-stones with a longer text. Category 1 stones date from the fifth or sixth centuries to the eleventh century but this stone cannot be more closely dated.

Bibliography

Edmonds (1844) 69-71 & fig.
Edmonds (1845) 56-8 & fig.
Blight (1856) page opp. p. 61.
Edmonds (1858*a*) 178-80 & fig.
Edmonds (1858*b*) 426.
Westwood (1858) 318.
Edmonds (1862) 60-2, 207 & fig.
Paull (1866-7*a*) xii.
Haddan & Stubbs (1869) 163.
(-) (1871-3*b*) 312.
Polsue (1872) 71.
Iago (1874-8) 363n.
Rhys (1875) 364-5.
Huebner (1876) no. 7, p. 3 & fig.
Rhys (1879) 212, 216, 405.
Buckley *et al.* (1885*a*) 267.
Buckley *et al.* (1885*b*) 335-6.
Soulsby (1885*a*) 76.
Soulsby (1885*b*) 248.
Langdon & Allen, J.R. (1888) 306-7, 318.
Borlase, W.C. (1893) 106.
Langdon & Allen, J.R. (1895) 51, 54, 59 & fig.
Holder (1896) col. 1191.
Rhys (1905) 37-8.
Daniell (1906) 240.
Greenbank (1906*b*) 187-8.
Langdon (1906) 420, *passim* & fig.
Jenner (1917) 75.
Dalton (1921) 64.
Jenner (1922-5) 57-8.
Henderson, C.G. (1925) 59.
Macalister (1929) 183.
Hencken (1932) 222, 224-5, 296.
Jenkin (1934) 29.
Macalister (1945) no. 479, pp. 457-8 & fig.
Thomas, I. (1947) 53-4, 62, 82.
Beckerlegge (1953) 173-7 & fig.
Jackson (1953) 168n, 188, 329.
Thomas, A.C. (1953) 125-30.
Thomas, A.C. (1957-8) 61.
Thomas, A.C. (1958) 33.
Best (1959) 438-9.
Thomas, A.C. (1961) 8-9, 13.
Fox (1964) 158-9.
(-) (1966) 51.
Thomas, A.C. (1967) 44.
Wall (1968) 176.
Pevsner (1970) 15, 172.
Radford (1971) 8.
Thomas, A.C. (1971*a*) 106 & fig.
Thomas, A.C. (1971*b*) 99, 106 & fig.

Appleby (1975) 112.
Laing (1975) 138.
Radford (1975) 4-5, 7.
Pearce (1978) 21-30, 66, 161, 178.
Pearce (1981) 169.
Thomas, A.C. (1981) 271-2 & fig.
Morris, R. (1983) 32.
Thomas, A.C. (1985*b*) 173.
Preston-Jones & Rose (1986) 155.
Thomas, A.C. (1986) 140 & fig.
Todd (1987) 249-50 & fig.

17 Indian Queens

The stone is now in the front garden of Indian Queens church. National Grid Reference SW 9162 5912. Examined 6 July 1984.

History

The stone was first mentioned in 1754 by W. Borlase; it was then 'about four miles East of Michel'.[1] It was still there in 1824,[2] and may have been also in 1842.[3] In 1859 Haigh said the stone was 'four miles from E. Michel';[4] this looks like a corruption of Borlase's statement and is not firm evidence as to the stone's location at that date. In August 1872 the stone was described as, 'In the vicinity of the inn', that is, the Indian Queen Inn.[5] It was then stated that the stone had 'been long lost sight of, [but] had lately been rediscovered by Mr. Iago'.[6] C.G. Henderson stated that when the stone was near the inn it marked the boundary between the parishes of St Columb and St Enoder,[7] but W.J. Stephens found no evidence of its having been a boundary stone.[8] In 1906 Langdon stated that the stone 'has been used as a gatepost', although neither he nor anyone else had mentioned this previously;[9] there is, however, a modern hole on the inscribed face. In 1930 Henderson noted that the stone would soon have to be moved 'on account of a road-widening scheme'.[10] Some years later, however, when the road was widened, the stone was left 'in the pathway, where it was an obstruction and in danger of damage'.[11] On 15 February 1939 it was moved about 0.8 km. into 'the enclosure of the Church of St. Francis',[12] that is, to its present position.

1. Borlase, W. (1754) 364.
2. Hitchins (1824) I, 446.
3. Redding (1842) 57n. Redding did not state that he had seen the stone.
4. Haigh (1858-9) 184.
5. (-) (1871-3*a*) xxvii.
6. (-) (1871-3*a*) xxvii.
7. Henderson, C.G. (1930) 68.
8. Stephens, W.J. (1939) 247.
9. Langdon (1906) 419.
10. Henderson, C.G. (1930) 69n.
11. Stephens, W.J. (1939) 247.
12. Stephens, W.J. (1939) 247.

Figure II.17 Indian Queens (photograph Woolf/Greenham Collection).

Description

The stone is a pillar-stone, complete and uncarved (fig. II.17). It measures 165 cm. in height, 35 to 50 cm. in width and 28 to 33 cm. in thickness.

Hitchins described the stone as 'about six feet high',[13] that is *c.* 180 cm., suggesting that only a small portion of the stone is now below ground level. The text is incised without framing-lines or panels on one face of the stone and appears to be primary. There is a modern hole on the same face. The letters measure 5.5 to 9 cm. and are very highly deteriorated; it is not even certain what script was used. The text, which may well be incomplete, is set in one line reading downwards and facing left.

Text

[C-VI.C-]

Discussion

The letter preceding the final C could be R. The text could then be read, [C-VIRC-] but is so deteriorated as to be unintelligible. W. Borlase's drawing and discussion suggest a reading, RVANI HIC IACIT, although he admitted, 'the letters are much worn, especially the second'.[14] The second letter is virtually illegible on his drawing. This reading was followed by most commentators until 1875 when Rhys said, 'to judge from its present state, the inscription may have been anything you please' although his 'own guess' was, [-]MAGLI HIC[-].[15] Langdon and Allen read only a few letters: 'only VA, or perhaps M, are now distinguishable'.[16] Macalister, however, read, CRVARIGI HI, and took the last two letters as the beginning of HIC IACIT.[17] In the light of the earlier evidence, Macalister's reading must be treated with caution. In my view the original text is not now recoverable.

The stone belongs to Category 1a, pillar-stones with a simple memorial text. Category 1 stones date from the fifth or sixth centuries to the eleventh century but this stone cannot be more closely dated.

Bibliography

Borlase, W. (1754) 364 & fig.
Polwhele (1803) II, 199-200.
Lysons, D. & Lysons, S. (1814) ccxxiii.
Hitchins (1824) I, 446-7.
Redding (1842) 57n.
Haigh (1858-9) 184, 191.
Brash (1869) 167n.
Iago *et al.* (1871-3) xlvi.

---

13. Hitchins (1824) I, 466.
14. Borlase, W. (1754) 364 & fig.
15. Rhys (1875) 366.
16. Langdon & Allen, J.R. (1895) 55.
17. Macalister (1945) 453.

(-) (1871-3*a*) xxvii.
Rhys (1875) 366.
Huebner (1876) no. 11, p. 4 & fig.
Brash (1879) 404.
Langdon & Allen, J.R. (1888) 306-8, 318.
Borlase, W.C. (1893) 183-4.
Langdon & Allen, J.R. (1895) 51, 55, 60.
Daniell (1906) 240.
Langdon (1906) 419, *passim* & fig.
Macalister (1929) 183-4 & fig.
Henderson, C.G. (1930) 55, 68-9.
Hencken (1932) 222, 295.
Jenkin (1934) 29.
Stephens, W.J. (1939) 247.
Macalister (1945) no. 474, pp. 452-3 & fig.
Nash-Williams (1950) 11n.
(-) (1966) 51.

18 Lancarffe

The stone is now built into the wall of a summer-house in the garden of Lancarffe, Bodmin. National Grid Reference SX 0828 6895. Examined 8 July 1984.

History

The stone was known to a Mr Dunn of Lancarffe from around 1912, lying in the bed of a stream. In 1928 the stone was removed to Bodmin but Mr Dunn recovered it and had it built into a new wall in the garden of Lancarffe house.[1] During one of these removals the stone was broken into two. This wall is probably the same one in which the stone is now set. Hencken, Pevsner and Weatherhill all refer to the stone's being built into the wall of an out-building of a farm, but there is no evidence that the stone was ever moved from Lancarffe garden.[2]

Description

The stone is set into a wall and the visible face is uncarved (fig. II.18). It is probably complete but is broken into two pieces. Originally it was probably an erect pillar-stone measuring 187 cm. in height and 19 to 25 cm. in width. The text is incised without framing-lines or panels on the visible face, the letters measuring 5.5 to 8 cm. in height. The text is legible and complete and appears to be primary. It is in two lines and originally it probably read downwards facing left, *see* Introduction, Section 4c. The text is in a predominantly capital script.

Text

DVNO[.]ATIHICIACIT
F/ILIME[.]CAGNI

1. Jenner & Henderson, C.G. (1929-32) 212.
2. Hencken (1932) 241, 292; Pevsner (1970) 44; Weatherhill (1985) 73.

Figure II.18 Lancarffe (photograph Woolf/Greenham Collection).

Discussion

The text reads, DVNO[.]ATI HIC IACIT FILI ME[.]CAGNI, probably, 'here lies [the body] of Duno[.]atus, son of Me[.]cagnus' with IACIT for IACET and FILI for FILII. Macalister read the names as DVNOCATI and MERCAGNI.[3] These readings are perfectly possible although the second could equally well be ME[S]CAGNI with the [S] set sideways. Jackson adopted the latter reading and took both names as Primitive Irish.[4] Padel, however, considered that DVNO[C]ATI could be Primitive Welsh/Cornish since its descendant, *Dincat*, occurs in the Llandaff Charters.[5] DVNOCATI occurs on a stone from Crickhowell, Wales.[6]

The Lancarffe stone belongs to Category 1b, pillar stones with a longer text. Category 1 stones date from the fifth or sixth centuries to the eleventh century; the Primitive Irish names (or name) suggest a date from the fifth or sixth century to the eighth century for this stone, a date which the use of horizontal I probably corroborates.

3. Macalister (1945) 435.
4. Jackson (1953) 171-2, 319. See also O'Brien (1973) 224-5.
5. Oliver Padel, in a personal communication. *Dincat* is a witness to Charter 203a; Davies (1979) 116, 160.
6. Macalister (1945) no. 327, pp. 314-16 & fig.; Nash-Williams (1950) no. 43, p. 69 & figs.

Bibliography

Jenner (1929) 378-9 & fig.
Macalister (1929) 184.
Jenner & Henderson, C.G. (1929-32) 210-12 & fig.
Hencken (1932) 241, 292.
Jenkin (1934) 30.
Macalister (1945) no. 457, pp. 435-6 & fig.
Jackson (1946) 523.
Nash-Williams (1950) 11n.
Jackson (1953) 171-2, 187-8, 319.
Fox (1964) 159.
(-) (1966) 50.
Evans (1967) 174, 210.
Pevsner (1970) 44.
Pearce (1978) 27, 162.[7]
Thomas, A.C. (1985*b*) 174.
Weatherhill (1985) 73 & fig.
Preston-Jones & Rose (1986) 157.
McManus (1991) 62, 93.

---

7. Pearce noted a stone from 'Bodmin' whose description suggests that the Lancarffe stone may have been intended.

19 Lanhadron

The stone is now in a hedgerow on Nunnery Hill near Lanhadron Farm, St Ewe. It is on the right-hand side of the unclassified St Ewe to Polgooth road, and is protected by an iron railing. National Grid Reference SW 9895 4785. Examined 3 July 1984.

History

The present stone is likely to be the base of the one described by one of Polwhele's correspondents in 1803: 'In the parish of St. Ewe there is a stone, which was erected perpendicularly in the midst of another square stone evidently placed there to receive it. It stands on a little bank contiguous to a common road'.[1] Both cross and base were said to be inscribed; Polwhele's correspondent described the text on the cross as 'too much obliterated to be decyphered' and the base as containing 'many characters, which are quite legible, but unknown to me'.[2] C.G. Henderson noted that on a map of the parish, printed in 1839, Lanhadron Cross was shown by the side of the road on top of Nunnery Hill.[3]

In 1880 Iago described the existing stone, that is, the base, thus: 'It lies on the brow of Nunnery Hill, sheltered by a hedge and almost wholly buried in the ground'; this description is confirmed by his illustration.[4] The base was unearthed for Iago's examination and then covered over again.[5] Subsequently it was unearthed, perhaps in 1895, since it was described then as 'By the road-side, on Nunnery Hill, buried in a hedge'.[6] At some time before 1929 it was surrounded by an iron railing.[7] The base remains in this position (fig. II.19(i)).

The cross-head and shaft were mentioned in a letter of July 1873 from T. Stephens to a Mr Roberts.[8] In this letter the cross was said to have been thrown down by a farmer looking for buried money. The letter added: 'Before my remembrance part of the pillar had been taken away, and also the cross that stood on the top of it'.[9] Neither cross-head nor shaft have

---

1. Quoted in Polwhele (1803) II, 199n-200n.
2. Quoted in Polwhele (1803) II, 200n.
3. Henderson, C.G. (1953-6b) 163; Henderson gave no further details and I have been unable to trace this map.
4. Iago (1878-81) 398 & fig.
5. Iago (1878-81) 398, 400.
6. Langdon & Allen, J.R. (1895) 51.
7. Macalister (1929) 184.
8. Quoted in Iago (1878-81) 398.
9. Quoted in Iago (1878-81) 398.

Figure II.19(i) Lanhadron (photograph Woolf/Greenham Collection).

been mentioned in print since then. The only drawing of what is presumably the cross-shaft is preserved in an eighteenth-century manuscript which belonged to J. Anstis[10] (fig. II.19(ii)). Some of the drawings are by Lhwyd but the one of Lanhadron is not certainly attributable to him. The drawing shows the Lanhadron cross-base and beside it a vertical column containing lettering. This is presumably the cross-shaft text.

Description

The existing stone is a complete, uncarved cross-base measuring 116 by 116 cm.; the socket to contain the cross measures 33 by 47 cm. The text is incised on the visible face within margins formed by lines incised around the socket. Three margins on each side are thus formed, the text being set in the middle margin which is *c.* 13 cm. in height. The letters measure 6 to 7 cm. in height and are set anti-clockwise around the stone, facing outwards. The text may have been complete but it is now too highly deteriorated to be certain. The script used is a predominantly insular one and the text is primary.

---

10. BL MS Stowe 1023, p. 47 (renumbered as p. 29). I am grateful to Professor A.C. Thomas for bringing this manuscript to my attention.

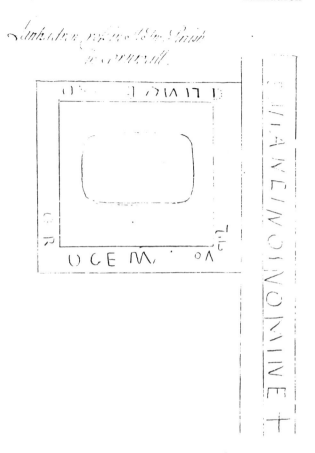

Figure II.19(ii)   Lanhadron (photograph BL MS Stowe 1023, p. 47, renumbered as p. 29, photograph by permission of the British Library).

Text

[LU...E-]
[-CR]
VCEM[+]
[-]

Discussion

The text reads, [LU...E-] [CR]VCEM [+-], the only complete and legible word being [CR]VCEM. The earliest drawing of the text is in the eighteenth-century manuscript mentioned above; this shows the text in a state similar to today.[11] The drawing published by Iago in 1880 shows the text in a condition only a little better than that of today.[12] Iago said: 'Most of the letters are much abraded, but a few of them are quite legible ... The word "Crucem" is quite clear'.[13] In spite of his drawing, and of these cautious words, Iago read the text as, ALSUE CURAVIT H' CRUCEM P' ANIMA SUA.[14] In 1888 Langdon and Allen read, ALSNE CURAVIT HANC CRUCEM PRO ANIMA SUA,[15] but in 1895 they read only, [-]CRUCEM[-].[16] Macalister read, LURATECUS FECIT CRVCEM + PRO ANIMA SUA.[17] In view of the evidence of the eighteenth-century drawing and of Iago's drawing and comments, the complete text is not now recoverable. The eighteenth-century drawing suggests that the text of the cross-shaft read vertically downwards with the letters facing left as: EMIANCINOINOMINE +. This text may have ended, - NOMINE +, but the rest cannot be reconstructed with any certainty.

The existing stone belongs to Category 2b, inscribed cross-bases. Category 2 stones date from the ninth to the eleventh century but this stone cannot be more closely dated.

Bibliography

Polwhele (1803) II, 199n-200n.
Iago (1878-81) 397-401 & figs.
Langdon & Allen, J.R. (1888) 313, 318.
Langdon & Allen, J.R. (1895) 51, 57, 60.
Hammond (1897) 279.
Daniell (1906) 241.
Langdon (1906) 420, *passim* & fig.
Henderson, C.G. (1925) 65.
Macalister (1929) 184-5 & fig.
Hencken (1932) 280-1, 297.
Benyon *et al.* (1937) 24-5, 88 & fig.
Macalister (1945) no. 480, pp. 458-9 & fig.
Henderson, C.G. (1953-6*b*) 163.
Sheppard (1967) 99.
Pool (1977) 140.
Higgitt (1986) 141.
Baird & White (unpub. 1961) vol. IV, D-G.[18]

---

11. BL MS Stowe 1023, p. 47 (renumbered as p. 29) & figs.
12. Iago (1878-81) 397-401 & figs.
13. Iago (1878-81) 399.
14. Iago (1878-81) 399.
15. Langdon & Allen, J.R. (1888) 313. On the same page they also gave the reading PREPARAVIT for CURAVIT.
16. Langdon & Allen, J.R. (1895) 57; there is no figure.
17. Macalister (1929) 184 & fig.; the word PRO is abbreviated.
18. There is no page numbering in this typescript.

20 Lanherne

The stone stands in the grounds of Lanherne Carmelite Nunnery, St Mawgan, outside a door to the chapel. National Grid Reference SW 8721 6592. Examined 6 July 1984.

History

The stone was first recorded in 1814 by Lysons and Lysons who stated that it 'originally stood in the Chapel-close of the barton of Roseworthy, in the parish of Gwinnear, from whence it was removed, some years since, to the garden of Lord Arundell's mansion-house, at Lanherne, where it now stands'.[1] In 1820 C.S. Gilbert stated that the cross had been moved to Lanherne 'a few years ago'.[2] In 1794 Lord Arundell gave the Manor of Lanherne to the Carmelite nuns, so the stone is likely to have been moved there before this date. Rickard gave the view of E. Rosevear that the stone was moved to Lanherne in medieval times;[3] in view of the evidence of Gilbert and of Lysons and Lysons, this seems unlikely. The stone has remained inside the nunnery garden since it was taken there.

Description

The stone is a cross, carved and complete except for a small portion of the cross-head. It is in a base, presumably modern, which is fixed into the ground.[4] It measures 151 cm. in height to the base, the shaft measuring 24 to 27 cm. in width and 17 to 20 cm. in thickness. Text (i) is incised without framing-lines but in a panel on the face of the stone at the bottom of the shaft (fig. II.20(i)). The panel measures 40.5 cm. in height by 21.5 cm. and the letters measure 3.5 to 8.5 cm. in height. Text (i) is complete and legible and is set in four lines reading horizontally. The space beneath the letters does not seem to have contained further text.

Text (ii) is incised without framing-lines but in a panel on the back of the stone at the bottom of the shaft (fig. II.20(ii)). The panel measures 28 cm. in height by 23 cm. and the letters measure 4 to 8 cm. in height. The text is

1. Lysons, D. & Lysons, S. (1814) ccxlv.
2. Gilbert, C.S. (1820) 700.
3. Rickard (1978-81) 168-9.
4. No base is mentioned in Langdon (1896) 357-9 & figs.

Figure II.20(i) Lanherne, text (i) (photograph
Woolf/Greenham Collection).

complete and legible and is set in two lines reading horizontally. The space
beneath the letters does not seem to have contained further text although
traces of what might have been a cross are visible. Both texts are primary
and both use a predominantly insular script.

Figure II.20(ii) Lanherne, text (ii) (photograph Woolf/
Greenham Collection).

Texts

(i)   + BRE
         ID[.I]
         MA
         H

(ii)   RŪ
         HOL

Discussion

Text (i) appears to read, + BREID [.I]MAH, although BSEID is equally possible. The lost letter could be B, E, R or perhaps E/T. Iago, reading + BS, suggested that this was a contraction for *beatus* and the text was therefore to be read, +B(EATUS) EID ET IMAH, that is, 'The Blessed Eid and Imah'.[5] This reading has been followed by many commentators although Macalister expressed doubt: 'the peculiarity of the names makes this open to question'.[6] The names are indeed peculiar; nor can I parallel the abbreviation +BS for *beatus*, although Lindsay noted *bi* and *běa*, both for *beati*.[7] The text may contain one or more personal names, perhaps BREID followed by E/T, Latin *et*, and [I]MAH. Such names are of unknown origin, unless [I]MAH is connected with the Irish *Imchadh*.[8] The name *Bredei* occurs in the *Pictish King-list*, a name taken by Jackson to be non-Celtic.[9]

Text (ii) reads RŪHOL, presumably for a name RUNHOL. The name probably contains Celtic *run-*,[10] since Old English *run-* is not certainly recorded as a first name-element.[11] A similar name was read on Sancreed II but that text is now highly deteriorated. Langdon stated that Iago conjectured that RUNHOL was the name of the carver of both crosses,[12] but this conjecture must be treated with great caution.[13]

The stone belongs to Category 2a, inscribed cross-shafts. Category 2 stones date from the ninth to the eleventh century; this stone is dated to the tenth or the eleventh century on artistic grounds.

---

5. Quoted in Langdon (1889a) 321.
6. Macalister (1949) 179.
7. Lindsay (1915) 421.
8. Jackson (1953) 173; O'Brien (1973) 225.
9. Jackson (1955) 143-4.
10. Cf. *Rúngal*: O'Brien (1973) 224.
11. The name *runstan* is recorded on a coin of Cnut, but Smart took this as 'probably an error for BRVNSTAN'; Smart (1981) 64.
12. Langdon (1896) 365.
13. See below, Entry 54, Sancreed II.

Bibliography

Lysons, D. & Lysons, S. (1814) ccxlv & figs.
Gilbert, C.S. (1820) 700.
Penaluna (1838) II, 75.
Hingston (1850) no. 18 & figs.[14]
Collins (1851) 275.
(-) (1851*b*) 190.
(-) (1856) 204.
Blight (1858*a*) 31 & figs.
Polsue (1870) 294 & fig. opp. p. vi.
Iago (1870-3) 484-5 & figs.
Iago *et al.* (1871-3) xlvi.
(-) (1871-3*a*) xxix.
Rhys (1875) 366-7.
Huebner (1876) no. 6, pp. 2-3 & figs.
Iago (1878-81) 399.
(-) (1886-9) 110-11.
Langdon & Allen, J.R. (1888) 312-13, 317.
Allen, J.R. (1889) 217, 222.
Langdon (1889*a*) 319, 320-1 & figs.
Langdon (1889*c*) 239-40 & figs.
Langdon (1890-1) 35 & *passim.*
Borlase, W.C. (1893) 107, 183-5.
Langdon (1894*b*) 315.
Langdon & Allen, J.R. (1895) 51, 57, 60 & figs.
Langdon (1896) 357-9, 365, *passim* & figs.
Daniell (1906) 244.
Langdon (1906) 419, *passim* & figs.
Henderson, C.G. (1925) 78.
Macalister (1929) 184.
Hencken (1932) 270, 276, 303.
Jenkin (1934) 32.
Dexter, T.F.G. & Dexter, H. (1938) 223-4 & figs.
Macalister (1949) no. 1047, pp. 178-9, 186 & figs.
Henderson, C.G. (1953-6*b*) 200.
Henderson, C.G. (1957-60*a*) 342.
Thomas, A.C. (1967) 104.
Pevsner (1970) 17, 116, 207 & fig.
Pearce (1978) 108, 178.
Sheppard (1978) 122.
Thomas, A.C. (1978) 78 & figs.
Rickard (1978-81) 168-9.
Pearce (1981) 216, 270 & fig.
Weatherhill (1981) 73.
Higgitt (1986) 141.
Preston-Jones & Rose (1986) 159.
Todd (1987) 296 & figs.

14. There is no page numbering in this book.

21 Lanivet

The stone is now inside Lanivet church, at the west end of the nave. National Grid Reference SX 0393 6420. Examined 9 July 1984 and 5 July 1985.

History

The stone was first mentioned in 1872 when it was 'In the wall of an old thatched cottage near the parish schoolroom' in Lanivet village.[1] It was then upside down and in two pieces.[2] In 1888 the stone was still in the wall,[3] but by 1895 it was 'Lying in the churchyard, in two pieces, by south porch'.[4] Langdon recorded it there in 1906 adding that the house where it had been found was 'near west end of church'.[5] In 1925 C.G. Henderson recorded the stone in the church;[6] Hencken was presumably in error in stating in 1932 that it was in the churchyard.[7]

Description

The stone is an incomplete pillar-stone containing no carving (fig. II.21). It is set in a modern base which is cemented to the floor. The stone measures 96 cm. in height to the base, 24 to 31 cm. in width and 22 to 34 cm. in thickness. The text is incised without framing-lines but inside a panel on one face of the stone. The panel measures 81 cm. by 16 to 19 cm. The text is slightly deteriorated and incomplete. The letters measure 8 to 12 cm. in height and are set in one line reading downwards and facing left. When I examined the stone in 1984 the letters had recently been chalked in. The text appears to be primary and is in a predominantly capital script.

1. Polsue (1872) vii.
2. Iago (1870–3) 486.
3. Langdon & Allen, J.R. (1888) 316.
4. Langdon & Allen, J.R. (1895) 51.
5. Langdon (1906) 416.
6. Henderson, C.G. (1925) 105.
7. Hencken (1932) 224.

Figure II.21 Lanivet (photograph Royal Commission on the Historical Monuments of England).

Text

A̲N̲N̲I̲C̲V
[F̲/I̲L-]

Discussion

The text reads, ANNICV [F/IL-], that is, 'Annicu [son]-'. The name is probably Latin and could be intended as either nominative or genitive. A stone from Abercar, Wales, contains the name [.]NNICCI in the genitive, which Nash-Williams suggested might be the same name.[8]

The Lanivet stone belongs to Category 1a, pillar-stones with a simple memorial text. Category 1 stones date from the fifth or sixth centuries to the eleventh century; the Latin name suggests a sixth- to eighth-century date for this stone.

Bibliography

Iago (1870-3) 486-7 & fig.
Iago *et al.* (1871-3) xlvi.
Polsue (1872) vii.
Iago (1874-8) 364n.
Huebner (1876) no. 18, p. 7 & fig.
Rhys (1879) 402-3.
Langdon & Allen, J.R. (1888) 307, 316.
Borlase, W.C. (1893) 183-4.
Langdon & Allen, J.R. (1895) 51, 55, 60 & fig.
Holder (1896) col. 157.
Langdon (1896) 23.
Daniell (1906) 241.
Langdon (1906) 416, *passim* & fig.
Henderson, C.G. (1925) 105.
Macalister (1929) 184.
Hencken (1932) 224, 300.
Macalister (1945) no. 465, p. 442 & fig.
Nash-Williams (1950) 69n.
(-) (1966) 50.
Pevsner (1970) 91.
Pearce (1978) 71, 179.
Morris, R. (1983) 25.
Weatherhill (1985) 73 & fig.
Todd (1987) 250.

---

8. Macalister (1945) no. 331, pp. 319-21 & fig.; Nash-Williams (1950) no. 41, p. 69 & figs.

22 Lanteglos

The stone is now in Lanteglos churchyard, near the south door of the church. National Grid Reference SX 0882 8233. Examined 15 July 1964, 30 September 1965, 10 July 1984, and 4 July 1985.

History

The stone was first recorded by Blight in 1858 at Lanteglos: 'This stone now props the side wall of an old barn'.[1] It was still in a farmyard on 'Castle Gough' estate in 1870,[2] but by 1875 was in 'the Rectory garden'.[3] In 1876 Maclean stated that the stone had 'recently been purchased by the Rev. J.J. Wilkinson, and set up in the Rectory grounds'.[4] Langdon recorded that 'about the year 1877' an uninscribed cross-head 'was fixed in its present incongruous position, on top of the Saxon inscribed stone which stands a few yards from the pond' in the Rectory garden.[5] This was also noted by G.F. Browne, in a letter to G. Stephens dated 27 November 1891;[6] the cross-head was presumably soon removed since it was not mentioned in 1895, nor in 1896 when the inscribed stone was described in detail.[7] In 1900 the stone was moved to its present position in the church-yard.[8] It is possible that this stone was the one noted (according to Iago) by Borlase 'about a mile west of Camelford, in the high road'.[9] Maclean recorded the tradition that the inscribed stone's original site had been 'near the earthworks at Castlegoff'; he continued: 'it is said that its base, with the socket therein, remained in situ within living memory, though now lost'.[10] The inscribed stone, being a pillar-stone, is unlikely ever to have stood in a base. A comparison of the descriptions given by Borlase and Maclean may, however, suggest that they were independently referring to the stone's original site.

1. Blight (1858a) 126.
2. Polsue (1870) 57.
3. Rhys (1875) 363.
4. Maclean (1876) 281.
5. Langdon (1896) 169.
6. Stephens, G. (1901) 101.
7. Langdon & Allen, J.R. (1895) 51, 58 & figs; (-) (1896a) 146-8.
8. Langdon (1906) 416. Information given in the church puts this date as 1907, presumably in error.
9. Iago (1890-1) 188, quoting 'Borlase MSS. Inscriptions, p. 89'. I cannot locate this reference.
10. Maclean (1876) 281.

Figure II.22(i)   Lanteglos, face (photograph Royal Commission on the Historical Monuments of England).

Figure II.22(ii) Lanteglos, left-hand side (photograph Woolf/Greenham Collection).

Description

The stone is a pillar-stone, complete and uncarved. It measures 222 cm. in height, 35 to 45 cm. in width and 16 to 20 cm. in thickness. Comparison with Blight's measurements suggests that some 20 cm. are now beneath the ground.[11] The text is probably complete, though rather deteriorated, and is incised without framing-lines or panels. The first two lines and the fourth are incised on one face of the stone (fig. II.22(i)) and, assuming this to be the face, the third line is incised on the left-hand side (fig. II.22(ii)). The letters, 7 to 10 cm. in height, all read downwards facing left. The text appears to be primary and is a predominantly capital script.

Text

ÆLSEL[.] 7 GENE[RE.]
[-E]ÞYS[.ESY–EL]
FORÆLWYNEY[SS.]UL 7[.OR]HEY
[-]

Discussion

The text now reads, + ÆLSEL[.] 7 GENE[RE.] [-E] ÞYS[.E] [SY-EL] FOR ÆLWYNEY[S] [S.]UL 7 [.OR] HEY[-]. The text has deteriorated since I first read it in July 1964.[12] Using both these readings, a text can be reconstructed: + ÆLSEL[Ð] 7 GENE[REÐ] [W]O[H]TE ÞYS[N]E [S]YB[STEL] FOR ÆLWYNEYS S[O]UL 7 [F]OR HEY[SEL], that is, ' + Aelsel[ð] and Gene[reð] made this ?family-stone [*or* ?place of peace] for Aelwine's soul and for ?themselves [*or* ?Hey[sel]]'. The language appears to be early Middle English but containing some odd forms. [W]O[H]TE is used for *worhte* or *worhton* in a position where a plural verb would be expected. [S]YB[STEL] is unrecorded but [S]YB- could be from Old English *sibb* 'relationship; peace' and [STEL] from Old English *steall* 'place' or *stela* 'support, stone'.[13] S[O]UL has no inflexional ending. HEY[SEL] could be an unrecorded, and curious, form of Middle English *he self* in a plural form, or it could be explained as an unrecorded name with HEY- from Old English *hyge-* and -[SEL] from Old English *-selð*.[14] The names AELSEL[Ð], AELWYNEYS and GENE[REÐ] can be explained although they look unusual:[15] AEL- appears in Domesday Book as a spelling of Old English

---

11. Blight (1858*a*) 126.
12. See Okasha (1971) no. 69, pp. 90-1. This published reading contains the error AELWYNES for AELWYNEYS.
13. Cf. Aelfric's *Se cinestôl stynt on þisum þrîm stelum*; Grein (1872) 20, line 18.
14. *Seld-* is however, to my knowledge, only recorded as a first name-element.
15. The forms of these names, and also of HEY[SEL], are obtained by combining my earlier and later readings.

aelf-, *ae͡ðel-*, *eald-*;[16] SEL[Đ] could be from Old English *-selð* (*see* above); -WYNEYS could be a form of the well-recorded Old English name element *-wine*, genitive singular *-wines*; and GENE[REÐ] could be a late spelling of the Old English name *eanred*, cf. Domesday Book *genred*.[17]

The stone belongs to Category 1b, pillar-stones with a longer text. Category 1 stones date from the fifth or sixth centuries to the eleventh century. On linguistic grounds this stone is unlikely to date from before the eleventh century. The use of English names is in accordance with this date.

Bibliography

Blight (1858*a*) 126 & fig.
Haddan & Stubbs (1869) 163.
Polsue (1870) 57.
Rhys (1875) 363-4.
Huebner (1876) no. 16, pp. 5-6, 89 & fig.
Maclean (1876) 281-2 & fig.
Iago (1878-81) 401.
Smith, W. & Cheetham (1880) 1978.
Iago (1883-5*a*) 278n.
Langdon & Allen, J.R. (1888) 313, 317.
Allen, J.R. (1889) 221.
Iago (1890-1) 188-9.
Langdon (1890-1) 91.
Borlase, W.C. (1893) 107, 185.
Langdon & Allen, J.R. (1895) 51, 58, 60 & figs.
Langdon (1896) 22, 169.
(-) (1896*a*) 146-8 & figs.
Stephens, G. (1901) 101-2 & figs.
Daniell (1906) 242.
Langdon (1906) 416, *passim* & figs.
Henderson, C.G. (1925) 109.
Macalister (1929) 184.
Hencken (1932) 265, 301.
Macalister (1945) 442-3.
Ellis, G.E. (1956-8*b*) 133-4.
Pevsner (1970) 94.
Okasha (1971) no. 69, pp. 90-1 & figs.
Ellis, P.B. (1974) 25.
Weatherhill (1985) 26, 74 & figs.
Todd (1987) 251.

16. Cf. Feilitzen (1937) 142 under *Al-*.
17. Feilitzen (1937) 118.

23 Lewannick I

The stone is now in Lewannick churchyard, to the west of the lych-gate. National Grid Reference SW 2759 8068. Examined 30 June 1984 and 6 July 1986.

History

The stone was found by Langdon on 7 June 1892 'on the south side of the churchyard, near a large tree'.[1] The stone was then 'apparently deeply buried'.[2] The stone has remained in the churchyard since it was found.

Description

The stone is an uncarved pillar-stone, slightly broken (fig. II.23). It now measures 122 cm. in height and 38 to 40 cm. in width with the broken thickness varying between 13 and 23 cm. When Langdon found the stone he gave its height as four feet (c. 120 cm.) above the ground and at least one and a half feet (c. 45 cm.) below.[3] This suggests that at least 43 cm. are now beneath the ground. Text (i) is incised without framing-lines or panels on the face of the stone. It is incomplete and highly deteriorated and the script is uncertain. The letters, 5 to 8 cm. in height, are set in four lines reading horizontally. This text appears to be primary. Text (ii), the ogham text, is incised vertically on the edge between the face and the left-hand side of the stone. This text is presumably primary but is now illegible. It is not now possible to be certain whether this text is complete or incomplete nor whether it reads upwards or downwards.

Texts

(i) [I]N[.EN]
     [.]VI[-]
     [MEM]
     [O..A]|
(ii) [ogham]: this text is now illegible.

---

1. Langdon (1892b) 251. The find was reported in the *Launceston Weekly News* on the Thursday preceding 27 June 1892.
2. Langdon (1892b) 251.
3. Langdon (1892b) 251.

Figure II.23 Lewannick I (photograph Royal Commission on the Historical Monuments of England).

Discussion

Text (i) probably reads, [I]N[.EN.]VI [-] [MEMO..A] with about two letters lost in the middle. It must be concluded to be virtually illegible. Langdon published drawings of the texts in several places.[4] Langdon described text (i) as 'quite distinct' and read it, INCENVI MEMORIA.[5] In 1929 Macalister said he had 'verified' Langdon's reading,[6] but by 1945 he admitted that it (whether he meant stone or text is uncertain) was 'in very bad condition';[7] nevertheless his drawing showed substantially the same text as Langdon's and he read INGENVI MEMORIA.[8] The traces of lettering surviving today are consistent with Langdon's reading. In view, however, of Macalister's comment, the text seems to have been in a deteriorated condition for many years. It cannot be reconstructed today with any certainty. Theories built upon the reading MEMORIA must therefore be treated with caution. Pearce, for example, translating MEMORIA as 'memorial shrine', said: 'it implies a grave which was the focus of pious observance',[9] while Bu'lock suggested the MEMORIA formula on this stone, as on others outside the south-west, was of North African origin.[10] Jackson, following the reading INGENVI, took this as a form of a Latin name *Ingenuus*,[11] but this reading also is far from certain. The feminine name INGENVA probably occurred on a Gaulish stone from Treves.[12] The name INGENVI is common and occurs on a Romano-British stone from Chester,[13] and probably on a stone from Llandanwg, Wales, although this reading is also uncertain.[14]

Text (ii) is now illegible. Langdon read it as, IGENAVI MEMOR, describing it as 'merely a repetition of the Latin legend'; his drawing supports this reading.[15] There are no early drawings other than Langdon's and his reading has been followed by almost all other commentators. McManus took text (i) as the primary text, text (ii) as a copy.[16] The lack of any early independent drawing of text (ii), along with its present illegibility, means that it cannot be reconstructed with any certainty, nor used as the basis for linguistic dating.[17]

---

4. For example, in Langdon (1892*b*) 251-2 & fig., in Langdon (1906) fig. 1, etc.
5. Langdon (1892*b*) 251.
6. Macalister (1929) 179.
7. Macalister (1945) 443.
8. Macalister (1945) 444.
9. Pearce (1981) 187.
10. Bu'lock (1956) 141.
11. Jackson (1953) 172, 175, 183, 366.
12. Le Blant (1856) no. 265, pp. 373-4 & fig. Only a portion of the stone was still in existence in 1856.
13. Collingwood, R.G. & Wright, R.P. (1965) no. 544, p. 181 & fig.
14. Macalister (1945) no. 416 (*recte* 415), pp. 392-3 & fig.; Nash-Williams (1950) no. 278, pp. 9, 169. Macalister gave a tentative reading of INTAENVI while Nash-Williams read IN[G(?)]ENVI.
15. Langdon (1892*b*) 251-2 & fig., quotation from p. 251. Langdon's drawing and reading were published many times; see Bibliography.
16. McManus (1991) 63.
17. Cf. Jackson (1953) 183.

The stone belongs to Category 1b, pillar-stones with a longer text. Category 1 stones date from the fifth or sixth centuries to the eleventh century. On the evidence of the ogham text, this stone is likely to date from the fifth or sixth to the eighth century. If the name were INGENVI, Latin *ingenuus*, this would corroborate a sixth- to eighth-century date for the stone.

Bibliography

Iago (1891-3) 214-15, & fig.
Langdon (1892*a*) 336-9 & fig.
Langdon (1892*b*) 251-2 & fig.
Langdon (1892-3) 285-8 & fig.
Borlase, W.C. (1893) 106-7.[18]
Iago (1893-5*b*) 173-4.
Iago *et al.* (1893-5) 119-21.
Langdon (1893-5*a*) 169.
Langdon (1893-5*b*) 280.
Langdon (1894*a*) 108-10 & fig.
Langdon (1894*b*) 315.
Langdon & Allen, J.R. (1895) 51, 53, 60 & fig.
(-) (1896*b*) 245-6, 248-51 & figs.
(-) (1897) 123.
Rhys (1905) 89.
Daniell (1906) 242.
Langdon (1906) 416, *passim* & figs.
Sedding (1909) 233-4.
Jenner (1922-5) 57-8.
Henderson, C.G. (1925) 119.
Hull (1926) 37-8.
Macalister (1929) 179.
Hencken (1932) 223, 226-7, 301 & fig.
Jenkin (1934) 29-30.
Macalister (1945) no. 466, pp. 443-4 & fig.
Jackson (1950) 199, 205, 208.
Nash-Williams (1950) 107n.
Jackson (1953) 141, 171-2, 175, 183, 366, 620n, 622.
Bu'lock (1956) 141.
Fox (1964) 160.
(-) (1966) 50.
Thomas, A.C. (1969-72) 259n.
Pevsner (1970) 101.
Thomas, A.C. (1971*a*) 107 & fig.
Thomas, A.C. (1971*b*) 103-6 & fig.
Laing (1975) 125.
Radford (1975) 5-8, 13.
Pearce (1978) 21-30, 68, 71, 89, 157, 161-2, 180 & fig.
Pearce (1981) 172, 186-8, 270.
Thomas, A.C. (1981) 79, 298.
Morris, R. (1983) 31.
Pearce (1985) 257-9.
Weatherhill (1985) 75 & fig.
Preston-Jones & Rose (1986) 155, 157.
Todd (1987) 250 & fig.
McManus (1991) 61-4, 97-9, 113, 117, 119-20, 124.

---

18. Borlase confused this stone with Southill.

24 Lewannick II

The stone is now inside Lewannick church, at the west end of the nave. National Grid Reference SX 2759 8071. Examined 30 June 1984 and 6 July 1986.

History

The stone was found in two pieces by F.H. Nicholls, a stone mason, on 17 July 1894 and 19 July 1894; when found the pieces were both built upside down into the walls of the north porch, one in the north wall, the other in the east wall.[1] In 1895 the stones were recorded as still in the wall of the north porch,[2] but by 1896 they had been removed from the wall and were 'placed together within the church'.[3] In 1906 Langdon described the stone as being in the church, adding, erroneously, that it had been found in the south porch.[4] In the same year the stone was said to be in the churchyard.[5] In 1932 Hencken also stated that the stone was in the churchyard.[6] In 1945 Macalister described the stone as 'leaning against the end pier of the south arcade, inside the church'.[7]

Description

The stone is an incomplete and uncarved pillar-stone now in two pieces (fig. II.24). It measures 150 cm. in height and 34 cm. in width; the thickness is broken and varies between 5 and 28 cm. Text (i) is incised without framing-lines or panels on the face of the stone and is incomplete. The letters are set in one line reading downwards facing left and measure 6 to 11 cm. in height. This text, which is only slightly deteriorated, appears to be primary and uses a predominantly capital script. There are two ogham texts, texts (ii) and (iii). Text (ii) is incised on the edge between the face and the left-hand side of the stone, text (iii) on that between the face and the right-hand side of the stone. Both texts (ii) and (iii) read vertically

---

1. Langdon (1894a) 110-11.
2. Langdon & Allen, J.R. (1895) 51.
3. (-) (1896b) 250.
4. Langdon (1906) 416.
5. Daniell (1906) 242.
6. Hencken (1932) 223.
7. Macalister (1945) 444.

Figure II.24 Lewannick II (photograph Woolf/Greenham Collection).

downwards and appear to be primary. Both are complete and only slightly deteriorated.

Texts

(i)   [-C]IA CI/TVLC[A]GNI
(ii)   [ogham] U[L]CAG[.I]
(iii) [ogham] [.L]CAG[.]I

Discussion

Text (i) reads, [-C] IACIT VLC[A]GNI, probably for, [HIC] IACIT VLC[A]GNI, that is, '[Here] lies [the body] of Ulc[a]gnus' with IACIT for IACET. Text (ii) reads, U[L]CAG[.I] and text (iii) reads, [.L]CAG[.]I. Both are renderings of the name ULCAGNI which occurs in text (i). It seems more likely that one person is commemorated, rather than more than one person with the same name. Jackson took the name as Primitive Irish.[8] The same name occurs on Nanscow and also on a stone from Llanfihangel-ar-Arth, Wales.[9] In the form ULCCAGNI the name occurs on an Irish ogham stone from Ballyhank.[10]

The stone belongs to Category 1b, pillar-stones containing longer texts. Category 1 stones date from the fifth or sixth centuries to the eleventh century. On the evidence both of the ogham texts and of the Primitive Irish name, this stone is likely to date from the fifth or sixth century to the eighth century.

Bibliography

Iago (1893-5b) 173-4.
Langdon (1893-5a) 169-71 & fig.
Langdon (1893-5b) 279-82 & fig.
Langdon (1894a) 110-11 & fig.
Langdon & Allen, J.R. (1895) 51, 53, 60 & fig.
Langdon (1896) 23, 25.
(-) (1896b) 245-6, 249-51 & figs.
Macalister (1897) 25.
(-) (1897) 123.
Macalister (1902) 148n.
Daniell (1906) 242-3.
Langdon (1906) 416, *passim* & figs.
Macalister (1907) 86.
Holder (1907-13) col. 22.

---

8. Jackson (1953) 179.
9. Macalister (1945) no. 370, pp. 352-3 & fig.; Nash-Williams (1950) no. 157, p. 115 & figs.
10. Macalister (1945) no. 100, p. 97 & fig.

Sedding (1909) 234.
Henderson, C.G. (1925) 119.
Hull (1926) 37-8.
Macalister (1929) 179.
Hencken (1932) 223, 226-7, 301.
Jenkin (1934) 29-30.
Macalister (1945) no. 467, p. 444 & fig.
Jackson (1950) 199, 205, 210.
Jackson (1953) 171n, 179, 187.
Fox (1964) 160.
(-) (1966) 50.
Evans (1967) 210.
Pevsner (1970) 101.
Laing (1975) 125.
Radford (1975) 5-6, 8, 13.
Pearce (1978) 21-30, 68, 71, 161-2, 180 & fig.
Pearce (1981) 172, 270.
Thomas, A.C. (1981) 298.
Pearce (1985) 257-9.
Weatherhill (1985) 75 & fig.
Preston-Jones & Rose (1986) 155, 157.
Todd (1987) 250.
McManus (1991) 8, 89, 97-8, 107, 125.

25 Lundy I

Figure II.25-8 A general view of the Lundy stones (photograph D.B. Hague).

The stone is now set with stones 26-28, Lundy II-IV, against an enclosure bank of Beacon Hill cemetery, Lundy Island. National Grid Reference SS 132 442.[1] Examined 2 July 1986.

History

The stone was discovered in 1905 when a new grave was being dug in the north west corner of the ruins of St Helen's Chapel on Beacon Hill.[2]

---

1. The National Grid Reference refers to Beacon Hill cemetery, not to the individual stone.
2. Gardner (1960) 56.

Figure II.25 Lundy I (photograph D.B. Hague).

Gardner said: 'it would seem that the stone had been incorporated in the wall at this point'.[3] The inscription was not noticed until 1923 at which date the stone was 'in a corner of the burial ground';[4] this is probably near the place where it had been found in 1905. In May 1981 the stone was moved to its present position.[5]

---

3. Gardner (1960) 56.
4. (-) (1923) 372.
5. Hague (1982); there is no page numbering in this pamphlet.

Description

The stone is a pillar-stone, incomplete and uncarved (fig. II.25). It measures 117 cm. in height, 42 cm. in width and 31 to 32 cm. in thickness. In 1923 the 'average length' of the stone was given as five and a half feet (*c.* 165 cm.),[6] suggesting that around 48 cm. are now beneath the ground. The text is incised without framing-lines or panels in two lines on one face of the stone. The text is incomplete and slightly deteriorated. The letters measure 7 to 16 cm. in height and read downwards facing left. The text appears to be primary and uses a predominantly capital script.

Text

[-.]GERNI
[-.T]I[.]ERNI

Discussion

The text now reads, [-.]GERNI [-.] [T]I[.]ERNI, where [T] is unusual in form. The first and second lost letters may both have been [I], while the third may have been [G] or [T]. The text is likely to have contained two personal names in the genitive, possibly originally joined by [FILI]. A possible reconstructed text is, [-I]GERNI [FILI] [T]I[G]ERNI, that is, '[the stone] of [-i]gernus, [?son] of [T]i[g]ernus'. If the second name was [T]I[G]ERNI, this is Celtic.[7] A name which may read TIGERN[I] occurs on a stone from Henfynyw, Wales;[8] the name TEGE[R]NOMALI occurs on the Cubert stone.

The Lundy I stone belongs to Category 1a, pillar-stones with a simple memorial text. Category 1 stones date from the fifth or sixth centuries to the eleventh century; the use of horizontal I might suggest a sixth- to eighth-century date for this stone.

Bibliography

(-) (1923) 372-3 & figs.
Chanter (1924-5) 308-9.
Jenner (1924-5) 74-5.
Loyd (1925) 22-4, 33 & figs.
Alexander (1937) 153-4.
Etherton & Barlow (1950) 43.

---

6. (-) (1923) 372.
7. Jackson (1953) 446-7.
8. Macalister (1949) no. 990, p. 139 & fig., reading TIGEIRN-; Nash-Williams (1950) no. 108, p. 95 & fig., reading TIGEI(?)R[N-; Jackson (1953) 446, reading TIGERN(I).

Pevsner (1952*a*) 116.
Gardner (1960) 55-64 & fig.
Gardner (1962) 23, 31-2.
Wilson (1964) 231.
(-) (1966) 51.
(-) (1968) 198 & fig.
Thomas, A.C. *et al.* (1969) 139, 142.
Grinsell (1970) 105.
Thomas, A.C. (1971*b*) 81-2, 110-11.
Laing (1975) 138.
Pearce (1978) 21-30, 70, 183 & fig.
Hague (1982).[9]
Gardner (1984) 128.
Langham, A. & Langham, M. (1984) 47.
Pearce (1985) 257-9.
Thomas, A.C. (1985*a*) 174.
Thomas, A.C. (1986) 140.
Todd (1987) 251.

---

9. There is no page numbering in this pamphlet.

26 Lundy II

The stone is now set against an enclosure bank of Beacon Hill cemetery, Lundy Island. National Grid Reference SS 132 442.[1] Examined 2 July 1986.

History

The stone was discovered by K.S. Gardner and A. Langham in 1961 during an investigation of Beacon Hill cemetery.[2] In May 1981 the stone was moved to its present position.[3]

Description

The stone is a pillar-stone, incomplete and carved only with what is probably a cross incised within a circle (fig. II.26). The stone measures 177 cm. in height, around 63 cm. in width and 5 to 15 cm. in thickness. Hague noted that the stone 'has been set up on a low concrete plinth incorporating a strip of lead',[4] but I could not see this. The text is incised without framing-lines or panels on the face of the stone; it is set in one line beneath the cross. The text is rather deteriorated and may be incomplete at the end where the stone is broken. The letters measure 10 to 15 cm. in height and read downwards facing left. The text appears to be primary and uses a predominantly capital script.

Text

[PO]TIT

Discussion

The text now reads, [PO]TIT, which may or may not be incomplete at the end. It is presumably a personal name, either in the nominative, that is,

---

1. The National Grid Reference refers to Beacon Hill cemetery, not to the individual stone.
2. Gardner (1962) 31.
3. Hague (1982). There is no page numbering in this pamphlet.
4. Hague (1982). There is no page numbering in this pamphlet.

Figure II.26 Lundy II (photograph Keith Gardner).

'[Po]tit', or perhaps in the genitive, that is '[the stone] of [Po]tit[us]'. The name [PO]TIT is probably Latin. A name probably to be read POTENTINI occurs on a stone from Brynkir, Wales;[5] this name is described as Latin by Nash-Williams but as Celtic by Jackson.[6]

---

5. Macalister (1945) no. 380, pp. 361-2 & fig.; Nash-Williams (1950) no. 84, p. 86 & fig.
6. Nash-Williams (1950) 8; Jackson (1953) 502.

The Lundy stone belongs to Category 1a, pillar-stones with a simple memorial text. Category 1 stones date from the fifth or sixth centuries to the eleventh century; the Latin name suggests a sixth- to eighth-century date for this stone.

Bibliography

Gardner (1962) 31-2.
Wilson (1964) 231.
(-) (1968) 198 & fig.
Thomas, A.C. *et al.* (1969) 139, 142 & fig.
Grinsell (1970) 105.
Thomas, A.C. (1971*b*) 81-2 & fig. opp. p. 145.
Laing (1975) 138.
Pearce (1978) 21-30, 70, 183 & fig.
Thomas, A.C. (1981) 165 & fig.
Hague (1982).[7]
Gardner (1984) 128.
Langham, A. & Langham, M. (1984) 47.
Pearce (1985) 257-9.
Thomas, A.C. (1985*a*) 174.
Thomas, A.C. (1986) 140, 142, 144.
Todd (1987) 251.

---

7. There is no page numbering in this pamphlet.

27 Lundy III

The stone is now set against an enclosure bank of Beacon Hill cemetery, Lundy Island. National Grid Reference SS 132 442.[1] Examined 2 July 1986.

History

The stone was found in 1962 by D.B. Hague during an investigation of Beacon Hill cemetery; it was 'lying in the ditch at the south end of the cemetery'.[2] In May 1981 the stone was moved to its present position.[3]

Description

The stone is a pillar-stone, probably incomplete and carved only with a cross incised within a circle (fig. II.27). The stone measures 97 cm. in height, 24 to 29 cm. in width and 27 to 32 cm. in thickness. Hague gave the total height of the stone as 125 cm.,[4] which suggests that around 28 cm. are now beneath the ground. The text is set beneath the cross on the face of the stone. The text is incised in two lines inside what is probably a panel: the stone has crumbled at both sides and there is now no sign of a left-hand vertical to the panel, although traces of a right-hand vertical can be seen. The text is probably complete but is rather deteriorated. The letters measure 4 to 8 cm. in height and read horizontally. The text appears to be primary and uses a predominantly capital script.

Text

RESG
EVT[A]

---

1. The National Grid Reference refers to Beacon Hill cemetery, not to the individual stone.
2. Gardner (1962) 32.
3. Hague (1982). There is no page numbering in this pamphlet.
4. Hague (1982). There is no page numbering in this pamphlet.

Figure II.27   Lundy III (photograph Keith Gardner).

Discussion

The text reads, RESGEVT[A] where the last letter could be [A] or [A/E]. It is presumably a feminine name in either the nominative, that is, 'Resgeut[a]' or in the genitive, that is, '[the stone] of Resgeut[a]'. The name may be Celtic; the name Celtic RES occurs on a stone from Llantwit Major, Wales.[5]

This stone belongs to Category 1a, pillar-stones with a simple memorial text. Category 1 stones date from the fifth or sixth centuries to the eleventh century but this stone cannot be more closely dated.

Bibliography

Gardner (1962) 32.
Wilson (1964) 231-2.
(-) (1968) 199 & fig.
Thomas, A.C. *et al.* (1969) 139, 142.
Grinsell (1970) 105.
Thomas, A.C. (1971*b*) 81-2.
Laing (1975) 138.
Pearce (1978) 21-30, 70, 183 & fig.
Pearce (1981) 186, 270.
Hague (1982).[6]
Gardner (1984) 128.
Langham, A. & Langham, M. (1984) 47.
Pearce (1985) 257-9.
Thomas, A.C. (1985*a*) 174.
Thomas, A.C. (1986) 140, 142.
Todd (1987) 251.

---

5. Macalister (1949) no. 1011, pp. 155-6 & figs; Nash-Williams (1950) no. 220, pp. 140, 142 & figs.
6. There is no page numbering in this pamphlet.

28 Lundy IV

The stone is now set against, and partly into, an enclosure bank of Beacon Hill cemetery, Lundy Island. National Grid Reference SS 132 442.[1] Examined 2 July 1986.

History

The stone was found in 1962 by D.B. Hague during an investigation of Beacon Hill cemetery; it 'was part of a complex of three [stones] formed in a triangle'.[2] It is possible that it was associated with 'two seemingly early graves'.[3] In May 1981 the stone was moved to its present position.[4]

Description

The stone is a pillar-stone, probably incomplete and carved only with what is probably a cross incised within a circle (fig. II.28). The stone measures 81 cm. in height, 8 to 29 cm. in width and about 25 cm. in thickness to where it is set into the bank. Hague said that the stone was about 100 cm. in height,[5] which suggests that some 20 cm. are now beneath the ground. The text is incised in one line on the face of the stone beneath the cross and above a horizontal framing-line. The text is slightly deteriorated but probably complete. The letters measure 5 to 6 cm. in height and read horizontally. The text appears to be primary and uses a predominantly capital script.

Text

TIMI

---

1. The National Grid Reference refers to Beacon Hill cemetery, not to the individual stone.
2. Gardner (1962) 32.
3. Thomas, A.C. *et al.* (1969) 142.
4. Hague (1982). There is no page numbering in this pamphlet.
5. Hague (1982). There is no page numbering in this pamphlet.

Figure II.28   Lundy IV (photograph D.B. Hague).

Discussion

The text reads, TIMI and is likely to be a personal name in the genitive, that is, '[the stone] of Timus'. The name may be Latin. The feminine name AEL[IA] TIMO occurred on a lost Romano-British stone from Risingham.[6]

This stone belongs to Category 1a, pillar-stones with a simple memorial text. Category 1 stones date from the fifth or sixth centuries to the eleventh century. If the name is Latin, this would suggest a sixth- to eighth-century date for the stone.

---

6. Collingwood, R.G. & Wright, R.P. (1965) no. 1209, p. 397 & fig.

Bibliography

Gardner (1962) 32.
Wilson (1964) 231-2.
(-) (1968) 199 & fig.
Thomas, A.C. *et al.* (1969) 139, 142.
Grinsell (1970) 105.
Thomas, A.C. (1971*b*) 81-2.
Laing (1975) 138.
Pearce (1978) 21-30, 70, 183.
Pearce (1981) 186, 270.
Hague (1982).[7]
Morris, R. (1983) 31.
Gardner (1984) 128.
Langham, A. & Langham, M. (1984) 47.
Pearce (1985) 257-9.
Thomas, A.C. (1985*a*) 174.
Thomas, A.C. (1986) 140.
Todd (1987) 251.

---

7. There is no page numbering in this pamphlet.

29 Lustleigh

The stone is now inside Lustleigh church, fastened to the west wall of the nave. National Grid Reference SX 7851 8127. Examined 28 June 1984 and 30 June 1985.

History

The stone was first noted in a manuscript of mid-eighteenth-century date, presented to the Bodleian Library, Oxford in 1757. The stone was then described as the 'threshold-stone of the South Door' of Lustleigh church.[1] The stone (*pace* Bate, and Chanter[2]) appears to have remained in this position, that is being used as the step of the inner doorway of the south porch, until 13 March 1979, when it was moved to its present position. Since the stone did not form part of the structure of the porch, it could have been inserted at any time before 1757.[3]

Description

The stone is an uncarved and incomplete pillar-stone in two pieces (fig. II.29). It measures 170 cm. in height, 36 to 38 cm. in width and 17 to 21 cm. in thickness. The text is incised without framing-lines but inside traces of a panel on the face of the stone. The text is legible but may not be complete. The letters, 6 to 10 cm. in height, are in two lines and read downwards facing left. The text appears to be primary and uses a predominantly insular script.

Text

DATUIDOC[-]
CONHINO[.-]

1. MS Bodl. 27866 (= MS Bodl. rolls 4) quoted in Madan (1905) 375.
2. Bate (1873-6) 392: 'built into the wall'; but cf. Bate (1876-8) 154: 'It lies at this time as when Lysons observed it, at the door of the main entrance into Lustleigh Church'; Chanter (1910) 482: 'formerly sill to church door'.
3. A point made by Swanton & Pearce (1982) 140.

Figure II.29 Lustleigh (photograph E.N. Masson Phillips).

Discussion

The text now reads, DATUIDOC[-] CONHINO[.-] and presumably contains two personal names. It is, however, uncertain how much, or indeed if any, further text is lost from the end and perhaps also from the beginning of each line. Both names appear to be nominative unless an ending is lost. It is uncertain whether one person, 'Datuidoc Conhino[.]', is named or whether name and patronymic are given, that is '[the stone of] Datuidoc, [son of] Conhino[.]'. Early drawings show the text in substantially the same state as it is today. For example, Lysons and Lysons' drawing suggests a text, D[A]TUIDOC CONHINOC, although they gave no reading.[4] Bate's

---

4. Lysons, D. & Lysons, S. (1822) cccviii & fig.

drawing and comments suggest a reading CATVIDOC CONRINO; he noted that Lysons and Lysons had added the C at the end of the second word.[5] A rubbing made by J.R. Allen also shows no sign of a final C on this word.[6] Macalister read, DATUIDOCI CONHINOCI FILIVS but admitted that the two final letters I 'have to be looked for'; of FILIVS he said: 'only the faintest ghosts are visible'.[7] The evidence of the early drawings suggests strongly that Macalister's reading of FILIVS, at least, should be abandoned. The names are both Celtic.[8] The DA- in DATUIDOC might suggest that this was a hypocoristic name in *do-*.[9]

The stone belongs to Category 1a, pillar-stones with a simple memorial text. Category 1 stones date from the fifth or sixth centuries to the eleventh century; the insular script used suggests a date from the eighth century onwards for this stone.

Bibliography

Polwhele (1797) I, 152.
Polwhele (1803) I, 146-8.
Lysons, D. & Lysons, S. (1822) cccviii & fig.
Halle (1851) 11-13.
Harding (1856) 83.
Thornton (1862) 335-6.
Haddan & Stubbs (1869) 162.
Iago (1871-3) 63n.
Bate (1873-6) 392.
Huebner (1876) no. 29, p. 11 & fig.
Bate (1876-8) 154 & fig.
Rhys (1880) 161-3 & fig.
Rhys (1882) 50 & fig.
Kerslake (1884) 109.
Parfitt (1884) 82.
(-) (1884*a*) 70.
(-) (1884*b*) 104.
Worth, R.N. (1886) 179-81, 318.
Holder (1896) cols 1101, 1150, 1296.
Crossing (1902) 157.
Madan (1905) 375.
McClure (1907) 730.
Chanter (1910) 482.
Macalister (1929) 192-3.
Alexander (1937) 153-4.
Macalister (1945) no. 490, pp. 469-70 & fig.
Nash-Williams (1950) 11n.
Pevsner (1952*b*) 200.
Jackson (1953) 189-90, 274, 279, 291, 521, 610, 646.
(-) (1966) 51.
Ellis, P.B. (1974) 28.

---

5. Bate (1876-8) 154 & fig.
6. Allen, J.R., BL Add. MS 37581, entry no. 10.
7. Macalister (1945) 469-70 & fig.
8. Jackson (1953) 189-90, 279, 610.
9. See Plummer (1910) II, 344.

Pearce (1978) 68, 71, 183.
Pearce (1981) 270.
Pearce (1982) 7.
Swanton & Pearce (1982) 139-43.
Pearce (1985) 257-9.
Woods (1988) 74, 78 & figs.

30 Lynton

The stone is now in the garden of Sixacre Farm, Lynton. National Grid Reference SS 7004 4824. Examined 3 July 1986.

History

The stone was discovered by Chanter in 1913: 'In February, 1913, I noticed that a large stone used as a hanging post for a gate near the old road from Parracombe to Lynton had some letters on it'.[1] Chanter noted that the gate was in one of the 'outer hedges of Lynton Common, which was enclosed about 1861' adding that, in his view, the stone was likely to have been found near to where it was utilised as a gatepost.[2] Chanter read his paper on 23 July 1913. When it was printed a postscript was added: 'Since the above was written the stone has been removed to the garden of Six Acre Farm, Lynton'.[3] This removal presumably took placing during the latter part of 1913; the stone has remained in the garden since then.

Description

The stone is an uncarved pillar-stone, probably complete (fig. II.30). It measures 128 cm. in height, 30 to 55 cm. in width and 14 to 29 cm. in thickness. Chanter gave the height of the stone when it was a gatepost as 'something over six feet six inches' of which over two feet were below ground.[4] This suggests that some 67 cm. are now beneath the ground. The text is incised without panels or framing-lines on a dressed portion of one face of the stone. The text is legible and probably complete. There are two modern holes on the inscribed face of the stone and it is possible, though unlikely, that one final letter has been lost in the making of one of these. The letters, measuring 4 to 10 cm. in height, are in two lines and read downwards facing left. When I examined the stone, the letters had recently been chalked in. The text appears to be primary and uses a predominantly capital script.

---

1. Chanter (1913) 270.
2. Chanter (1913) 272-3, quotation from p. 272.
3. Chanter (1913) 275.
4. Chanter (1913) 272.

Figure II.30   Lynton (from Chanter (1913) plate opposite p. 271).

Text

CAVVDIF/IL/IVS
CIVI[L]I

Discussion

The text reads, CAVVDI FILIVS CIVI[L]I, that is, '[the stone] of Cauudus, son of Civi[l]is' where the nominative FILIVS is used for the genitive *filii*. The name CAVVDI may be Celtic,[5] while the name CIVI[L]I is Latin.

This stone belongs to Category 1a, pillar-stones with a simple memorial text. Category 1 stones date from the fifth or sixth centuries to the eleventh century; the Latin name suggests that this stone dates from the sixth to the eighth century, a date which the use of horizontal I probably corroborates.

Bibliography

Chanter (1913) 270-5 & fig.
Haverfield (1914) 41-2 & fig.
Haverfield (1918) xxxii-xxxiii, xxxviii & fig.
Dalton (1921) 64.
Alexander (1937) 153-4.
Vowles (1939) 13.
Fox (1964) 159.
(-) (1966) 51.
Grinsell (1970) 104-5, 210 & fig.
Radford (1975) 5.
Pearce (1978) 21-30 & fig.
Pearce (1981) 171.
Pearce (1985) 257-8.

---

5. See Chanter (1913) 273-4.

31 Madron I

The stone is now in a field on a moor about 3 km. from Morvah. The field is on the left-hand side of a track that leads off to the right from the unclassified Madron to Morvah road. National Grid Reference SW 4268 3530. Examined 5 July 1984 and 2 July 1985.

History

In a letter dated 15 October 1700, Lhwyd described the stone as 'a large moor-stone in a common, called *Gwn mên Screpha*, in *Maddern* parish'.[1] In a letter dated 5 January 1711/12 from the Rev. S. Lobb to Moyle, the stone was described as lying 'just by a Road, which leads from *St. Ives* to *St. Just*'.[2] Lobb added: "tis certain it has lain, as now it does, time out of mind'.[3] In 1754 W. Borlase described the stone as lying, 'In a croft about half a mile to the North West of Lanyon'.[4] The stone was recorded lying in the same place up to and including 1824.[5] Around 1825 it was placed erect.[6] All the descriptions, from 1700 onwards, seem to refer both to the same place and to the stone's present location. Since the stone is now about 1.5 km. from the road, and does not appear to have been moved, it seems likely that the road mentioned by Lobb has been re-routed. It may be that Lobb was referring to the 'Old St Ives Road', the route of which was discussed by Weatherhill.[7]

In 1849 the stone was again thrown down due to the landowner's having 'dug around and beneath it, in the hope of finding buried treasure'.[8] In the stone's prostrate position the text was said to be hidden.[9] The stone was described as prostrate by Blight in 1861 although his own drawing of the stone, published in 1856, shows it erect.[10] In the summer of 1861 Halliwell described it as 'in an inclined position, fallen down on one side of the pit', but with the text visible.[11] Polsue said that the stone was re-erected around 1862.[12] The stone was apparently erect on 15 August 1871

---

1. Lhwyd (1700a); this part of this work has no page numbering.
2. Quoted in Moyle (1726) 201-2.
3. Quoted in Moyle (1726) 202.
4. Borlase, W. (1754) 357.
5. Hitchins (1824) I, 434; see also Bibliography.
6. (-) (1849) 494: 'about twenty-four years ago'.
7. Weatherhill (1981) 78-81.
8. (-) (1849) 494.
9. Edmonds (1858a) 182.
10. Blight (1861) 20; Blight (1856) 67 & fig.
11. Halliwell (1861) 95.
12. Polsue (1870) 221.

Figure II.31   Madron I (photograph E.N. Masson
Phillips).

at which date Iago described it as having had the letters painted blue.[13]
Jennings recorded that the field in which the stone stands was called in his
day the 'Pillar Field'.[14]

Description

The stone is an uncarved pillar-stone, probably complete (fig. II.31). It
measures 191 cm. in height, 27 to 55 cm. in width and 30 to 39 cm. in

---

13. Iago (1871-3) 68.
14. Jennings (1936) 11.

thickness. Measurements taken when the stone was prostrate suggest that *c.* 109 cm. is now below ground and that the buried part is wider than the part now visible.[15] The text is incised without framing-lines or panels on one face of the stone. The text is legible and probably complete. The letters, 6 to 13 cm. in height, are in two lines reading downwards facing left. The text appears to be primary and uses a predominantly capital script.

Text

RIALOBRANI
[-]CVNOVALI[-]

Discussion

The text now reads, RIALOBRANI [-] CVNOVALI[-]. Moyle read the text as, RIALOBRANI CUNOVALI FILI, a reading supported by the drawing which accompanies it.[16] W. Borlase read a similar text.[17] A photograph preserved by J.R. Allen clearly shows FILI at the end of the second line, the last letter being a horizontal I.[18] The stone is set so deeply into the ground that the letters read by Moyle as FILI are now buried. Iago's drawing shows a text, RIALOBRANI + + CVNOVALI FILI,[19] the two crosses corresponding to traces still visible at the beginning of the second line. The original reading is likely to have been, as Moyle suggested, RIALOBRANI CVNOVALI FILI, that is, '[the stone] of Rialobranus, son of Cunovalus', perhaps with two crosses.[20] The names RIALOBRANI and CVNOVALI are Celtic.[21]

The stone belongs to Category 1a, pillar-stones with a simple memorial text. Category 1 stones date from the fifth or sixth centuries to the eleventh century; the use of horizontal I might suggest a sixth- to eighth-century date for this stone.

Bibliography

Lhwyd (1700*a*).[22]
Lhwyd (1702) 248.

---

15. Lobb, quoted in Moyle (1726) 201, said the stone measured 10 feet. In 1856 it was said to be 9 feet, 10 inches: (-) (1856) 181. In 1861, however, Halliwell measured it as 8 feet, 4 inches: Halliwell (1861) 95-6.
16. Moyle (1726) 204 & fig.
17. Borlase, W. (1754) 357 & fig.
18. Allen, J.R., BL Add. MS 37580, entry no. 57.
19. Iago (1871-3) 67-9 & fig.
20. The two crosses were discussed by Iago; Iago (1871-3) 69.
21. Jackson (1953) 457, 459, 649. Cf. also Rhys (1879) 359, 406; Bergin (1932) 141; Evans (1967) 271; O'Brien (1973) 223.
22. This part of this work has no page numbering.

Moyle (1726) 190-2 (letter of 15 October 1711); 195 (letter of 10 December 1711); 196-204 & fig. (letter of 17 January 1711/12 quoting letter of 5 January 1711/12).
Borlase, W. (1754) 357-9 & fig.
Gough (1789) I, 13.
Polwhele (1803) I, 144-6.
Lysons, D. & Lysons, S. (1814) ccxxii & fig.
Gilbert, C.S. (1817) 187-8.
Hitchins (1824) I, 434-5.
Paris (1824) 125-6.
Gilbert, D. (1838) II, 122; III, 79-80.
Redding (1842) 172 & fig.
Courtney (1845) 157.
(-) (1849) 494.
(-) (1851*b*) xxvi, 168.
Wright, T. (1852) 455.
Blight (1856) 67, page opp. p. 61 & fig.
(-) (1856) xxvi, 181.
Edmonds (1858*a*) 182-3 & fig.
Haigh (1858-9) 184.
Blight (1861) 19-21.
Halliwell (1861) 95-6.
Edmonds (1862) 64-5, 212-3 & fig.
Wilkinson (1862) 52.
Blight (1865) 147.
Paull (1866-7*a*) xi.
Harding (1867) 21.
Polsue (1868) 115.
Borlase, W.C. (1869) 36.
Haddan & Stubbs (1869) 163.
Polsue (1870) 209, 221.
Iago (1871-3) 67-9 & fig.
Polsue (1872) vi & fig. (frontispiece).
(-) (1873) 74-5.
Huebner (1876) no. 2, pp. 1, 89 & fig.
Brash (1879) 403.
Rhys (1879) 86, 359, 379, 404, 406.
Lach-Szyrma (1883-5) 375.
Lukis (1885) 15, 26 & fig.
Langdon & Allen, J.R. (1888) 305-10, 317.
(-) (1888-92) 23-4.
Loth (1890) 44, 46.
Rhys (1890-1) 647.
Borlase, W.C. (1893) 182-3.
Langdon & Allen, J.R. (1895) 51, 55, 60 & fig.
Holder (1896) col. 1196.
(-) (1903-5) 330.
Holder (1904) col. 1181.
Rhys (1905) 70.
Daniell (1906) 239.
Langdon (1906) 419, *passim* & fig.
Jenner (1922-5) 56-62.
Macalister (1929) 179.
Hencken (1932) 222, 227, 302.
Jenkin (1934) 29 & fig.
Jennings (1936) 11 & fig. opp. p. 80.
Macalister (1945) no. 468, pp. 445-6 & fig.
Nash-Williams (1950) 11n.
Jackson (1953) 457.
Thomas, A.C. (1954) 17-18.

Thomas, A.C. (1957-8) 61.
Fox (1964) 160.
Russell (1964) 93.
(-) (1966) 51.
Evans (1967) 271.
Thomas, A.C. (1968) 2.
Pevsner (1970) 111.
Russell (1971) 82.
Thomas, A.C. (1971a) 65 & fig.
O'Brien (1973) 223.
Ellis, P.B. (1974) 19.
Radford (1975) 4-5, 12-13.
Maxwell (1976) 10.
Pool (1977) 140.
Mandach (1978) 230-1 & fig.
Pearce (1978) 29 & fig.
Thomas, A.C. (1980) 108.
Pearce (1981) 169-72, 175, 270 & fig.
Weatherhill (1981) 63, 70, 79-80 & fig.
Weatherhill (1985) 25-6, 105 & figs.
Thomas, A.C. (1986) 68, 77 & fig.
Todd (1987) 249-51 & fig.
McManus (1991) 102, 104, 113.
Pool (undated) 13 & fig.

32 Madron II

The stone is now inside Madron church, fixed to the floor at the west end of the south aisle. National Grid Reference SW 4533 3182. Examined 5 July 1984 and 2 July 1985.

History

The stone was discovered in January 1936, 'hidden in the south-west wall of the church ... under nine layers of plaster'.[1] Around 1936, it was photographed while still in the wall.[2] By 1949 it had been removed from the wall and was in the church.[3]

Description

The stone is a pillar-stone containing carving (fig. II.32); it is now incomplete.[4] It measures 179 cm. in height, 20 to 35 cm. in width and 27 to 33 cm. in thickness. The text is incised in three lines on the visible face of the stone. It is set without framing-lines but in a panel which is c. 26 cm. wide and probably went from end to end of the stone. The text is probably complete but much of it is now highly deteriorated; it is not even certain what script is used. The letters, 7 to 10 cm. in height, read downwards facing left. The text appears to be primary.

Text

NR
QON[F.]LI[-]
[.....]NN[A/R]L[..]

Discussion

About 15 letters are lost from the lacuna in the second line. In the third line, the first group of lost letters could be [F/I] or [E.] followed by [H/E] or

1. Jennings (1936) 45-6.
2. Jennings (1936) fig. opp. p. 80.
3. Macalister (1949) 179.
4. Jennings (1936) 45.

Figure II.32   Madron II (photograph Madron Parish Church).

[N/E]. The text appears to read, NR QON[F.]LI [-]NN[AR]L[..]. QON[F.]LI could perhaps be a name in the genitive or a name followed by [FI]LI; neither of these is certain and none of the rest of the text can be interpreted. Macalister read the first part of the text, up to and including [F.]LI, upside down as HADNOBVIS.[5] He read the remainder of the text as, FILIA. . . GVENNCREST with 'a slight suggestion of an initial CV' in the lacuna.[6] The text as it is today does not seem to support Macalister's reading.

5. Macalister (1949) 179.
6. Macalister (1949) 179.

The stone probably belongs to Category 1a, pillar-stones with a simple memorial text. Category 1 stones date from the fifth or sixth centuries to the eleventh century but this stone cannot be more closely dated.

Bibliography

Jennings (1936) 11, 45-6 & fig. opp. p. 80.
Macalister (1949) no. 1048, p. 179 & fig.
Russell (1964) 93.
Thomas, A.C. (1968) 2 & fig.
Thomas, A.C. (1969-72) 259 & fig.
Russell (1971) 82.
Maxwell (1976) 10.
Pearce (1978) 28, 71, 180 & fig.
Weatherhill (1981) 70 & fig.

33 Madron III

The stone is now lost.

History

In 1949 Macalister described the stone as 'built into the N. wall of the N. aisle, west of the entrance door'.[1] In 1968 A.C. Thomas described the stone in this position;[2] he did not, however, personally examine it.[3] In 1981 Weatherhill also recorded the stone in this position although he did not state that he had examined it there.[4] No-one else has ever recorded the stone. It seems likely that Macalister did see an inscribed stone; he may have recorded it as being in Madron church when it was in fact in a different church. I have made a careful search for this stone, in Madron and elsewhere, but have failed to locate it.

Description and Text

From Macalister's description and drawing the stone appears to have been uncarved and probably incomplete (fig. II.33). Macalister described it as having 'a tenon worked at one end' and gave its measurements as '3'9½" x 0'9"',[5] that is, 114 by 27 cm. The text was set in one line without framing-lines or panels on the visible face of the stone. The text appears to have been legible but incomplete. It is unclear whether or not it was primary. Macalister noted that if the stone 'were set in a stand, the inscription would run downward'.[6] The text appears to have used a predominantly insular script, described by Macalister as 'the most cursive-looking script I have ever seen in any lapidary inscription'.[7] Macalister read the text as, URITIN FILI SN.., and said there was no indication of further text. From his drawing, a reading URITN, or URI + N, followed by F/IL/I M-, seems just as likely.

1. Macalister (1949) 179.
2. Thomas, A.C. (1968) 1.
3. Professor A.C. Thomas, in a personal communication.
4. Weatherhill (1981) 70.
5. Macalister (1949) 179.
6. Macalister (1949) 179.
7. Macalister (1949) 179-80.

Figure II.33   Madron III (from Macalister (1949) fig. 1049).

Discussion

Macalister read, URITIN FILI SN.., but, as noted above, other readings are also possible. The text might have contained personal names joined by FILI but, until this stone is located, nothing further can be conjectured about its text.

The stone is unclassifiable since it is lost and no adequate description or drawing exists. Such stones cannot be dated.

Bibliography

Macalister (1949) no. 1049, pp. 179-80 & fig.
Thomas, A.C. (1968) 1.
Weatherhill (1981) 70.

34 Mawgan

The stone now stands on a piece of grass at the meeting of three roads in the centre of Mawgan village. National Grid Reference SW 7071 2486. Examined 4 July 1984.

History

The stone was first described by Sir R. Vivian in a letter to Moyle dated 5 May 1715. Vivian stated that the stone 'stands upright in the High-way, where two Lanes meet, in the Parish of *Mawgan*, in *Meneag*, not a quarter of a Mile from the Parish-Church'.[1] It has remained there since then. Langdon recorded that the stone was 'believed to be *in situ*'.[2]

Description

The stone is an uncarved pillar-stone, probably complete (fig. II.34). G.E. Ellis observed a hole at the top of the stone and suggested that it might have been a socket-hole;[3] however, I could not find any hole. It measures 180 cm. in height, 35 to 52 cm. in width and 28 to 49 cm. in thickness. The text is incised without framing-lines or panels and reads downwards facing left, the letters measuring *c.* 13 cm. in height. The text is set in two lines on one face of the stone and appears to be primary. The text is so highly deteriorated that it is not certain whether or not it is complete, nor what script is used. Traces of what could have been further lettering occur on one side of the stone, the right-hand side if the text is taken to be on the face of the stone. The Ordnance Survey symbol has been incised on the back of the stone.

Text

[-C̲.E̲.V̲N̲-]
[-]

---

1. Quoted by Moyle in a letter of 9 June 1715 to W. Musgrave; Moyle (1726) 249.
2. Langdon (1906) 419.
3. Ellis, G.E. (1952-3*a*) 61.

Figure II.34   Mawgan (photograph Herbert Hughes).

Discussion

The first lacuna probably held seven or eight letters, the second perhaps four. The text is now so deteriorated as to be virtually illegible, but a photograph taken in 1936 shows that the lower line was still legible then.[4] From the photograph it seems to have read, [.E]NAIVS. The earliest drawing known to me is that published by Moyle. This shows a text in two lines reading, GNEGVMI FILI ENANS.[5] W. Borlase's drawing and description suggest a reading, CNEGVMI FIL [.]ENANS,[6] and Gough gave a similar text.[7] Rhys read, CLEGVMI FILI GENAIVS,[8] and Iago, CNEGVMI FILI GENAIVS.[9] Iago's text seems to give a reading consistent with earlier drawings and readings and is perhaps to be translated as, '[the stone] of Cnegvmus, son of Genaius'. If the second name was in the nominative it could alternatively be translated, 'Genaius son of Cnegvmus'. *Gen-* is a well-attested element in Gaulish names, of either Celtic or Latin origin.[10] The origin of the other name is unknown. Macalister observed marks above the text which he interpreted as α, ω and M for *Maria*.[11] In view of the evidence of the early drawings these can be disregarded.

The stone belongs to Category 1a, pillar-stones with a simple memorial text. Category 1 stones date from the fifth or sixth centuries to the eleventh century but this stone cannot be more closely dated.

Bibliography

Moyle (1726) 242 (letter of 10 March 1714/15); 248-50 & fig. (letter of 9 June 1715).
Borlase, W. (1754) 359-60 & fig.
Gough (1789) I, 14 & fig.
Polwhele (1803) II, 200.
Lysons, D. & Lysons, S. (1814) ccxxii.
Gilbert, C.S. (1817) 187.
Penaluna (1819) 176.
Gilbert, C.S. (1820) 780-1.
Hitchins (1824) I, 443.
Penaluna (1838) II, 70-1.
Redding (1842) 57n.[12]
(-) (1851*b*) 213.
(-) (1856) 230.
Haigh (1858-9) 184.
Haddan & Stubbs (1869) 163.

---

4. See fig. II.34.
5. Moyle (1726) 248-50 & fig.
6. Borlase, W. (1754) 359 & fig.
7. Gough (1789) I, 14 & fig.
8. Rhys (1875) 368.
9. Iago (1883-5*a*) 282-3 & fig.
10. Evans (1967) 203-7.
11. Macalister (1945) 447.
12. Redding erroneously described this stone in a location corresponding to that of Gulval I.

Polsue (1870) 280.
Rhys (1875) 368.
Huebner (1876) no. 5, p. 2 & fig.
Brash (1879) 404.
Rhys (1879) 216.
Iago (1883-5a) 276-84 & fig.
Langdon & Allen, J.R. (1888) 307-8, 317.
Iago (1892-8) 38.
Borlase, W.C. (1893) 182-3.
Langdon (1893) 107.
Langdon & Allen, J.R. (1895) 51, 55, 60.
Holder (1896) cols 1051, 1997.
Langdon (1896) 6 & *passim*.
Rhys & Brynmor-Jones (1900) 17.
Daniell (1906) 241.
Langdon (1906) 419, *passim* & fig.
Macalister (1929) 179.
Hencken (1932) 265, 303.
Jenkin (1934) 30.
Macalister (1945) no. 469, pp. 446-7 & fig.
Ellis, G.E. (1952-3a) 61.
Henderson, C.G. (1957-60a) 337.
Beckerlegge (1959-61) 281-2.
Dowson (1966) 79.
(-) (1966) 51.
Pevsner (1970) 114-15.
Weatherhill (1985) 63 & figs.
Preston-Jones & Rose (1986) 157.

35 Nanscow

The stone is now in the garden of Nanscow Farm, St Breock. National Grid Reference SW 9689 7080. Examined 12 July 1984.

History

The stone was first described in 1846 by Kent. On 22 January he stated that it 'now supplies the place of a gate-post, at a spot a few miles distant from Padstow... The proprietor of the land promises to remove it to a more secure situation'.[1] In 1856 the stone was 'at the mowhay gate, Nanscowe'.[2] Nanscow Farm is some 8 km. from Padstow so it is possible but by no means certain that the location described by Kent was on or near the farm. Polsue described the stone as a 'gatepost at Nanscowe Mowhay' although neither Iago's drawing of 1872, a copy of which was reproduced by Polsue, nor Langdon's drawing published in 1889 show the stone in use as a gatepost.[3] In 1895, however, the stone was again stated to be a gatepost at Nanscow;[4] it is not clear whether this refers to the Mowhay gate or to another gate. In 1906 the stone was still described as a gatepost.[5] In 1929, Macalister described it as 'on the left-hand side of the garden walk leading to the farmhouse',[6] probably, *pace* Pevsner and Weatherhill,[7] its present position. In 1858, in an ambiguous reference, Kent may have suggested that a cremation burial had been associated with the stone.[8]

Description

The stone is an uncarved pillar-stone, probably complete (fig. II.35). It measures 125 cm. in height, 24 to 37 cm. in width and 20 to 28 cm. in thickness. Comparison with the measurements given by Kent suggests that

---

1. Kent *et al.* (1846*b*) 77.
2. Whitley *et al.* (1856) 25.
3. Polsue (1872) legend beneath frontispiece; the drawing is by Iago and is identical to the drawing published in Iago (1871-3) 70-1 & fig. Langdon's drawing was published in Allen, J.R. (1889) figs opp. p. 70.
4. Langdon & Allen, J.R. (1895) 51.
5. Langdon (1906) 419.
6. Macalister (1929) 185.
7. Pevsner (1951) 140: 'used as a gatepost at Nanscowe Farm'; this was repeated in Pevsner (1970) 160. Cf. also Weatherhill (1985) 76.
8. Kent (1858) 24.

Figure II.35   Nanscow (photograph Herbert Hughes).

some 55 cm. are now beneath the ground.[9] The texts are incised without framing-lines or panels and are both legible. Both contain one line and read downwards facing left. Text (i) may be incomplete at the end; it is set on the face of the stone with letters measuring 10 to 18 cm. in height. Text (ii) is complete and is set on the left-hand side of the stone with letters measuring 11 to 14 cm. in height. Both texts appear to be primary and both use a predominantly capital script.

Texts

(i)   VLCAGNIFI[L-]

(ii) SEVERI

Discussion

Taken together the texts now read, VLCAGNI FI[L-] SEVERI, where part of the [L] of FI[L] is beneath the ground. Several early drawings show the word FI[L] as FILI.[10] This is likely to have been the reading, the final [I] as well as part of the [L] of FI[LI] (for FILII) being now buried. The text can then be translated, '[the stone] of Ulcagnus, son of Severus'. Jackson took VLCAGNI as a Primitive Irish name.[11] The same name occurs on Lewannick II and also on a stone from Llanfihangel-ar-Arth, Wales.[12] SEVERI is a Latin name.[13] The same name occurs on a stone from Newchurch, Wales, although the text on this stone has been re-cut.[14] The name SEVERVS occurs on a Gaulish stone from Viviers and also occurred on a lost Gaulish stone from Treves.[15]

The Nanscow stone belongs to Category 1a, pillar-stones with a simple memorial text. Category 1 stones date from the fifth or sixth centuries to the eleventh century. The Primitive Irish name suggests a date from the fifth or sixth century to the eighth century for this stone; the Latin name is in accordance with such a date and the use of horizontal I probably also corroborates it.

---

9. Kent *et al.* (1846*b*) 77.
10. For example, Kent *et al.* (1846*b*) 77 & fig.; Iago (1871-3) 70-1 & fig.
11. Jackson (1953) 171.
12. Macalister (1945) no. 370, pp. 352-3 & fig.; Nash-Williams (1950) no. 157, p. 115 & figs.
13. Jackson (1953) 518n; Rhys (1879) 402.
14. Macalister (1945) no. 373, p. 356; Nash-Williams (1950) no. 171, p. 118 & figs.
15. Le Blant (1865) no. 484, pp. 210-11 & fig.; Le Blant (1856) no. 240, p. 345.

Bibliography

Kent *et al.* (1846*a*) 49.
Kent *et al.* (1846*b*) 77 & figs.
Whitley *et al.* (1856) 25-6.
Kent (1858) 24-5.
Haigh (1858-9) 183-4.
Smirke *et al.* (1861) 177.
Haddan & Stubbs (1869) 163.
Iago (1871-3) 70-1 & fig.
Polsue (1872) fig. (frontispiece).
Rhys (1875) 364.
Huebner (1876) no. 14, p. 5 & figs.
Rhys (1879) 359, 402.
Langdon & Allen, J.R. (1888) 306-8, 318 & figs.
Allen, J.R. (1889) figs opp. p. 70.
Loth (1890) 47.
Iago (1890-1) 237.
Borlase, W.C. (1893) 106.
Langdon (1893) 107.
Langdon (1893-5*a*) 170.
Langdon (1893-5*b*) 282.
Langdon & Allen, J.R. (1895) 51, 55, 60 & figs.
(-) (1896*b*) 251.
Rhys (1905) 89.
Daniell (1906) 242.
Langdon (1906) 419, *passim* & figs.
Holder (1907-13) col. 22.
Sedding (1909) 234.
Jenner (1922-5) 58.
Macalister (1929) 185.
Hencken (1932) 222, 227, 293.
Jenkin (1934) 29.
Macalister (1945) no. 472, p. 450 & figs.
Jackson (1950) 210.
Nash-Williams (1950) 11n, 115n.
Jackson (1953) 171, 518.
Fox (1964) 159.
(-) (1966) 51.
Evans (1967) 210.
Pevsner (1970) 160.
Reed, J. & Reed, B. (1971) 107.
Radford (1975) 5-6, 8.
Pearce (1978) 24, 161.
Thomas, A.C. (1985*b*) 173.
Weatherhill (1985) 76 & figs.
McManus (1991) 62.

36 Parracombe

The stone is now lost.

History

The stone was recorded in 1797 by Polwhele but even then was lost.
Polwhele stated:

> Badcock, in his notes on Chapple, mentions a *Stone* near *Holywell*,
> on the borders of *Exmoor* . . . 'I have searched for this stone, says
> he, and employed others in the same pursuit. At last I was
> informed, to my great mortification, that about ten or twelve years
> since, it was made the foundation of a little bridge, on the rivulet
> where it originally stood.'[1]

The bridge was widened in 1864 but Chanter and Worth, writing in 1905,
thought it probable that the stone was still there.[2] Grinsell recorded that
the bridge was partially destroyed in 1952, 'so it is doubtful whether this
stone can ever be recovered'.[3] The tradition of an inscribed stone built
into the bridge is, however, still known in the village.

Description and Text

The description of the stone and its text come from Polwhele who was
quoting Badcock:

> "The man who erected this bridge, said, 'there were nearly twenty
> letters on it - that they had an indenting between them, and were
> not of the common figure; for many persons, who examined them,
> pronounced them to be *Greek*'".[4]

No further description of the stone or of the text was given.

---

1. Polwhele (1797) I, 151. I cannot locate the Rev. Samuel Badcock's 'Notes on Chapple'. See Chanter & Worth, R.H. (1905) 377, 380-1, 386-7.
2. Chanter & Worth, R.H. (1905) 387.
3. Grinsell (1970) 105.
4. Polwhele (1797) I, 151.

Discussion

No drawing, to my knowledge, exists of this lost stone, nor was any reading of the text published. The stone is unclassifiable since it is lost and no adequate description or drawing exists. Such stones cannot be dated.

Bibliography

Polwhele (1797) I, 151-2.
Chanter & Worth, R.H. (1905) 380-1, 386-7.
Chanter (1913) 275.
Grinsell (1970) 105, 210.
Pearce (1978) 29.

37 Penzance

The stone is now in Penlee Memorial Gardens, beside the entrance door to the museum, Penlee House. National Grid Reference SW 4705 3005. Examined 11 July 1984.

History

Until 1829 the cross stood at 'the north-east corner of the Green Market'.[1] In September 1829, during road-widening, the cross was moved a few metres to stand at the junction of Greenmarket and Causewayhead.[2] The inscription was discovered in 1829 when the cross was moved.[3] Halliwell recorded that the house on this corner was demolished in the summer of 1861 but that the cross remained there; he continued: 'it is said that the Corporation intend to remove it into a more conspicuous position near the Town Hall'.[4] The cross was subsequently moved, before 1870, to the western end of the Market House where Langdon recorded that, 'In this position the back and lower portion of the sides are concealed'.[5] This explains why Blight and Langdon both mentioned the text on the back but did not show the back of the stone in their drawings.[6] On 15 July 1899 the cross was moved to the Morrab Gardens and in the summer of 1953 to its present position. Pool suggested that the original site of the cross may have been one of the two places with the field-name 'Park-an-Grouse' (Cross Field), one of which, on the north side of Alverton, is near to Green-market.[7]

Description

The stone is a complete cross with carving on all sides of the shaft. Photographs of the stone taken when it was being moved show it broken at the bottom and suggest that there must be only a small portion of shaft inside the modern base.[8] The stone measures c. 215 cm. to the base and

---

1. Millett (1888-92) 350.
2. Pool (1974) 8, 215n.
3. Courtney (1845) 18; Blight (1856) 3.
4. Halliwell (1861) 24, 28-9, quotation from p. 29.
5. Polsue (1870) 136; Langdon (1896) 308.
6. Blight (1856) 3 & fig.; Langdon (1896) 308-10 & figs.
7. Pool (1974) 8.
8. See fig. II.37(i).

Figure II.37(i) Penzance, text (i) (photograph Penzance Town Council).

the shaft measures 47 to 56 cm. in width and 23 to 25 cm. in thickness. The texts are both incised low down on the shaft, without framing-lines but inside panels; both read downwards facing left.

Text (i) is set on the back of the shaft in two panels which together measure 44 cm. in height (to the break) by 21.5 cm. (fig. II.37(i)). This text

Figure II.37(ii) Penzance, text (ii) (photograph Penzance Town Council).

is in three lines with letters measuring 2.5 to 6.5 cm. in height. Text (i)(a) is legible and complete; text (i)(b) is legible but incomplete although it is unlikely that any text is hidden inside the modern base. Text (i) appears to be primary and uses a predominantly insular script.

Text (ii) is set on the right-hand side of the shaft in two panels which together measure 61 cm. in height by 16 cm. (fig. II.37(ii)). This text is complete but highly deteriorated. It appears to be primary but it is uncertain what script is used. The text is set in four lines, the letters measuring 4 to 6 cm. in height.

Texts

(i) (a) [.]MBUIN
[-]UMQ:
[-.]TNI
(b) FO[-]
P[-]
C[-]

(ii)   (a)   [R̲E̲.. + .]
             [C̲R̲-]
       (b)   D + [.]
             [..]

Discussion

Text (i)(a) reads, [-.]MBUIN[-]UMQ: [.]TNI, although the first I could be an L; text (i)(b) reads, FO[-]P[-]C[-]. It is not clear whether these texts are to be read together or separately. The dots after Q could perhaps indicate the end of a word or, possibly, an abbreviation.[9] I cannot interpret the rest of text (i). Macalister was the first to publish a drawing of the texts, in 1929, and this drawing shows text (i) in substantially the condition it is today.[10] Macalister's drawing and commentary suggest a reading of text (i)(a) as, CVMBUIN|UICUMQ:|ENITHI; he read text (i)(b) as I do.[11] Clearly Macalister was right in rejecting Blight's reading of the text.[12] He concluded that text (i) was 'impossible to interpret',[13] a conclusion with which I agree.

Text (ii)(a) reads, [RE.. + .CR-] with three or four letters lost after the final [R], and must be concluded to be illegible. Macalister's 1929 drawing substantiates his reading, REGIS + RI|CATICRUX.[14] It is my view that there is insufficient room on the stone for such a text, especially for the second line; in the light of the state of this text today, Macalister's reading must be treated with caution. It seems to me most inadvisable to build upon Macalister's reading of this text theories concerning the existence of early kings of Cornwall, as for example, the following: 'A native ruling family survived west of the Tamar long enough to set up the early tenth century cross, now in Penlee Gardens, Penzance, the inscription on which seems to have referred to a King Riocatus or Ricatus'.[15] Text (ii)(b) reads, D + [. . .], which I cannot interpret. It may have been part of text (ii)(a) or a separate text. Macalister's 1929 drawing shows a similar text to mine which Macalister admitted 'I can make nothing of . . .'.[16]

The stone belongs to Category 2a, inscribed cross-shafts. Category 2 stones date from the ninth to the eleventh century; this stone is dated to the tenth or eleventh century on artistic grounds.

---

9. Cf. Q: on the Jarrow dedication stone, Okasha (1971) no. 61, pp. 85-6 & fig.
10. Macalister (1929) 185-8 & figs.
11. Macalister (1929) 186-7 & fig.
12. Blight (1856) 3; Macalister (1949) 181.
13. Macalister (1929) 187.
14. Macalister (1929) 188 & fig.
15. Pearce (1978) 168.
16. Macalister (1929) 188 & fig.

Bibliography

Courtney (1845) 17-18.
Blight (1856) 3 & fig.
Halliwell (1861) 24, 28-9.
Polsue (1870) 236.
Iago (1878-81) 397n.
Iago (1888-92) 387.
Millett (1888-92) 350-1.
Langdon (1890-1) 62 & *passim*.
Langdon (1896) 308-10, *passim* & figs.
Daniell (1906) 245.
Langdon (1906) 419 & *passim*.
Macalister (1929) 185-8 & figs.
Hencken (1932) 248, 268-70, 306.
Jenkin (1934) 31.
Dexter, T.F.G. & Dexter, H. (1938) 42-4, 69, 119-23, 126-7 & figs.
Macalister (1949) no. 1051, pp. 180-2 & figs (figs numbered 1052).
Thomas, A.C. (1954) 18.
Ellis, G.E. (1956-8a) 1.
Russell (1964) 93-4.
Thomas, A.C. (1967) 97.
Pevsner (1970) 139.
Russell (1971) 82, 88.
Rowe, L. (1973) & fig.[17]
Pool (1974) 7-8, 215n & figs.
Maxwell (1976) 10.
Pearce (1978) 168 & fig.
Pearce (1981) 177.
Weatherhill (1981) 63, 72 & fig.
Weatherhill (1985) 26.
Higgitt (1986) 141.
Preston-Jones & Rose (1986) 159.
Thomas, A.C. (1986) 67.
Todd (1987) 195.
Pool (undated) 16 & fig.

17. There is no page numbering in this book.

38 Perranporth

The stone is now lost.

History

The stone was recorded in 1932 by Hencken 'built upside down into wall of St. Pieran's oratory'.[1] St Pieran's oratory is now covered with sand; in 1980, when it was last uncovered, the inscribed stone was observed by Dr L. Olson and O.J. Padel. They considered that the letters might be of any date and were not necessarily early Christian.[2]

Description and Text

The description of the stone and its text are taken from Hencken: 'Perranporth, built upside down into wall of St. Pieran's oratory . . .*rn*. . . and below . . .*fa*. . .'.[3] Hencken gave no further details of the stone or of the text.

Discussion

No interpretation of such a fragmentary text is possible. The stone is unclassifiable since it is lost and no adequate description or drawing exists. Such stones cannot be dated.

Bibliography

Hencken (1932) 224, 260-1, 306.
Macalister (1949) no. 1052, p. 182.
Warner (1963) 71.
(-) (1966) 51.

---

1. Hencken (1932) 224.
2. Oliver Padel, in a personal communication.
3. Hencken (1932) 224.

39 Phillack I

The stone is now in Phillack churchyard, to the east of the church and set against the wall of an outhouse. National Grid Reference SW 5655 3842. Examined 2 July 1984.

History

The stone was discovered in 1856 when the church was being rebuilt. Edmonds, quoting information from the Rector, the Rev. F. Hockin, stated that it 'was one of the foundation stones of the late church near the south-eastern corner of the chancel'.[1] In 1858 Edmonds said that it 'now stands outside the wall of the "vestry," in the south-eastern corner of the church-yard'.[2] This is presumably the stone's present position.

Description

The stone is an uncarved pillar-stone, probably complete (fig. II.39). It measures 156 cm. in height, 40 to 50 cm. in width and 30 to 38 cm. in thickness. Comparison with Edmond's measurements suggests that some 76 cm. are now beneath the ground.[3] The text is incised without framing-lines or panels on the visible face of the stone. The text is rather deteriorated and may not be complete. The letters, 3 to 7 cm. in height, are in two lines and read downwards facing left. The text appears to be primary and the script used is predominantly insular in form.

Text

CLO[-]
MO[BRA]TTI

Discussion

The text now reads, CLO[-] MO[BRA]TTI, with about six letters lost from the lacuna. Soon after the stone was found Edmonds said that 'the

---

1. Edmonds (1862) 207.
2. Edmonds (1858a) 181.
3. Edmonds (1858a) 181.

Figure II.39   Phillack I (photograph Herbert Hughes).

inscription appears to be illegible'.[4] However drawings by Iago and Langdon support their readings of, respectively, CLOTUALI MOGRATTI,[5] and CLOTUALI MOBRATTI.[6] The text can probably be reconstructed as, CLO[TUALI] MO[BRA]TTI, that is, '[the stone] of Clo[tualus], [son] of Mo[bra]ttus', or perhaps, '[the stone] of Clo[tualus] Mo[bra]ttus'. Macalister was the first to read FILI on the stone.[7] The evidence from the early drawings and from the present state of the text suggests that FILI is unlikely ever to have been visible on the stone. The name CLO[TUALI] is Celtic.[8] The name MO[BRA]TTI is probably Primitive Irish, the prefix *mo-* being found in the formation of hypocoristic Irish names.[9]

The stone belongs to Category 1a, pillar-stones with a simple memorial text. Category 1 stones date from the fifth or sixth centuries to the eleventh century. The Primitive Irish name suggests a date from the fifth or sixth century to the eighth century for this stone; the insular script used suggests that a date in the eighth century is more likely than an earlier one.

Bibliography

Edmonds (1858a) 181.
Edmonds (1862) 63, 207.
Paull (1866-7a) xii.
Iago (1871-3) 59-67 & fig.
Polsue (1872) 69 & fig. (frontispiece).
(-) (1873) 95.
Rhys (1875) 365-6.
Huebner (1876) no. 230, p. 88 & fig.
Rhys (1879) 358, 379, 405.
(-) (1884-8) 230.
Loth (1890) 43.
Iago (1892-8) 38.
Borlase, W.C. (1893) 107.
Langdon & Allen, J.R. (1895) 52, 55, 60 & fig.
Holder (1896) col. 1046.
Holder (1904) col. 628.
Daniell (1906) 240.
Langdon (1906) 419, *passim* & fig.
Sedding (1909) 336.
Rhys (1918) 193.
Henderson, C.G. (1925) 165.
Macalister (1929) 188.
Hencken (1932) 265, 306.
Macalister (1945) no. 471, pp. 449-50 & fig.
Nash-Williams (1950) 11n.
Jackson (1953) 274, 646.
Henderson, C.G. (1957-60b) 407.

4. Edmonds (1858a) 181.
5. Iago (1871-3) 59-67 & fig.
6. Langdon & Allen, J.R. (1895) 55 & fig.
7. Macalister (1929) 188; Macalister (1945) 449-50 & fig.
8. Jackson (1953) 646; Evans (1967) 180, 269-71.
9. See Vendryes (1937) 254-68.

Thomas, A.C. (1961) 13, 21 & fig.
(-) (1966) 51.
Evans (1967) 180, 271.
Pevsner (1970) 141.
Rowe, L. (1973) & fig.[10]
Radford (1975) 6.
Pascoe (1976) 97.
Pearce (1978) 21-30, 71, 181.
Thomas, A.C. (1985b) 173.

---

10. There is no page numbering in this book.

40 Phillack II

The stone is built into the outside gable of the porch on the south side of Phillack church, some 3.5 m. from the ground. National Grid Reference SW 5654 3841. Examined 2 July 1984.

History

The stone was discovered in 1856 when the church was being rebuilt. Edmonds stated that it was found 'forming part of the walls' of the church and that it was then rebuilt into 'the wall of the new church porch, directly over the apex of the arch of the doorway'.[1] This is its present position. Langdon recorded further information from the Rev. Canon Hockin who was vicar of Phillack in 1856: 'Mr. Hockin was not present when the stone was discovered, but the contractor informed him that he found it in the south wall, flush with the inside face, and plastered over'.[2]

Description

The stone is some 15 cm. in height by some 25 cm. in width. Having been used as building material, it may be incomplete. The visible face of the stone contains a circle carved in relief with the one-letter text incised inside it without further panels or framing-lines (fig. II.40). The letter is some 12 cm. in height and is set horizontally. The text is legible and complete. There is no evidence as to whether or not the text is primary.

Text

☧

Discussion

The text reads ☧, the *chi-rho* symbol in its 'Constantine' form. C.G. Henderson in his discussion of this text inserted a note of caution: 'The Chi-Rho

---

1. Edmonds (1858a) 181.
2. Langdon (1893) 101.

Figure II.40   Phillack II (photograph Woolf/Greenham Collection).

monogram over the south porch (if genuine) is of great value'.[3] If genuine, the 'Constantine' form of the *chi-rho* would suggest an early date, perhaps the fifth century; on the Continent this form of *chi-rho* dates from the fourth to fifth century.[4]

The stone belongs to Category 3d, *chi-rho* stones.

Bibliography

Edmonds (1858a) 181 & fig.
Edmonds (1862) 63, 207 & fig.
Haddan & Stubbs (1869) 163n.
Polsue (1872) 68.
(-) (1873) 95.
Huebner (1876) 1 & fig.
(-) (1884–8) 229.
Lach-Szyrma (1886–9) 56.
Allen, J.R. (1887) 87 & fig.
Langdon & Allen, J.R. (1888) 308–9, 317.
Iago (1890–1) 254.
Langdon (1890–1) 92.
(-) (1892) 2.
Borlase, W.C. (1893) 183–4.
Langdon (1893) 97–108 & figs.

3. Henderson, C.G. (1925) 165.
4. Hamlin (1972) 24.

Langdon & Allen, J.R. (1895) 52, 55, 60 & fig.
Langdon (1896) 23.
(-) (1896*b*) 256.
McGovern (1904) 7.
Langdon (1906) 419, *passim* & figs.
(-) (1906*a*) 182.
Sedding (1909) 171, 335.
Jenner (1917) 75.
Henderson, C.G. (1925) 165.
Hencken (1932) 222, 224, 306.
Thomas, I. (1947) 53, 82.
Thomas, A.C. (1957-8) 61.
Henderson, C.G. (1957-60*b*) 407.
Thomas, A.C. (1961) 9, 13 & fig.
(-) (1966) 51.
Wall (1968) 176 & fig.
Pevsner (1970) 16, 141.
Hamlin (1972) 25.
Rowe, L. (1973) & fig.[5]
Pascoe (1976) 97.
Pearce (1978) 28, 66, 70-1, 88, 181 & figs.
Pearce (1981) 186-7 & fig.
Thomas, A.C. (1981) 165, 270 & fig.

---

5. There is no page numbering in this book.

41 Plymstock

The stone is now in the grounds of Plymstock Telephone Exchange, 46 Stentaway Road, Plymouth, on a grass bank near the entrance to the grounds. National Grid Reference SX 5186 5364. Examined 17 July 1964 and 25 June 1984.

History

The stone was recorded by Phillips in 1939. It was then in a field 'north of Stentaway House, adjoining the road from Plymstock to Billacombe' and had been in that position 'within the memory of two generations, at least'.[1] The inscription was first observed in 1946 when the stone was moved to the boundary-wall of the same field.[2] It was moved a few metres back to its present position some time between 1964 and 1978. It is possible, but by no means certain, that the inscribed stone is the cross first noticed by Gribble in 1883.[3]

Description

The stone is an incomplete carved cross with no base (fig. II.41). It measures 168 cm. in height, 40 cm. in width and 15 cm. in thickness. The text is incised in one line low down on one face of the shaft of the cross. It is set inside two horizontal framing-lines, some 26 cm. apart, which thus form a panel with the edges of the shaft. The text is probably complete although traces below the line of text suggest the possibility of further text now lost. The text is now highly deteriorated although it was quite legible in 1964. The letters, which are in a predominantly capital script, measure 6 to 15 cm. in height and read horizontally. It is uncertain whether or not the text is primary.

Text

[ELE℞]

---

1. Phillips (1939) 232.
2. Phillips (1950) 105-6.
3. Gribble (1884) 42.

Figure II.41   Plymstock (photograph E.N. Masson
Phillips).

Discussion

The text now reads, [ELEᛈ], perhaps for [ELEW] or [ELEP]. When I
examined the text in July 1964 it was perfectly legible and then read ELEᛈ,
which I took as ELEW with the Old English runic letter ᛈ = W.[4] Neither
ELEW or ELEP make sense as single words; previously I suggested that
ELEW might be a form of an unrecorded Old English personal name
*ELEWYN(N).[5] ELEW could be incomplete or abbreviated or with the rune

---

4. Okasha (1971) 106.
5. Okasha (1971) 106.

Ᵽ standing for its rune-name *wyn*, as on a coin of Edward the Elder where Ᵽberht occurs for *wynbeorht*.[6] The element *el-*, though not *ele-*, occurs in Domesday Book as an occasional spelling for the Old English elements *aelf-aeðel-* etc.[7] The name *eleᵽine* for *aethelwine* occurs on a coin of Cnut.[8]

The stone belongs to Category 2a, inscribed cross-shafts. Category 2 stones date from the ninth to the eleventh century; if the name is English, it would be in accordance with such a dating.

Bibliography

Gribble (1884) 42.[9]
Phillips (1938) 303.[10]
Phillips (1939) 232 & fig.
Phillips (1950) 105-6.
Phillips (1954) 184-5 & figs.
Okasha (1971) no. 101, p. 106 & fig.
Phillips (1979) 141 & fig.
Todd (1987) 299.

---

6. Smart (1981) 83.
7. Feilitzen (1937) 142, 172, 182.
8. Smart (1981) 12.
9. This work does not certainly refer to the inscribed cross.
10. This work does not certainly refer to the inscribed cross.

42 Porthgwarra

The stone is now lost.

History

The stone recorded only in an eighteenth-century manuscript which belonged to J. Anstis: 'A Corner Stone in the Court Wall of hor Gwera, or the Higher Cove in St. Levans pish, within a Quarter of a Mile of the Lands End'.[1]

Figure II.42 Porthgwarra (BL MS Stowe 1023, p. 39, renumbered as p. 25, photograph by permission of the British Library).

Description and Text

The description and text are taken from the drawing in Anstis' manuscript (fig. II.42). No measurements are given. The stone appears to be uncarved, although only one face is shown. The stone is shown lying, with its left-hand side broken. The text is set in one line inside a panel and reads horizontally. The text is legible but incomplete at the beginning where the stone is broken. It uses a predominantly capital script. It is unclear whether

---

1. BL MS Stowe 1023, p. 39 (renumbered as p. 25).

or not the text is primary. The text reads: [-]HS.SPED, with a small horizontal line above the H.

Discussion

No interpretation of a lost text of such a fragmentary nature is possible. The stone is unclassifiable since it is lost and no adequate description or drawing exists. Such stones cannot be dated.

Bibliography

Hogg (1960-1) 246-7.
Russell (1971) 82.
Maxwell (1976) 10.
Pool (1977) 140.
BL MS Stowe 1023, p. 39 (renumbered as p. 25) & fig.

43 Redgate

The stone now stands, alongside a carved, uninscribed stone, in a grass enclosure in a field; this field is on the left-hand side of the unclassified road from St Cleer to Redgate, about 1.5 km. from St Cleer. National Grid Reference SX 2361 6883. Examined 7 July 1985.

History

The stone has always stood in the same field as it stands today. It was recorded there three times in the early seventeenth century. In 1600 Camden stated: '... duo cippi ... alter barbaris characteribus iam fugientibus inscribitur'.[1] In 1602 Carew said: 'There are two moore [presumably 'moor' not 'more'] stones, pitched in the ground, very neere together ... In this latter, are graued certaine letters'.[2] Norden, who died *c.* 1626, recorded that on 'the craggie *Moores* ... standeth a monument of verie greate antiquitie, called *The other haulfe stone*'.[3]

Around 1680, during 'the latter End of the Reign of King CHARLES II' according to Hals, some tin miners, looking for treasure, dug around the stone and found underground a 'spacious Vault, wall'd about and arch'd over with Stones, having on the Sides thereof two Stone Seats'.[4] Hals reported that when the miners abandoned their attempt, the earth around the stone fell into the pit and the stone fell over.[5] The stone remained lying down for over 150 years. In 1849 Spence said it had been 'Until very lately ... lying in a deep pit and nearly covered with brambles, moss, etc.'.[6] Spence organised an excavation and also had the stone re-erected in the same field. Spence recorded that the underground chamber was considered by some to be tin mine workings but that he thought that it was a chapel.[7] In 1932 further excavations were conducted but without disturbing the stone. Andrew described these excavations in detail, concluding that the underground chamber was not a chapel but was '*made by men who came to search for treasure and stayed a while to prospect for tin*'.[8] Andrew suggested that this work pre-dated the accounts by Carew and Camden;[9] it is possible, however, that the chamber was dug between 1600 and 1680.

---

1. Camden (1600) 155. This is the earliest edition of Camden to mention the stone.
2. Carew (1602) 128v-129r.
3. Norden (1728) 58.
4. Hals (?1750) 46-7.
5. Hals (?1750) 47.
6. Spence (1849) 212-13.
7. Spence (1849) 214.
8. Andrew (1933-6) 112-39, quotation from p. 125.
9. Andrew (1933-6) 125.

Figure II.43   Redgate (photograph Royal Institution of Cornwall)

Description

The stone appears to have formed the lower part of a carved cross-shaft but it is now incomplete (fig. II.43). It has no base; Langdon in fact described it as a 'cross-base'.[10] The stone measures 140 cm. in height, 67 to 85 cm. in width and 54 cm. in thickness. Lysons and Lysons recorded the height of the stone as six feet (*c.* 180 cm.) which suggests that 40 cm. of the shaft are now beneath the ground.[11] The text is incised on one face of the stone. It is set without framing-lines but set inside a panel measuring 66 by 59 cm. The text is complete, legible and primary. The text is set in five lines reading horizontally. It uses a predominantly insular script and the letters vary between 5 and 14 cm. in height.

Text

DONI
ERT:RO
GAVIT
PROA[.]
IMA

Discussion

The text reads, DONIERT : ROGAVIT PRO A[.]IMA where the last word is presumably A[N]IMA. This can be translated as, 'Doniert requested [this cross *or* prayers] for [his] soul'. Camden first suggested that DONIERT was to be identified with Dumnarth, or Dumgarth, who is recorded in the Welsh Annals *sub anno* 875: 'Dumgarth rex Cerniu [id est Cornubiæ] mersus est'.[12] This identification has been accepted, although sometimes with reservations, by many scholars. In my view this identification is possible but certainly no more than possible. The name DONIERT is Celtic; the spelling *-i-* for original *-g-* suggests that it is Primitive Welsh/Cornish.[13]

The stone belongs to Category 2a, inscribed cross-shafts. Category 2 stones date from the ninth to the eleventh century but this stone cannot be more closely dated.

10. Langdon (1896) 377.
11. Lysons, D. & Lysons, S. (1814) ccxxii-ccxxiii. Hals' measurement of eight feet is either an over-estimate or Hals was confused with the height of the uninscribed stone; see Hitchins (1824) I, 439.
12. Camden (1607) 139. The quotation from the Welsh Annals is from BL MS Harley 3859 dating from *c.* 1100, edited by Williams: Williams (1860) 15. The variant spellings *Dumnarth* and *Cerneu*, quoted by Williams, are from the thirteenth-century Public Record Office MS E. 164/1. See also Hughes (1980) 67-85.
13. Jackson (1953) 421-3, 439. I am grateful to Oliver Padel for drawing to my attention the significance of the spelling with *-i-*.

216   *Entries*

Bibliography

Camden (1600) 155.
Carew (1602) 128v-129r & fig.
Camden (1607) 139 & fig.
Cressey (1668) 746.
Speed (1676) 21 & fig.
Lhwyd (1700*b*).[14]
Moyle (1726) 185, 187-8 (letter of 22 August 1711); 237-8 & fig. (letter of 10 March 1714/15, quoting letter of 30 November 1700).
Norden (1728) 58-9 & figs.
Hals (?1750) 46-8 & fig.
Borlase, W. (1754) 360-3 & fig.
Gough (1789) I, 5, 17 & figs.
Britton & Brayley (1801) 388.
Polwhele (1803) II, 195-7.
(-) (1807) 717-18.
Lysons, D. & Lysons, S. (1814) ccxxii-ccxxiii, ccxlvi.
Gilbert, C.S. (1817) 203.
Bond (1823) 195-202 & figs.
Hitchins (1824) I, 439-43.
Gilbert, D. (1838) I, 178-95 & fig.
Penaluna (1838) I, 108.
Redding (1842) 57 & fig.
Spence (1849) 211-15 & fig.
Hingston (1850) no. 47 & figs.[15]
Collins (1851) 76.
Coppard (1851) 205.
(-) (1851*b*) 193.
Coppard (1853) 73-4.
(-) (1856) 208.
Blight (1858*a*) 128 & fig.
Smirke *et al.* (1861) 177.
Wilkinson (1862) 52.
Paull (1866-7*a*) xi.
Polsue (1867) 202, 205-6.
(-) (1869) xxii, xxiv.
Iago (1871-3) 67.
Rhys (1875) 369-70.
Huebner (1876) no. 22, p. 8 & fig.
Iago (1878-81) 399.
Langdon & Allen, J.R. (1888) 311-13, 318.
Allen, J.R. (1889) 129, 217, 220-1.
Langdon (1889*a*) 319, 325-7 & figs.
Langdon (1889*c*) 239.
Langdon (1890-1) 36, 87 & *passim*.
Borlase, W.C. (1893) 184-5.
Langdon & Allen, J.R. (1895) 52, 57, 60 & fig.
Langdon (1896) 377-9, *passim* & figs.
Norway (1897) 211-12.
Rhys (1905) 74.
Daniell (1906) 244, 290.
Langdon (1906) 419, *passim* & fig.

14. This part of this work has no page numbering.
15. This book has no page numbering.

(-) (1910-11*b*) 281-4 & figs.
Rhys (1918) 193.
Jenner (1919) 137.
Henderson, C.G. (1925) 41.
Macalister (1929) 188.
Andrew (1932) 25-7.
Hencken (1932) 268, 271, 295.
Nance (1933*a*) 36.
Nance (1933*b*) 10.
Andrew (1933-6) 112-39 & fig.
Nance (1936) 15-16.
Macalister (1949) no. 1054, p. 184 & fig. (fig. numbered 1055).
Ellis, G.E. (1952-3*b*) 177-9 & figs.
Jackson (1953) 421.
Radford (1953) 23.
Thomas, A.C. (1957-8) 69.
Allen, J. (1967) 13.
Thomas, A.C. (1967) 104.
Pevsner (1970) 15, 16-17, 163-4.
Thomas, A.C. (1971*a*) 65 & fig.
Ellis, P.B. (1974) 19.
Radford (1975) 14.
Pearce (1978) 168 & fig.
Thomas, A.C. (1978) 76-9 & figs.
Pearce (1981) 177, 270.
Weatherhill (1981) 63.
Weatherhill (1985) 26, 35 & fig.
Higgitt (1986) 141.
Preston-Jones & Rose (1986) 159.
Thomas, A.C. (1986) 67-8 & fig.
Todd (1987) 295.

44 Redruth

The stone is now lost.

History

The stone was recorded by W. Borlase in 1740: 'In the Eastern wall at the back of the Altar on the outside of the Church, there is a Stone . . . with the following Inscr:'[1]. The present nave of St Euny's Church was rebuilt around 1770,[2] and it is likely that the inscribed stone was lost, or perhaps re-used in building, at that time. It has not been certainly recorded since 1740. It is possible, but no more than possible, that the stone was the one referred to by Penaluna in 1819: 'Within the fence of the plantations of the vicarage, is an ancient stone, which deserves the attention of the curious'.[3] Tangye suggested that the inscribed stone may originally have been associated with the 'prominent existing section of a *lan*'.[4]

Description and Text

The description and text are taken from Borlase's description and drawing (fig. II.44). The stone appears to have been an uncarved pillar-stone. It is not clear whether it was complete or incomplete. Presumably it originally stood erect, measuring three feet, six inches in height by ten inches in width, that is, 105 by 25 cm. The text was set in two lines, apparently without framing-lines or panels, on the visible face of the stone. It is unclear whether or not the text was either complete or primary. From the drawing, the letters appear to be legible but with three lost at the end of the second line. The script seems to be a predominantly capital one. The stone was apparently built into the wall so that the letters read horizontally. Originally it probably read downwards facing left, *see* Introduction, Section 4c. From the drawing, the text apparently read:

MAVOUIH
VITO[-]

1. Borlase, W. (unpub. 1740) 52.
2. Penaluna (1819) 218. Subsequently Penaluna gave this date as 1761: Penaluna (1838) II, 191.
3. Penaluna (1819) 219-20. Penaluna repeated this in 1838; Penaluna (1838) II, 191.
4. Tangye (1985) 171.

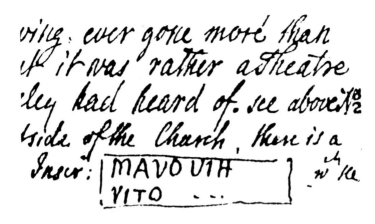

Figure II.44 Redruth (BL MS Egerton 2657, p. 52, renumbered as p. 59, photograph by permission of the British Library).

Discussion

The text probably read, MAVOUIH VITO[-]. A.C. Thomas suggested that the H might have been a misreading by W. Borlase of F/I or, less likely, of L/I and that the text therefore contained two personal names joined by FILI.[5] This suggestion is certainly a plausible hypothesis. Such personal names are not recorded but parallels can be suggested. A Celtic name, probably reading MAVOHE[NI] occurs on a stone from Llanboidy, Wales;[6] personal names beginning VIT- are well recorded, for example St Clement VITALI.

The stone presumably belonged to Category 1a, pillar-stones with a simple memorial text. Category 1 stones date from the fifth or sixth centuries to the eleventh century but this stone cannot be more closely dated.

Bibliography

Penaluna (1819) 219-20.[7]
Penaluna (1838) II, 191.[8]
Tangye (1985) 171-2.
Thomas, A.C. (1985*b*) 173-4 & fig.
Borlase (unpub. 1740) 52 & fig.

---

5. Thomas, A.C. (1985*b*) 174.
6. Macalister (1945) no. 365, pp. 349-50 & fig.; Nash-Williams (1950) no. 149, p. 113 & figs. See Jackson (1953) 440, 521.
7. Penaluna may or may not have been referring to the inscribed stone.
8. Penaluna may or may not have been referring to the inscribed stone.

45 Rialton

The stone is now at Rialton Barton, St Columb Minor. It is built at ground level into an exterior wall of an outbuilding. National Grid Reference SW 8499 6292. Examined 6 July 1984 and 4 July 1985.

History

The stone was first mentioned in 1814 by Lysons and Lysons who stated that it 'supports a shed in a back-court at Rialton-house'.[1] In 1817 C.S. Gilbert said that he had known of the stone since 1809, adding that it 'supports the roof of a linhay in the great court at Rialton Priory'.[2] According to C.G. Henderson, Rialton House, Rialton Priory and Rialton Court are alternative names for the same building, as opposed to Rialton Barton, which was built around 1866.[3] In 1852 T. Wright recorded that the stone 'stands in the parish of St. Columb Minor ... it is five feet high'.[4] This seems to imply that the stone was erect and had not then been built into a wall. Wright repeated this statement in subsequent editions of his work, in 1861 and 1875. This lessens its value as evidence since by August 1867 the stone had been 'built into the wall of a stable'.[5] In 1875 Rhys recorded the stone at 'a farmhouse called Upper Rialton ... in the wall of an outhouse'.[6] Upper Rialton is presumably Rialton Barton and the stone is likely to have been in its present position since 1867. Rhys stated that the walls at Upper Rialton contained 'stones brought from the neighbouring house, which was formerly a priory, now a farm house'.[7] Henderson also recorded this,[8] although the present occupants of Rialton Barton are not aware of any other early stones.[9]

Description

The stone is a pillar-stone, probably complete, with its visible face uncarved (fig. II.45). If it were standing erect it would measure 166 cm. in

---

1. Lysons, D. & Lysons, S. (1814) ccxxiii.
2. Gilbert, C.S. (1817) 195.
3. Henderson, C.G. (1936) 6.
4. Wright, T. (1852) 455.
5. Paull (1866-7b) 365.
6. Rhys (1875) 367.
7. Rhys (1875) 367.
8. Henderson, C.G. (1936) 6.
9. In a personal communication from William Carlyon of Rialton Barton.

Figure II.45   Rialton (photograph Royal Institution of Cornwall).

height and 40 to 56 cm. in width; 166 cm. bears comparison with Gilbert's 'five feet'[10] (*c.* 150 cm.) suggesting that little was lost when the stone was built into the wall. The text is incised without framing-lines or panels on the visible face of the stone. It is complete and legible. The letters are set in two lines and measure 5 to 10 cm. in height. Originally the letters probably read downwards facing left, *see* Introduction, Section 4c. The text appears to be primary and uses a predominantly capital script. There are some further marks at the left-hand edge of the face of the stone, to the left of the present second line. These seem to me more likely to be accidental scratches than letters.

Text

BO[N]EMIMORI
TRIBVNI

Discussion

The text reads BO[N]EMIMORI TRIBVNI. There are now no traces of any letters before TRIBVNI although Rhys read . . .ILLI there,[11] as did Langdon and Allen, a reading supported by Langdon's drawing.[12] This was expanded by Macalister to (F)ILLI.[13] The two earliest drawings, by Lysons and Lysons in 1814 and by C.S. Gilbert in 1809, show no lettering at this point.[14] There are traces of marks visible today but they do not much resemble letters. In view of this, and of the evidence of the early drawings, it seems to me unlikely that any text is lost. There are some problems in interpreting the text as it is today. First, BO[N]EMIMORI could be a Latin name *Bo[n]emimor(i)us* or it could be two words, MIMORI for MEMORIA 'memorial' or 'memory' either with a Latin name *Bonus, Bona* or with a Latin adjective *bonus, -a, -um.* BONA, which Nash-Williams took as a name, occurs on an inscription from Caerwys in Wales.[15] The formula *bone memoriæ,* 'of good memory' is very common in Gaulish inscriptions.[16] Second, TRIBVNI could be a Latin name *Tribun(i)us* or a title *tribunus* 'tribune'. The name TREBONI occurred on a now lost Romano-British stone from Hadrian's Wall.[17] Third, it is not clear whether the two

10. Gilbert, C.S. (1817) 195.
11. Rhys (1875) 367.
12. Langdon & Allen, J.R. (1895) 55 & fig.
13. Macalister (1945) 455 & fig.
14. Lysons, D. & Lysons, S. (1814) ccxxiii; Gilbert, C.S. (1817) 195 & fig., drawing dated 1809.
15. Macalister (1945) no. 402, pp. 377-8 & fig.; Nash-Williams (1950) no. 184, p. 126 & fig.; in my view BONA could be an adjective here too.
16. See Introduction, Section 5, Gaulish.
17. Collingwood, R.G. & Wright, R.P. (1965) no. 2019, p. 618.

words refer to one person or to two. A likely interpretation of the text is, '[the stone] of the tribune (or, of Tribun(i)us) of good memory'.

The stone probably belongs to Category 1b, pillar-stones with a longer text. Category 1 stones date from the fifth or sixth centuries to the eleventh century. The Latin name or title might suggest a sixth- to eighth-century date for this stone, a date which the use of horizontal I probably corroborates.

Bibliography

Lysons, D. & Lysons, S. (1814) ccxxiii & fig.
Gilbert, C.S. (1817) 195 & fig.
Hitchins (1824) I, 448.
Wright, T. (1852) 455.
Haigh (1858-9) 184.
Paull (1866-7b) 364-5.
Smirke (1866-7) xiii.
Grover (1867) 225-6.
Polsue (1867) 241.
Haddan & Stubbs (1869) 163.
Iago (1870-3) 485-6.
Iago et al. (1871-3) xlvi.
(-) (1871-3a) xxix.
Whitley (1874-8) 203.
Rhys (1875) 367-8.
Huebner (1876) no. 13, p. 5 & fig.
Rhys (1879) 403.
Langdon & Allen, J.R. (1888) 306-8, 318.
Iago (1890-1) 235-7.
Langdon (1890-1) 92.
Iago (1892-8) 38.
Borlase, W.C. (1893) 106.
Langdon & Allen, J.R. (1895) 52, 55, 60 & fig.
Langdon (1896) 23.
Rhys (1905) 57-8.
Daniell (1906) 241.
Langdon (1906) 420, passim & fig.
Jenner (1922-5) 58.
Macalister (1929) 188.
Hencken (1932) 223, 227, 295.
Jenkin (1934) 29.
Macalister (1945) no. 476, pp. 454-5 & fig.
Jackson (1946) 523.
Nash-Williams (1950) 11n.
Fox (1964) 159.
(-) (1966) 51.
Pevsner (1970) 152.
Radford (1975) 5, 13.
Preston-Jones & Rose (1986) 157.

46 St Clement

The stone is now in St Clement churchyard, on the south side of the church, near the south door. National Grid Reference SW 8509 4386. Examined 3 July 1984.

History

The stone was first mentioned in 1754 by W. Borlase who said: 'This Stone serves, at present, to hang a gate to, on the Vicarage of St. Clement's'.[1] It was illustrated in this position by Haslam.[2] In 1845 Haslam noted: 'The Cross ... thanks to the Rev. C.M. Gibson, the Vicar of St. Clement's, ... is released from the servile position which it long occupied as a gate post'.[3] When rescued by Gibson, the stone was presumably moved to the rectory garden where it was recorded in 1863.[4] It remained there until it was moved to its present position on 8 November 1938.[5]

Description

The stone is a cross, complete and containing carving (fig. II.46). The face of the stone shows evidence of its having been used as a gatepost. The shaft of the cross measures 226 cm. in height and the head some 40 cm.; the shaft measures 36 to 40 cm. in width and 26 to 37 cm. in thickness. It is likely that the stone was originally an inscribed pillar-stone and was subsequently made into a cross. The text is incised, without framing-lines or panels, on the face of the shaft. It is complete and legible. The letters, 6 to 14 cm. in height, are in one line and read downwards facing left. The text appears to be primary and the script used is a predominantly capital one. In addition traces of an ogham text, set on the edge of the left-hand side and the front of the shaft, were observed by Macalister.[6] There is no trace of any ogham text today.

---

1. Borlase, W. (1754) 356.
2. In Kent *et al.* (1846*b*) 77-8 & fig.
3. Haslam (1845) 30; paper read 7 November 1845.
4. Jones (1863) 287.
5. The guidebook to the church erroneously gives this date as 1922: Bampfield & O'Flynn (1981) 8.
6. Macalister (1929) 181-2 & fig.; Macalister (1945) 451-2 & fig.

Figure II.46 St Clement (photograph Herbert Hughes).

Text

IGN̲IOCVITALIFILITORRICI

Discussion

The text reads, IGNIOC VITALI FILI TORRICI, that is, 'Ignioc. [The stone] of Vitalus, son of Torricus', with FILI for FILII. It has been suggested many times that the first word, IGNIOC, presumably a name, is a text later than the rest. There is some evidence to support this: the letters of IGNIOC are smaller than the rest; the script of IGNIOC includes one certainly insular form, G, and another that is possibly insular, N, while the rest of the text uses only capitals; IGNIOC does not fit well into the grammatical structure of the rest of the text. Individually, features such as these are not uncommon in south-western inscriptions; taken together, they may suggest, but certainly do not prove, that IGNIOC was a later addition. IGNIOC could have been added at the time when the stone was made into a cross or it could pre-date this.

TORRICI is a Celtic name, perhaps a hypocoristic form.[7] The -OC of IGNIOC suggests that it too may be Celtic. VITALI is presumably the common Latin name VITALIS.[8] Jackson's discussion of this name and of VITALIANI seems to imply that he took them as Celtic names, although elsewhere he described VITALIANI as Latin.[9] VITALIANI occurs on a stone from Nevern, Wales.[10] The name VITALIS occurs on three Gaulish stones, from Arles, Treves and Paris;[11] it also occurs on a Romano-British stone from Cirencester.[12] The name VITALIN occurs on an Irish ogham stone from Ballinvoher.[13] Macalister saw traces of an ogham text on the St Clement stone but his reading is highly conjectural and in my view it is unlikely that the stone ever contained an ogham text.[14]

The stone probably belongs to Category 1c, pillar-stones which were later re-cut to form crosses. Category 1 stones date from the fifth or sixth centuries to the eleventh century. In their original form, Category 1c stones are likely to pre-date the period of the ninth to eleventh century since the re-cutting of the stones to form crosses may date from then. If the name VITALI is Latin, this suggests a sixth- to eighth-century date for the stone, a date which the use of horizontal I probably corroborates.

---

7. Cf. Jackson (1953) 610 and Rhys (1879) 358, 405; see also Plummer (1910) II, 344.
8. Rhys (1879) 405.
9. Jackson (1953) 290-2; 183.
10. Macalister (1945) no. 445, pp. 423-4 & fig.; Nash-Williams (1950) no. 354, p. 197 & figs.
11. Le Blant (1865) no. 535, p. 271 & fig.; Le Blant (1856) no. 301, pp. 406-7 & fig.; Le Blant (1856) no. 202, pp. 277-81 & fig.
12. Collingwood, R.G. & Wright, R.P. (1965) no. 111, p. 34 & fig.
13. Macalister (1945) no. 166, p. 160 & fig.
14. Macalister (1929) 181-2 & fig.; Macalister (1945) 451-2 & fig.

Bibliography

Borlase, W. (1754) 356 & fig.
Gough (1789) I, 15.
Polwhele (1803) I, 146-8.
Lysons, D. & Lysons, S. (1814) ccxxi.
Gilbert, C.S. (1817) 196.
Hitchins (1824) I, 432-3.
Penaluna (1838) I, 110.
Redding (1842) 57n.
Haslam (1845) 30.
Kent *et al.* (1846*a*) 49.
Kent *et al.* (1846*b*) 77-8 & fig.
Haslam (1847) 308-9 & fig.
(-) (1851*b*) 142.
Wright, T. (1852) 455.
Whitley *et al.* (1856) 26.
(-) (1856) 154.
Blight (1858*a*) 125 & fig.
Haigh (1858-9) 184-5.
Smirke *et al.* (1861) 177.
Jones (1862) 139.
Jones (1863) 287-8, 290 & fig.
Barham (1866-7) 56.
Paull (1866-7*a*) xi.
Polsue (1867) 214.
Haddan & Stubbs (1869) 163.
Iago (1871-3) 61n.
Polsue (1872) iv.
Huebner (1876) no. 9, pp. 3-4 & fig.
Rhys (1879) 359, 405.
(-) (1884*c*) 204 & fig.
Allen, J.R. (1887) 98.
Langdon & Allen, J.R. (1888) 307-9, 318.
Loth (1890) 48.
Iago (1890-1) 237.
Langdon (1890-1) 91.
Borlase, W.C. (1893) 182.
Langdon (1893-5*b*) 280.
Langdon & Allen, J.R. (1895) 50, 53, 59 & fig.
Langdon (1896) 6, 22.
Rhys (1896) 285.
Macalister (1902) 122.
Holder (1904) col. 1893.
Daniell (1906) 240.
Langdon (1906) 419, *passim* & fig.
Sedding (1909) 328.
Jenner (1922-5) 58.
Henderson, C.G. (1925) 41-2.
Diack (1927) 229n, 232.
Macalister (1929) 181-2 & fig.
Hencken (1932) 241, 243, 266, 295.
Jenkin (1934) 30-1.
Macalister (1945) no. 473, pp. 451-2 & fig.
Jackson (1950) 199.
Nash-Williams (1950) 11n.
Jackson (1953) 171n, 290, 610.
Henderson, C.G. (1953-6*a*) 76.
Best (1959) 437.

(-) (1966) 51.
Pevsner (1970) 164-5.
Laing (1975) 125.
Radford (1975) 4, 10, 13.
Mandach (1978) 230 & fig.
Pearce (1978) 21-30, 71, 178 & fig.
Bampfield & O'Flynn (1981) 8.
Pearce (1981) 171 & fig.
Thomas, A.C. (1985*b*) 174.
Weatherhill (1985) 26, 50 & fig.
Harvey (1987) 47.

47 St Columb Major

The stone is now in St Columb Major churchyard, beside the south door of the church. National Grid Reference SW 9129 6366. Examined 6 July 1984, 4 July 1985 and 8 July 1986.

History

The stone was first recorded in 1858 by Blight: 'This Cross stands without the church-yard wall at St. Columb; ... this stone has recently been used as a gate-post'.[1] In August 1872 the stone was recorded 'in a garden adjoining' the churchyard.[2] It was still outside the churchyard in 1875.[3] By 1895 the stone was: 'Standing in the churchyard, near the south porch',[4] that is, in its present position. Macalister described the stone as 'much abraded, apparently by footwear'.[5] The sole evidence for the stone's having lain flat is if it is identified with a stone described by Godwin in 1853: 'The stone lying between the jambs of this doorway [i.e. the inner doorway of the south porch] is evidently antecedent to the date of the present structure. It appears to be sepulchral, the remains of a cross enclosed within a circle being still visible'.[6] This description could refer to the inscribed stone. The history of the stone between 1858 and 1895 given above, however, makes this seem unlikely. In 1896 Langdon appears to have known of three stones: the inscribed cross-slab in the churchyard, the cross in the churchyard which had been a gatepost, and a cross-slab which had been a step to a doorway but which was then inside the church.[7] The last is presumably the stone referred to by Godwin. Macalister seems to have confused these stones and his description 'abraded ... by footwear' can therefore be disregarded.

Description

The stone is a complete slab carved with a cross (fig. II.47). It measures 134 cm. in height, 64 to 65 cm. in width and 23 to 26 cm. in thickness.

---

1. Blight (1858a) 10.
2. (-) (1871-3a) xxviii.
3. Rhys (1875) 366.
4. Langdon & Allen, J.R. (1895) 50.
5. Macalister (1929) 182.
6. Godwin (1853) 322.
7. Langdon (1896) 6, 22, 23. Alternatively it is possible that Langdon's descriptions on pp. 6 and 22 refer to the same stone; Macalister's confusion, however, remains.

Figure II.47   St Columb Major (photograph Woolf/
Greenham Collection).

Comparison with Blight's measurements suggests that some 31 cm. is now beneath ground.[8] The text is incised without framing-lines or panels on the face of the slab. The letters, 7-12 cm. in height, are set in three lines and read horizontally. The text is now illegible and no further description of it is possible.

Text

The text is now illegible.

Discussion

Since it was first published the text seems to have been hard to read. The earliest drawing of the stone, by Blight, published in 1858, shows only traces of letters and Blight said then: 'it evidently bore an inscription, which is now almost entirely obliterated'.[9] Langdon's drawing shows only traces of lettering and he noted: 'Only a very few letters of the inscription are now left'.[10] C.G. Henderson also said that, 'Remains of ancient lettering can be traced but not deciphered'.[11] Macalister, however, read, IACONIVS adding, 'as soon as the letters are seen at all, they are perfectly easy to read'.[12] The traces of letters remaining today are not inconsistent with Macalister's reading. Nevertheless, in view of the earlier evidence, this reading must be treated with great caution and the text considered as now irrecoverable.

The stone belongs to Category 3c, cross-slabs, but it cannot be dated.

Bibliography

Blight (1858*a*) 10 & fig.
Polsue (1867) 236.
(-) (1871-3*a*) xxviii.
Rhys (1875) 366.
Langdon & Allen, J.R. (1895) 50, 53, 59.
Langdon (1896) 6.
Langdon (1906) 419, *passim* & fig.
Macalister (1929) 182.
Henderson, C.G. (1930) 54.
Hencken (1932) 241-2, 295.
Macalister (1945) no. 475, pp. 453-4 & figs.
Henderson, C.G. (1953-6*a*) 92.
Best (1959) 437.
(-) (1966) 51.
Pearce (1978) 27.

---

8. Blight (1858*a*) 10.
9. Blight (1858*a*) 10 & fig.
10. Langdon (1906) 419 & fig.
11. Henderson, C.G. (1930) 54.
12. Macalister (1945) 454 & fig.

48 St Endellion

The stone is now about 1.5 km from St Endellion. It stands on a piece of grass at the junction where two unclassified roads, one to St Minver and one to Roscarrock, leave the unclassified road from Portquin to St Endellion. National Grid Reference SW 9900 7972. Examined 10 July 1984, 4 July 1985 and 25 September 1987.

History

The stone was probably recorded in 1753, according to M. Henderson: 'In 1753 a James Tregeare collected notes for Borlase . . . He referred to a cross standing on the boundary of Roscarrock Barton, between Roscarrock and St Endellion Church "... with a barbarous inscription on the spill of same"'.[1] The stone was certainly recorded in 1821. G.E Ellis quoted an extract from the diary of J.A. Trevan for 1821 where Trevan noted: 'At the junction of the roads above Roscarrock higher-town gate, stood in a great stone pedestal, a square granite post' which had 'been thrown down and broken within these few years'.[2] In 1873 Maclean recorded that the stone had been 'removed by the late Mr. Symons of Gonvena to Doydon Head, near Port Quin, on the western side of the creek, where he had erected a summer-house, and where the stone yet remains'.[3] The stone remained on Doydon Head until 'the end of 1932' when it was replaced in its original position, where it still is.[4]

Description

The stone is a pillar-stone probably complete but in two pieces, cemented into a circular base (fig. II.48). It appears to be uncarved, although a cross in relief has been noted on the back of the stone.[5] I looked for this cross but could not see it. There is a hole at the top of the stone which Ellis suggested might have been a socket-hole.[6] The two pieces together

---

1. Henderson, M. (unpub. 1985) 362. No reference is given for the quotation from Tregeare.
2. Quoted in Ellis, G.E. (1954-5a) 65.
3. Maclean (1873) 485.
4. Willmott (1933) 17.
5. See, for example, Hencken (1932) 223, 242-3 & figs; Ellis, G.E. (1954-5a) 66.
6. Ellis, G.E. (1952-3a) 61; Ellis, G.E. (1954-5a) 66.

Figure II.48 St Endellion (photograph E.N. Masson Phillips).

measure 149 cm. in height, the width being 30 to 31 cm. and the thickness 19 to 21 cm.

The texts are incised on one face of the stone and both appear to be primary. Text (i) is set at the top of the stone and reads horizontally; its one letter is 33 cm. in height. This text is legible and complete. Beneath it is incised an arc of a circle enclosing the top of text (ii); there are no further framing-lines or panels on the stone. Text (ii) is set in two lines reading downwards and facing left, the letters being 9 to 10 cm. in height. Text (ii) is highly deteriorated and might not be complete. The script used appears to be predominantly capital in form with many ligatures.

Texts

(i)   ☧

(ii) [BR..ACNIIH/C/IAC/IT]
      [-US]

Discussion

Text (i) reads ☧, the *chi-rho* symbol in its monogram form. About 12 to 14 letters are lost from the lacuna in text (ii) and further text might have been lost at the end of the second line. Text (ii) probably reads, [BR..ACNI IHC IACIT -US], perhaps '[the body] of [Br..acnus] lies here [-]' with [IHC] for HIC and [IACIT] for IACET. This text has always been hard to read. In 1821 Trevan described the inscriptions as 'now almost obliterated' and in 1873 Maclean described the stone as 'in very bad condition', a statement to some extent confirmed by Iago's drawing which accompanies it.[7] Nevertheless, Maclean read text (ii) as 'without doubt, BROEAGAN HIC IACIT' perhaps followed by NADOTTI FILIVS, although these two words are described as 'very doubtful'.[8] In 1895 Langdon and Allen read, BROCAGNI IHC IACIT | NADOTTI FILIVS although the accompanying drawing suggests that their reading of the second line was largely conjectural.[9] In 1929 Macalister said of Langdon and Allen's reading of the second line, 'I can say no more than that I found nothing to contradict it',[10] but later he accepted their reading.[11] If the reading were NADOTTI, the first element might be *nad-* as occurs in Irish names.[12] Jackson, following Macalister's reading, took BROCAGNI as a Celtic name, either Primitive Irish or Primitive Cornish.[13] The name BROCAGNI occurs on a stone from Llangeler, Wales,[14] and in ogham on an Irish stone from Dunalis.[15] In 1821 Trevan described the stone as containing inscriptions 'on two sides'.[16] It is possible that he was referring to texts (i) and (ii) on one face and the cross in relief which has been observed on the opposite face; alternatively he could have seen a text totally lost by the time of Maclean's detailed description in 1873. Macalister suggested that there might also be an ogham text

7. Trevan, quoted in Ellis, G.E. (1954-5*a*) 65; Maclean (1873) 485-6, quotation from p. 486.
8. Maclean (1873) 485.
9. Langdon & Allen, J.R. (1895) 58 & fig.
10. Macalister (1929) 183.
11. Macalister (1945) 457.
12. Plummer (1910) II, 366; O'Brien (1973) 277-8.
13. Jackson (1953) 566, 665n.
14. Macalister (1945) no. 372, pp. 354-6 & fig.; Nash-Williams (1950) no. 160, p. 116 & figs.
15. Macalister (1945) no. 316, p. 304 & fig.
16. Quoted in Ellis, G.E. (1954-5*a*) 65.

on the stone.[17] There is no sign of any ogham text today and in my view this can be disregarded.

The stone belongs to Category 1b, pillar-stones with longer texts. Category 1 stones date from the fifth or sixth centuries to the eleventh century. On the evidence of the monogram *chi-rho* symbol, this stone is likely to date from the sixth to the eighth century.

Bibliography

Iago (1870-3) 483.
Maclean (1873) 485-6 & figs.
Iago (1874-8) 364n.
Huebner (1876) no. 15, p. 5 & figs.
Rhys (1879) 402.
Langdon & Allen, J.R. (1888) 306-10, 318.
Borlase, W.C. (1893) 183-4.
Langdon & Allen, J.R. (1895) 51, 58, 59 & figs.
Holder (1896) cols 616-17.
Langdon (1896) 5-6.
Baring-Gould (1899-1900) 110.
Holder (1904) col. 672.
Rhys (1905) 87-8.
Daniell (1906) 241.
Langdon (1906) 420, *passim* & figs.
Jenner (1917) 75.
Macalister (1929) 183.
Hencken (1932) 223, 242-3, 296 & figs.
Willmott (1933) 17-18.
Jenkin (1934) 30.
Macalister (1945) no. 478, pp. 456-7 & fig.
Jackson (1950) 199.
Ellis, G.E. (1952-3a) 61.
Jackson (1953) 171n, 463, 566, 665n.
Ellis, G.E. (1954-5a) 65-7 & figs.
Fox (1964) 160.
(-) (1966) 51.
Wall (1968) 177 & fig.
Thomas, A.C. (1969-72) 259 & fig.
Pevsner (1970) 169.
Hamlin (1972) 25.
Laing (1975) 125.
Radford (1975) 10-11, 13.
Pearce (1978) 26-8, 162 & fig.
Thomas, A.C. (1980) 108.
Pearce (1981) 172, 187 & fig.
Thomas, A.C. (1981) 165 & fig.
Weatherhill (1985) 26, 82 & figs.
Thomas, A.C. (1986) 141 & fig.
Harvey (1987) 47.
McManus (1991) 107.
Baird & White (unpub. 1961) vol. IV, D-G.[18]
Henderson, M. (unpub. 1985) no. 187, pp. 362-3 & figs.

---

17. Macalister (1929) 183.
18. There is no page numbering in this typescript.

49 St Hilary

The stone is now in St Hilary churchyard, to the south of the church, beside the gate. National Grid Reference SW 5503 3127. Examined 5 July 1984 and 3 July 1985.

History

The stone was found in 1853 after the destruction of St Hilary church by fire in March 1853. Blight recorded that the stone 'was found at the north-west angle of the chancel, 2 feet below the level of the floor. From its position, it is probable that it was used as a foundation stone'.[1] By 1858 the stone was described as: 'placed close to the church-yard gate, on the right hand side of the walk leading to the church porch'.[2] This is its present position.

Description

The stone is a pillar-stone containing carving and is probable complete (fig. II.49). It measures 193 cm. in height, 35 to 52 cm. in width and 26 cm. in thickness. Comparison with Blight's measurements suggests that only 4 or 5 cm. of the stone are now beneath the ground.[3] The text is incised without framing-lines or panels on the visible face of the stone. The text is legible and complete. The letters, 9 to 14 cm. in height, are set in two lines and read downwards facing left. The text appears to be primary and uses a predominantly capital script.

Text

N[.] NOTI
[..] NOTI

---

1. Blight (1856) 68.
2. Edmonds (1858a) 181-2.
3. Blight (1856) 68.

Figure II.49 St Hilary (photograph Herbert Hughes).

Discussion

The text appears to read, N[.] NOTI [..] NOTI, perhaps '[the stone] of Notus, [son] of Notus' with some marks or letters preceding the text. The name is presumably Latin; Holder, however, taking [-]NOTI as an incomplete name, regarded it as Celtic.[4] The marks or letters have been interpreted in various ways, for example, as mason's marks made by Notus,[5] as the letters CONG and CONG to give a reading CONGNOTI CONGNOTI,[6] and as α, ω and M = Maria.[7] In my view it is not clear whether these marks were letters, some of an odd form, or were intended as decoration.

The stone belongs to Category 1a, pillar-stones with a simple memorial text. Category 1 stones date from the fifth or sixth centuries to the eleventh century; the use of a Latin name, if such it is, would suggest that this stone dates from the sixth to the eighth century.

Bibliography

Blight (1856) 68 & figs.
Edmonds (1858a) 181-2 & fig.
Edmonds (1862) 63-4, 213 & fig.
Paull (1866-7a) xi.
Polsue (1868) 189.
Iago (1871-3) 61n.
Huebner (1876) no. 4, p. 2 & fig.
Rhys (1879) 405.
Cornish (1880-4) 174.
(-) (1880-4b) 99.
Langdon & Allen, J.R. (1888) 319.
Iago (1888-92) 387.
Iago (1892-8) 35-9 & fig.
Teague *et al.* (1892-8) 118-22 & fig.
Borlase, W.C. (1893) 182-3.
Iago (1893-5a) 111-12 & fig.
Langdon & Allen, J.R. (1895) 51, 54, 59 & fig.
Holder (1904) col. 776.
Daniell (1906) 239.
Langdon (1906) 420, *passim* & fig.
Jenner (1924-5) 275.
Henderson, C.G. (1925) 83.
Macalister (1929) 179.
Hencken (1932) 241, 298.
Jenkin (1934) 30.
Macalister (1945) no. 481, pp. 460-1 & fig.
Thomas, I. (1947) 54.
(-) (1966) 51.
Pevsner (1970) 178.
Pearce (1978) 71, 179.
Weatherhill (1985) 108.

---

4. Holder (1904) col. 776.
5. Blight (1856) 68.
6. Iago (1892-8) 37-9.
7. Macalister (1945) 460.

50 St Just I

The stone is now lost.

History

The stone was first recorded in 1842 by the Rev. J. Buller who found it near St Helen's Chapel, Cape Cornwall. Buller stated:

> The cross ... was rescued a few years since by him who records the fact, from the artificial water course which passes near [that is, near the chapel], in which it was immersed. It may now be seen preserved as a valuable relic in the chancel of the parish church with a brass plate denoting its ancient locality.[1]

Haslam drew the stone and published this drawing in 1845 and again in 1847.[2] In 1847 the stone was still in the church, 'in a recess in the chancel'.[3] In 1858 Blight said, referring to Buller, that the stone had been placed in the chancel, and published a drawing of the stone which is not Haslam's initialled drawing.[4] Blight did not illustrate the stone in his first edition of this work, published in 1856. This suggests that he drew the stone, or acquired the drawing, between 1856 and 1858. In 1868 Polsue reported that the stone was no longer in the church.[5] In 1890-1, Iago stated that the stone was down the vicarage well.[6]

In 1893 Langdon suggested that this stone was one of the two crosses that the Rev. G.C. Gorham, vicar of St Just from 1846 to 1850, threw down the vicarage well; only one of these was recovered and Langdon suggested that the inscribed stone was still down the well.[7] There is a discrepancy in date between Gorham's finally leaving St Just in 1850 and Blight's publishing his drawing of the stone in 1858. Langdon, without giving any evidence, said: 'Although Blight illustrates this stone, I am in a position to state that he never saw it'.[8] It seems to me that the balance of probability is that the stone was lost between 1858 and 1868, and its loss was not

---

1. Buller (1842) 45.
2. Haslam (1845) 29 & fig.; Haslam (1847) 304 & fig.
3. Haslam (1847) 303.
4. Blight (1858b) 61 & fig.
5. Polsue (1868) 293.
6. Iago (1890-1) 255.
7. Langdon (1893) 105.
8. Langdon (1893) 104.

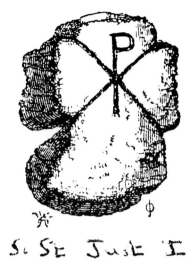

Figure II.50   St Just I (from Haslam (1847) 304).

therefore due to the machinations of Gorham. In 1909 and again in 1964 it was implied, clearly in error, that the stone was still in existence.[9] M. Henderson recorded a local tradition that the stone is down a well under the floor of the old kitchen of the vicarage, and not down either of the wells in the vicarage garden, both of which were searched in vain in May 1970.[10]

Description and Text

The description and text are taken from Haslam's description and drawing (fig. II.50). The stone, which was probably complete, was shaped like a small cross but uncarved except for the text. Haslam said it had 'the appearance of having been a gable-cross'.[11] It measured 'about eleven inches by nine',[12] that is, about 27 by 22 cm. The text was set horizontally, without framing-lines or panels, on the one face of the stone illustrated. It was legible and presumably complete. It is unclear whether or not it was primary. The text read ☧, that is, the *chi-rho* symbol.

---

9. Sedding (1909) 170-1, although on p. 335 the stone is said to be lost; Vosper (1964) 257.
10. Henderson, M. (unpub. 1985) 496.
11. Haslam (1847) 304.
12. Haslam (1847) 304.

Discussion

Both the early drawings of this stone show the *chi-rho* monogram in its early, 'Constantine', form. On the Continent this form of *chi-rho* dates from the fourth to the fifth century,[13] and this stone may have been fifth-century in date. The stone belongs to Category 3d, *chi-rho* stones.

Bibliography

Buller (1842) 45.
Haslam (1845) 29 & fig.
Haslam (1846a) 235.
Haslam (1847) 304 & fig.
(-) (1851b) 170.[14]
Blight (1856) viin.
(-) (1856) 183.
Blight (1858b) 61 & fig.
Blight (1861) 179 & fig.
Edmonds (1862) 199.
Polsue (1868) 293.
Haddan & Stubbs (1869) 163n.
Huebner (1876) 1 & fig.
Allen, J.R. (1887) 86-7 & fig.
Langdon & Allen, J.R. (1888) 308-9, 319.
Iago (1890-1) 254-5.
Langdon (1890-1) 92n.
(-) (1892) 2.
Langdon (1893) 97-108 & fig.
Langdon & Allen, J.R. (1895) 51, 55, 60 & fig.
Langdon (1896) 5, 271n.
(-) (1896b) 256.
McGovern (1904) 7.
Langdon (1906) 420, *passim* & fig.
(-) (1906a) 181-2.
Sedding (1909) 170-1, 335.
Jenner (1917) 75.
Macalister (1929) 179.
Hencken (1932) 222-4, 266-7, 300 & fig.
Thomas, A.C. (1957-8) 61.
Henderson, C.G. (1957-60a) 240.
Russell (1958-9) 101.
Vosper (1964) 257, 262.
(-) (1966) 51.
Nicolas (1968) 26-7 & fig.
Wall (1968) 175 & fig.
Russell (1971) 81.
Hamlin (1972) 25.
Rowe, L. (1973) & fig.[15]
Maxwell (1976) 10.

---

13. Hamlin (1972) 24.
14. It is not clear whether this reference and the following one, two editions of the same book, are describing St Just I or St Just II: 'in the church a Roman Christian monument with ☧', (-) (1851b) 170.
15. There is no page numbering in this book.

Pearce (1978) 21-30, 66-7, 88, 178 & fig.
Pearce (1981) 187 & fig.
Henderson, M. (unpub. 1985) 496.

51 St Just II

The stone now stands in the north aisle of St Just church. National Grid Reference SW 3714 3144. Examined 2 July 1984 and 2 July 1985.

History

In 1834 the Rev. J. Buller found the stone built into the wall of the chancel of the church; when he wrote in 1842, the stone had been 'placed in the wall on the north side of the altar'.[1] It remained there, being recorded in 1893 in use 'as the credence table',[2] until it was 'removed from the sanctuary into the north aisle, where it lay for some time on the floor just below the pulpit'.[3] Peter in 1899 was the first to record it in its present position.[4]

Description

The stone is an uncarved pillar-stone, probably complete, set into a modern base. It measures 104 cm. in height to the base, 34 to 37 cm. in width and 21 to 29 cm. in thickness. Text (i) is incised without framing-lines in an open-ended panel, measuring 66 by 26 cm., on one face of the stone (fig. II.51(i)). Text (i) is legible and complete. Its one letter is 21 cm. in height and reads horizontally. Text (ii) is incised without framing-lines or panels on one side of the stone, the left-hand side if text (i) is taken as being on the face of the stone (fig. II.51(ii)). Text (ii) is legible and complete. Its letters, 5 to 12 cm. in height, are in two lines reading downwards and facing left. Text (ii) uses a predominantly capital script. Both texts appear to be primary.

Texts

(i)   Ᵽ
(ii) NI
      SELVSI̲C̲IACIT

---

1. Buller (1842) 19-21, quotation from p. 21.
2. Langdon (1893) 102.
3. (-) (1906*d*) 183.
4. Peter (1899-1900) 186, paper read 1899; cf. Langdon (1906) 420: 'used as a credence table till 1901'.

Figure II.51(i)   St Just II, text (i) (photograph E.N. Masson Phillips).

Discussion

Text (i) reads ☧, the *chi-rho* symbol in its monogram form. Text (ii) can be read, SELVS IC IACIT, that is, 'Selus lies here' with IACIT for IACET. The letters IC might be a spelling of HIC or a double ligature I/H/C for HIC. The letters NI are smaller in size and are set above the rest of this text. If contemporary, they may have been intended to be inserted into the text to correct a spelling error. The name would then read SELNIVS or SENILVS.[5] The name SENILVS, and probably also SELVS, would be Latin

---

5. This suggestion was first published by Rhys: Rhys (1874*b*) 333.

Figure II.51(ii) St Just II, text (ii) (photograph Herbert Hughes).

but SELNIVS is less easy to explain. The name SENLS for SENILIS occurs on a Romano-British stone from Hadrian's Wall.[6]

The St Just stone belongs to Category 1b, pillar-stones with longer texts. Category 1 stones date from the fifth or sixth centuries to the eleventh century. On the evidence of the monogram *chi-rho* symbol, this stone is likely to date from the sixth to the eighth century, a date which the use of horizontal I probably corroborates. If the stone does contain a Latin name, this would also be in accordance with such a date.

Bibliography

Buller (1842) 19-21 & figs.
Haslam (1845) 29-30 & fig.
Haslam (1846a) 235.
Haslam (1847) 303-4 & fig.
(-) (1851b) 170.[7]
(-) (1856) 183.
Edmonds (1858a) 180 & figs.
Blight (1861) 174-5.
Blight (1862) 539 & fig.
Edmonds (1862) 62, 210 & figs.
Blight (1865) 28 & fig.
Grover (1867) 227 & fig.
Polsue (1868) 290.
Haddan & Stubbs (1869) 162.
Rhys (1874b) 333.
Huebner (1876) no. 1, p. 1 & fig.
Rhys (1879) 406.
(-) (1880-4a) 18.
Lach-Szyrma (1886-9) 56.
Allen, J.R. (1887) 87-8 & fig.
Langdon & Allen, J.R. (1888) 306-8, 319.
Ranken (1888-92) 313.
Loth (1890) 47.
Iago (1890-1) 237, 254.
Langdon (1890-1) 92.
(-) (1892) 2.
Iago (1892-8) 38.
Borlase, W.C. (1893) 182-3.
Langdon (1893) 97-108 & figs.
Langdon & Allen, J.R. (1895) 51, 55, 60 & figs.
Langdon (1896) 5-6, 24.
(-) (1896b) 256.
Peter (1899-1900) 186-7 & fig.
McGovern (1904) 7.
Daniell (1906) 456.
Greenbank (1906a) 183.
Langdon (1906) 420, *passim* & figs.
(-) (1906a) 182.

---

6. Collingwood, R.G. & Wright, R.P. (1965) no. 1665, p. 252 & fig.
7. It is not clear whether this reference and the following one, two editions of the same book, are describing St Just I or St Just II: 'in the church a Roman Christian monument with Ⲣ', (-) (1851b) 170.

(-) (1906*b*) 182-3.
(-) (1906*c*) 183.
(-) (1906*d*) 183-4.
Sedding (1909) 170-1, 335.
Jenner (1917) 75.
Jenner (1919) 128.
Brown (1921) 92 & fig.
Dalton (1921) 65.
Jenner (1922-5) 58.
Henderson, C.G. (1925) 87.
Collingwood, W.G. (1927) 1.
Macalister (1929) 179.
Hencken (1932) 223, 225, 300.
Jenkin (1934) 29-30.
Dexter, T.F.G. & Dexter, H. (1938) 271-2 & fig.
Macalister (1945) no. 483, pp. 461-2 & figs.
Thomas, A.C. (1954) 18.
Thomas, A.C. (1957-8) 61.
Henderson, C.G. (1957-60*a*) 242.
Russell (1958-9) 101.
Best (1959) 439.
Fox (1964) 160.
Vosper (1964) 262 & fig.
(-) (1966) 51.
Nicholas (1968) 29.
Wall (1968) 177 & fig.
Thomas, A.C. (1969-72) 259 & fig.
Pevsner (1970) 16, 183.
Russell (1971) 81.
Thomas, A.C. (1971*a*) 77 & fig.
Hamlin (1972) 25.
Rowe, L. (1973) & fig.[8]
Radford (1975) 9.
Maxwell (1976) 10.
Pearce (1978) 27-30, 70, 88, 161, 179 & figs.
Pearce (1981) 187, 270 & fig.
Thomas, A.C. (1981) 165 & fig.
Weatherhill (1981) 74 & figs.
Weatherhill (1985) 26, 108 & figs.

8. There is no page numbering in this book.

52 St Kew

The stone is now inside St Kew church, at the west end of the nave. National Grid Reference SX 0215 7687. Examined 10 July 1984 and 6 July 1986.

History

The stone was found in 1924 by the vicar, the Rev. H. Dalton Jackson, when 'the bridge spanning the brook just below the church was widened'.[1] Macalister stated that: 'At one time it was apparently used as a footbridge, but it was lost in the bed of a stream flowing past the church, and recovered in 1924';[2] Macalister does not, however, give any evidence to support this assertion that the stone had been a footbridge. By 1927 the stone was in the churchyard and by 1932 it was inside the church.[3] Hencken noted that the stone appeared to have been used as a gatepost in modern times.[4]

Description

The stone is an uncarved pillar-stone, broken at top and bottom (fig. II.52). It measures 72 cm. in height, 30 to 37 cm. in width and 30 to 39 cm. in thickness. Text (i) is incised in one line on the visible face of the stone. This text is set without framing-lines in an open-ended panel about 40 cm. in length. It is legible, probably complete and appears to be primary. The letters measure 6 to 9 cm. in height and read downwards facing left, assuming the panel to have been closed at the top and open-ended at the bottom. The script used is a predominantly capital one. Text (ii), the ogham text, is incised on the upper part of the edge between the visible face and the right-hand side of the stone. Originally the text probably read vertically downwards. This text is incomplete and slightly deteriorated but is probably primary.

Texts

(i)   IV[S]TI
(ii)   [ogham] [-]STI̲

---

1. Doble (1927) 14.
2. Macalister (1945) 462.
3. Doble (1927) 14; Hencken (1932) 242.
4. Hencken (1935) 156-7.

Figure II.52   St Kew (photograph Herbert Hughes).

Discussion

Text (i) reads, IV[S]TI, with an odd form of insular S. This can be inter-preted, '[the stone] of Iu[s]tus'. Text (ii) reads, [-]STI, but is now too incomplete to be intelligible. It is possible, but by no means certain, that it is a rendering of text (i). The name IV[S]TI is Latin.[5] The name IUSTI may also have occurred on a lost stone from Plourin in Brittany.[6] The name IVSTI also occurs on a stone from Ystradfellte, Wales.[7] In the form IVSTVS it occurs twice on a Gaulish stone from Narbonne,[8] and IVSTV- also occurs on a broken stone from St Éloi.[9] In the form IVSTVS, the name occurs on a Romano-British stone from Caerleon.[10]

The stone belongs to Category 1a, pillar-stones with simple memorial texts. Category 1 stones date from the fifth or sixth centuries to the eleventh century. On the evidence of the ogham text this stone is likely to date from the fifth or sixth century to the eighth century. The Latin name is in accordance with this dating.

Bibliography

(-) (1922-5) 351-2.
Doble (1927) 14.
Hencken (1932) 242-4, 300.
Jenkin (1934) 30.
Hencken (1935) 156-8 & figs.
Macalister (1945) no. 484, p. 462 & fig.
Jackson (1950) 199, 205, 208.
Jackson (1953) 171-2, 187.
Fox (1964) 159.
(-) (1966) 51.
Pevsner (1970) 185.
Laing (1975) 125.
Pearce (1978) 26, 71, 161, 179 & fig.
Pearce (1981) 172, 188-9.
Ashbee (1982) 181.
Bernier (1982) 161.
Weatherhill (1985) 82 & fig.
Olson & Padel (1986) 44.
Preston-Jones & Rose (1986) 157.
McManus (1991) 61-2, 64, 98, 113.

---

5. Jackson (1953) 172.
6. Bernier (1982) 161.
7. Macalister (1945) no. 344, p. 331 & fig.; Nash-Williams (1950) no. 73, p. 82 & figs.
8. Le Blant (1865) no. 621, pp. 476-80 & fig.
9. Le Blant (1856) no. 113, p. 200 & fig.
10. Collingwood, R.G. & Wright, R.P. (1965) no. 322, p. 110 & fig.

53 Sancreed I

The stone is now in Sancreed churchyard, near the south door of the church. National Grid Reference SW 4202 2934. Examined 2 July 1984, 2 July 1985 and 1 July 1986.

History

The inscribed cross-shaft was found in 1881 by the vicar, the Rev. R. Basset Rogers, during restoration of the church: 'It was built horizontally into the upper and eastern part of the wall of the aisle'.[1] Rogers took a carved, uninscribed cross-head, attached to a portion of shaft, from where it was fixed to the churchyard wall and cemented it on to the inscribed shaft. This uninscribed cross-head with its portion of shaft had been illustrated on the churchyard wall by Blight.[2] Rogers then placed his composite cross 'on the right-hand side of the gateway leading to the vicarage, which adjoins the churchyard'.[3] On 13 June 1894, at Langdon's instigation, the cross was removed from there, placed in a base, and erected in its present position.[4] Langdon held that the cross-head and shaft had originally come from the same monument but that a small portion of shaft was missing.[5] The inscription was first observed by Langdon at some time before 1895,[6] perhaps when the cross was moved in June 1894.

Description

The stone is a carved cross in a modern base, reconstructed as described above (fig. II.53). The cross measures about 180 cm. in height to the base, the shaft measuring 33 cm. in width and 19 cm. in thickness. The text is incised in two lines low down on the face of the shaft. It is set without framing-lines in a panel measuring 17 by 17 cm. The text is probably complete but highly deteriorated; it is primary and uses a predominantly insular script. The letters measure 4 to 6 cm. in height and read horizontally.

---

1. In an account given by Rogers to Langdon, quoted in Langdon (1896) 363.
2. Blight (1856) 21 & fig.
3. Langdon (1896) 363.
4. Langdon (1896) 362-3.
5. Langdon (1896) 363-4 & figs.
6. The first work to mention the inscription was Langdon & Allen, J.R. (1895).

Figure II.53 Sancreed I (photograph Royal Commission on the
Historical Monuments of England).

Text

R[-]
[HO.]

Discussion

The text now reads, R[-HO.] with two or three letters lost from the lacuna. The text may have been a personal name. Langdon's drawing of the stone suggests that the text has always been in poor condition; Langdon, however, read the text as RUNHŌ, which he later expanded to RUNHŌ[L](?).[7] Even if the reading were Ō, this would be an unparalleled abbreviation for OL. Langdon, following Iago, compared the similar text RŪHOL, presumably for RUNHOL, on the Lanherne stone, text (ii), conjecturing that this might be the name of the man who carved both crosses.[8] In view of the deteriorated condition of the Sancreed text, even in Langdon's time, and the improbability of Ō, even if this were the reading, standing for OL, this conjecture must be treated with caution. It seems to me to be quite inadmissible to use this identification as even part of an argument for dating a series of Cornish crosses.[9] In 1906, though not in his earlier and fuller account of the stone, Langdon noted, 'Possibly there may have been other letters at the top of the shaft', a suggestion which his 1906 drawing to some extent substantiates.[10] I do not think, however, that there was any further text in this position.

The stone belongs to Category 2a, inscribed cross-shafts. Category 2 stones date from the ninth to the eleventh century; this stone is dated to the tenth or eleventh century on artistic grounds.

Bibliography

Langdon & Allen, J.R. (1888) 313, 319 & figs.
Langdon (1889*a*) 319, 329-30.
Langdon (1890-1) 35, 92 & *passim*.
Langdon & Allen, J.R. (1895) 52, 57, 60 & fig.
Langdon (1896) 359-60, 362-5, *passim* & figs.
Daniell (1906) 244.
Langdon (1906) 420, *passim* & fig.
(-) (1910-11*a*) 37 & fig.
Macalister (1929) 189.
Hencken (1932) 270, 276-7, 307 & figs.
Dexter, T.F.G. & Dexter, H. (1938) 223, 225 & figs.
Macalister (1949) no. 1058, p. 186 & fig. (fig. numbered 1059).
Thomas, A.C. (1954) 18.

---

7. Langdon (1896) 364 & fig.; Langdon (1906) 420 & fig.
8. Langdon (1896) 365.
9. Cf., for example, Thomas, A.C. (1978) 78-9.
10. Langdon (1906) 420 & fig.; cf. Langdon (1896) 362-5 & figs.

Henderson, C.G. (1957-60*b*) 436.
Russell (1962) 111.
Thomas, A.C. (1967) 104.
Pevsner (1970) 207.
Russell (1971) 82, 89.
Rowe, L. (1973) & fig.[11]
Maxwell (1976) 10.
Pearce (1978) 68, 181.
Thomas, A.C. (1978) 78 & fig.
Weatherhill (1981) 73 & figs.
Higgitt (1986) 141.
Todd (1987) 296 & figs.
Pool (undated) 16 & fig.

---

11. There is no page numbering in this book.

54 Sancreed II

The stone is now in Sancreed churchyard. It stands to the left of the path leading from the south gate to the south door of the church. National Grid Reference SW 4202 2933. Examined 2 July 1984 and 2 July 1985.

History

This stone was described and illustrated by Lysons and Lysons in 1814; it was then in 'Sancreet church-yard'.[1] No inscription was seen until Langdon discovered it some time in or before 1895.[2] He described how he and the vicar, the Rev. R. Basset Rogers, had the cross dug up, unearthing some 100 cm. of the shaft which contained the text.[3] On 14 June 1895 the cross was placed in 'an old circular cross-base' brought from Treganhoe farm nearby; it was then set up in its present position in, or close to, the position it had previously occupied.[4] Baird and White noted a suggestion that the stone might originally have been a memorial stone and that it was subsequently turned upside down and made into a cross.[5] If text (i) really read upwards (*see* Description below), this might lend support to the suggestion; however the traces of text (ii) suggest that this at least was a primary text.

Description

The stone is a complete, carved cross set into a base as described above. It now measures 228 cm. in height, the shaft measuring 27 to 29 cm. in width and 25 to 28 cm. in thickness. The base is now buried beneath the ground, along with some 42 cm. of shaft. This is calculated using Langdon's measurements of the height of the cross as eight feet, three inches (c. 247.5 cm.) to the base with nine inches (c. 22.5 cm.) inside the base.[6] Text (i) is incised in a space beneath a panel of carving at the bottom of the left-hand side of the shaft (fig. II.54(i)). Text (ii) is incised in a panel in the corresponding space on the face of the shaft (fig. II.54(ii)). The corresponding spaces

1. Lysons, D. & Lysons, S. (1814) ccxlv & fig.
2. Langdon & Allen, J.R. (1895) 52, 55, 60 & fig. Earlier works by Langdon do not mention the inscription.
3. Langdon (1896) 360-1.
4. Langdon (1896) 360-1, quotation from p. 361.
5. Baird & White (unpub. 1961); there is no page numbering in this typescript. Cf. also Hencken (1932) 224.
6. Langdon (1896) 361.

Figure II.54(i)   Sancreed II, text (i) (photograph Woolf/
Greenham Collection).

on the back and right-hand side of the shaft probably never contained texts.

Text (i) is set in one line, probably without framing-lines, and is incomplete. It is unclear whether or not the text is primary. The letters are *c.* 6 cm. in height and read upwards facing right or downwards facing left. The text is so highly deteriorated as to be virtually illegible and it is not certain what script is used. Text (ii) consists of only small traces of what

Figure II.54(ii) Sancreed II, text (ii) (photograph Woolf/
Greenham Collection).

may have been letters in an open-ended panel measuring 21 cm. in width.
The position of text (ii) suggests that it was primary but no further description of it is possible.

Texts

The texts are now illegible.

Discussion

Langdon's drawings, made soon after the texts were first observed, suggest that the texts were in a deteriorated state then; nevertheless Langdon read text (i) as FILIVS IC adding that he found the letters 'quite distinct'.[7] Indeed he saw traces of a further line of text above FILIVS IC but could decipher only an M or N.[8] Macalister read even more: EROCAV[I]|FILIVS IC.[9] The traces of letters visible today are consistent with Langdon's reading but, in view of the evidence of his drawing, this text cannot be considered certain, and Macalister's first line seems to me conjectural. Langdon read text (ii) as, INCX|X; he admitted, however, that these letters were 'markings . . . which may be the remains of an inscription now almost obliterated', a statement supported by his drawing.[10] Of this text Macalister commented, 'presumably reading IACIT, though I cannot identify the letters'.[11] In my view it is not even certain that there was a text here. Macalister read a third line of text on the back of the shaft: [-]RCAS| [-]O[-],[12] of which text Langdon recorded nothing. In view of the evidence of Langdon's drawings, this 'text' can be disregarded.

The stone belongs to Category 2a, inscribed cross-shafts. Category 2 stones date from the ninth to the eleventh century but this stone cannot be more closely dated.

Bibliography

Lysons, D. & Lysons, S. (1814) ccxlv & fig.
Hingston (1850) no. 5 & fig.[13]
Blight (1856) 18 & figs.
Blight (1862) 537.
Blight (1865) 26.
Polsue (1872) 139.
Langdon & Allen, J.R. (1888) 314, 319 & figs.
Langdon (1889a) 319, 328-9.
Langdon (1890-1) 35 & *passim*.
Langdon & Allen, J.R. (1895) 52, 55, 60 & fig.
Langdon (1896) 359-62, *passim* & figs.
Daniell (1906) 245, 455.
Langdon (1906) 420, *passim* & figs.
(-) (1910-11a) 37.

---

7. Langdon (1896) 362 & fig.
8. Langdon (1896) 362.
9. Macalister (1929) 189.
10. Langdon (1896) 361 & fig.
11. Macalister (1929) 189.
12. Macalister (1929) 188.
13. There is no page numbering in this book.

Macalister (1929) 188-9.
Hencken (1932) 224, 307.
Dexter, T.F.G. & Dexter, H. (1938) 198-200 & figs.
Macalister (1949) no. 1057, pp. 185-6 & fig. (fig. numbered 1058).
Henderson, C.G. (1957-60*b*) 436.
Russell (1962) 111.
(-) (1966) 51.
Pevsner (1970) 207.
Russell (1971) 82, 89.
Rowe, L. (1973) & fig.[14]
Maxwell (1976) 10.
Pearce (1978) 27, 68, 181 & fig.
Weatherhill (1981) 73 & figs.
Higgitt (1986) 141.
Pool (undated) 16 & fig.
Baird & White (unpub. 1961) vol. X, R-S.[15]

---

14. There is no page numbering in this book.
15. There is no page numbering in this typescript.

55 Sourton

The stone stands on the grass verge near the junction where the A 386, Torrington to Tavistock road, meets the A 30, Okehampton to Launceston road. National Grid Reference SX 5458 9159. Examined 27 June 1984, 7 July 1985 and 25 September 1987.

History

The stone was first mentioned by Bate in 1874 who said it was 'on the Okehampton Road';[1] subsequently Bate recorded that the stone was, 'Near the village of Sourton, on the high road from Tavistock to Okehampton'.[2] In 1984 and 1985 I examined the stone on a grass bank on the left-hand side of the road about 6.5 km. south of Okehampton. It stood at the junction of the A 386, Torrington to Tavistock road, and the A 30, Okehampton to Launceston road, National Grid Reference SX 5474 9179. This may have been the same position as that in which the stone was first recorded. The stone was moved in November 1986 during construction of the Okehampton by-pass and was kept in Okehampton Castle. It was placed in its present position in 1993. When it was moved in 1986, no observable archaeological context was found, suggesting that it may have been moved before.[3] This was supported by the fact that the Ordnance Survey mark was found to have been incised on the part that had been below the ground.

Description

The stone is a roughly shaped cross with a long shaft and may be complete (fig. II.55). It probably contained some carved decoration on and near the cross-arms, although this is now highly deteriorated. The stone now measures 332 cm. in height but when it stood beside the road about 147 cm. of shaft were beneath the ground. The shaft measures 39 to 45 cm. in width and 25 to 29 cm. in thickness; the width across the cross-arms is 50 cm. Immediately beneath the cross-arms are incised four modern letters, H O T L, one on each side of the stone. These refer to the names of nearby towns and indicate that the stone served as a sign-post in modern times.

---

1. Bate (1873-6) 392, paper read 19 November 1874.
2. Bate (1876-8) 155.
3. I am most grateful to Frances Griffith, Sites and Monuments Register, Devon County Council, for supplying me with this information.

Figure II.55 Sourton (photograph Exeter City Museums).

The Ordnance Survey mark is also incised on the face of the stone, towards the lower end of the shaft.

Text (i) is incised on the face of the stone, beneath the modern letter H. It is set horizontally, without framing-lines or panels, and its one letter measures about 18 cm. in height. It is complete and only slightly deteriorated. Text (ii) is incised in three lines on the face of the stone, beneath text (i). Text (ii) is highly deteriorated and may not be complete.

It is incised in a predominantly capital script without framing-lines or panels. The letters measure 7 to 12 cm. in height and read downwards facing left. Both texts appear to be primary and the stone seems likely to have originally been a pillar-stone which was subsequently made into a cross, a suggestion first put forward by Bate.[4]

Texts

(i)   ℞

(ii) [.R]INCIP[I]
      [..R.-]
      A/V[.]DE[..]

Discussion

Text (i) reads ℞, the *chi-rho* symbol in its monogram form. Text (ii) reads, [.R]INCIP[I] [-] AV[.]DE[..]. The letters AV[.], at the beginning of the third line, could alternatively be read as AN. This text is now too deteriorated to be interpreted with any certainty. Soon after the stone was first recorded, Bate described text (ii) as 'almost illegible', a description supported by his drawing.[5] Rhys, however, read, PRINCIPI DIRIVI ANDETI (or AVDETI), describing the PR as 'only a guess'.[6] Baring-Gould read, PRINCIPI FILIVS AVDEI, a reading supported by his drawings,[7] while Macalister read, PRINCIPI IVRIVCI AVDETI, a reading which his drawings support.[8] In view of the state of the text today and of these conflicting readings, the text is not now recoverable.

The stone belongs to Category 1c, pillar-stones which were later re-cut to form crosses. Category 1 stones date from the fifth or sixth centuries to the eleventh century. In their original form, Category 1c stones are likely to pre-date the period of the ninth to the eleventh century since the re-cutting of the stones to form crosses may date from then. The carving may be contemporary with the re-cutting but the monogram *chi-rho* symbol is presumably contemporary with the stone in its original form and suggests a sixth- to eighth-century date; such a date is probably corroborated by the use of horizontal I.

4. Bate (1876-8) 156.
5. Bate (1876-8) 156 & fig.
6. Rhys (1918) 191-2.
7. Baring-Gould (1918) 196 & figs.
8. Macalister (1929) 193-4 & figs.

Bibliography

Bate (1873-6) 392.
Bate (1876-8) 155-6 & fig.
Crossing (1902) 118-19 & fig.
Baring-Gould (1918) 196-8 & figs.
Rhys (1918) 191-2.
Macalister (1929) 193-4 & figs.
Phillips (1937) 336-7.
Phillips (1938) 339.
Macalister (1945) no. 491, pp. 470-1 & figs.
Nash-Williams (1950) 11n.
Fox (1964) 159-60, 162.
(-) (1966) 51.
Evans (1967) 147.
Wall (1968) 177-8 & fig.
Thomas, A.C. (1969-72) 259 & fig.
Hamlin (1972) 25.
Pearce (1978) 21-30 & fig.
Pearce (1981) 172.
Thomas, A.C. (1981) 165 & fig.
Pearce (1985) 257-8, 274.
Thomas, A.C. (1986) 77 & figs.
Woods (1988) 79 & figs.

56 Southill

The stone is now in Southill churchyard, near the front gate, on the left of the path leading from the gate to the church. National Grid Reference SX 3288 7261. Examined 27 June 1984 and 7 July 1985.

History

The stone was discovered on 3 September 1891 by Wills while searching for a lost cross recorded by Blight. The stone was then in a rockery, 'in an oblique position at the eastern end of the Rectory garden'.[1] Wills added: 'The present gardener told me that when the rockery was formed, about fifteen years ago . . . he assisted in removing the inscribed stone from Pigs' Court, a short distance below the Rectory (where it was built into an old wall), to its present site'.[2] Iago recorded that the stone was dug up, washed and re-erected in the Rectory grounds on 4 November 1891.[3] In 1932 it was in the Rectory garden but in 1945 Macalister recorded it 'at the entrance to the churchyard'.[4] *Pace* Pearce, this is presumably its present position.[5]

Description

The stone is an uncarved pillar-stone, probably incomplete. It measures 168 cm. in height, 26 to 34 cm. in width and 25 to 33 cm. in thickness. Comparison with measurements of the stone given when it was dug up suggest that some 77 cm. of the stone are beneath the ground.[6]

The text is incised without framing-lines or panels on one face of the stone, under a double arc (fig. II.56). The text is slightly deteriorated but probably complete. The letters are in two lines and read downwards facing left. The letters measure 8 cm. in height and the cross preceding the text measures 16 cm. in height by 12 cm. The text appears to be primary and uses a predominantly capital script.

---

1. Wills (1891) 324.
2. Wills (1891) 326.
3. Iago (1893-5*a*) 110.
4. Hencken (1932) 242; Macalister (1945) 464.
5. Pearce (1978) 71: 'In the rectory garden'.
6. Langdon (1893) 107: 'The total length of the stone is 8 ft. 2 in.'.

Figure II.56 Southill (photograph A. Gimblett).

Text

CVM<u>RE</u>G<u>N</u>I
<u>F</u>/<u>I</u>LIMAVCI

Discussion

The text now reads, + CVMREGNI FILI MAVCI, that is, '[the stone] of Cumregnus, son of Maucus', with FILI for FILII. The name CVMREGNI is presumably Latin. Fox suggested that this name 'embodies a royal title' but this is not certain.[7] The element MAV- of the name MAVCI suggests that this name might be Celtic.[8] Early drawings, for example that by Iago,[9] show the cross preceding the text as a *chi-rho* symbol in its monogram form. The traces remaining today are consistent with either an ordinary cross or a *chi-rho* monogram.

The stone belongs to Category 1a, pillar-stones with a simple memorial text. Category 1 stones date from the fifth or sixth centuries to the eleventh century. If the stone did contain the monogram *chi-rho* symbol, this would suggest a sixth- to eighth-century date for the stone. The Latin name is in accordance with such a dating and the use of horizontal I probably also corroborates it.

Bibliography

Wills (1891) 324-6 & figs.
Iago (1891-2) 158-60 & fig.
Allen, J.R. (1892) 172.
(-) (1892) 2.
Langdon (1893) 97-108 & fig.
Iago (1893-5a) 109-11 & fig.
Langdon & Allen, J.R. (1895) 52, 55, 60 & fig.
Langdon (1896) 5.
(-) (1896b) 254-7 & fig.
(-) (1897) 123.
Holder (1904) col. 484.
Daniell (1906) 241.
Langdon (1906) 423, *passim* & fig.
Jenner (1917) 75.
Jenner (1922-5) 58.
Henderson, C.G. (1925) 178.
Macalister (1929) 179.
Hencken (1932) 242, 308.
Macalister (1945) no. 486, pp. 464-5 & fig.
Nash-Williams (1950) 11n.
Fox (1964) 160.
(-) (1966) 51.
Wall (1968) 177 & fig.
Thomas, A.C. (1969-72) 259 & fig.
Pevsner (1970) 214.
Hamlin (1972) 25.
Radford (1975) 7, 10, 13.
Pearce (1978) 28, 71, 181 & fig.

---

7. Fox (1964) 160.
8. Cf. Jackson (1953) 440-1.
9. Iago (1891-2) 158-9 & fig.

Thomas, A.C. (1980) 108.
Pearce (1981) 169, 187 & figs.
Thomas, A.C. (1981) 165 & fig.
Thomas, A.C. (1985*b*) 174.
Todd (1987) 245.

57 Stowford

The stone is now in Stowford churchyard, on a grass bank to the right of the gate. National Grid Reference SX 4329 8700. Examined 25 June 1984.

History

The stone was first recorded in 1838 by Kempe who said: 'much praise is due to the Rev. Mr. Johnes, who caused this curious relic to be taken up from the road side and preserved in the church-yard'.[1] In 1851 the stone was described as measuring 'about 5 feet in length'.[2] This seems to imply that the stone was then lying rather than erect; however, the word 'length' is used on occasion in the nineteenth century to describe vertical height, so this deduction is not certain. In May 1870, W.C. Borlase described the stone in the churchyard, 'standing on the top of the hedge, to the right of the entrance gate'.[3] In spite of the word 'hedge', Borlase's description and the accompanying illustration suggest that the stone was probably then in its present position. Burnard, however, stated in 1895 that, 'The Rev. S. Baring-Gould believes it was found in a hedge, and placed in its present position a good many years ago'.[4] Baring-Gould identified the inscribed stone with the 'Long Stone' mentioned in 1628 when it had stood 'near where is the church porch'.[5] He continued: 'On this occasion [presumably 1628] it was cast down and put across a drain to serve as a footbridge' remaining there until the then rector set it up in the churchyard.[6] In my view this identification is possible but by no means certain.

Description

The stone is an uncarved pillar-stone, probably complete (fig. II.57). It measures 160 cm. in height, 39 cm. in width and 43 cm. in thickness. The text is incised without framing-lines or panels on one face of the stone. The text is probably complete but slightly deteriorated; it uses a predominantly insular script with some odd letter forms. The letters, 6 to 15 cm. in height,

---

1. Kempe (1838) 45.
2. (-) (1851a) 424.
3. Borlase, W.C. (1868-70) 236 & fig.
4. Burnard (1895) 229.
5. Baring-Gould (1918) 195-6, quotation from p. 196.
6. Baring-Gould (1918) 196.

Figure II.57   Stowford (photograph Patricia Broch Associates).

are in one line and read downwards facing left. The text appears to be primary.

Text

[G]U[.G]L̲E̲[S]

Discussion

The text probably reads, [G]U[.G]LE[S] where the bracketed letters are legible but unusual in form. Various readings of the text have been suggested. Alexander read, GUNIGLEI(?),[7] while Chanter gave three possibilities, GURGLES, GUMGLEI and GUNGLEL.[8] The text is presumably a Celtic name; Rhys, in comments suggesting a reading GURGLES, compared the Welsh name *Gwrlais*.[9]

The stone belongs to Category 1a, pillar-stones with a simple memorial text. Category 1 stones date from the fifth or sixth centuries to the eleventh century. This text uses insular script which suggests a date from the eighth century onwards for this stone.

Bibliography

Kempe (1838) 45 & fig.
(-) (1851a) 423-4 & fig.
Smirke *et al.* (1861) 177-8.
Borlase, W.C. (1868-70) 236-7 & figs.
Bate (1873-6) 392.
Rhys (1875) 362.
Huebner (1876) no. 28, p. 11 & fig.
Worth, R.N. (1886) 179-81.
Burnard (1895) 228-9 & fig.
Holder (1896) col. 2045.
Chanter (1910) 481.
Baring-Gould (1918) 195-8 & fig.
Rhys (1918) 192.
Macalister (1929) 193.
Alexander (1937) 153-4.
Macalister (1949) no. 1060, p. 187 & fig. (fig. numbered 1061).
Pevsner (1952a) 147.
(-) (1966) 51.
Radford (1969) 81.
Radford (1975) 6, 13.
Pearce (1978) 21-30, 71, 183.
Pearce (1985) 257-9.
Todd (1987) 250.

---

7. Alexander (1937) 154.
8. Chanter (1910) 481.
9. Rhys (1875) 362.

58 Tavistock I

The stone is now in the garden of Tavistock vicarage.[1] National Grid Reference SX 481 742.[2] Examined 27 June 1984 and 4 July 1986.

History

The stone was first recorded by Bray who saw it in 1804. He recorded information from his father that, some 20 years earlier, the stone had been lifted from the pavement at West Street, Tavistock, as it had 'become so worn and slippery as to be dangerous to horses'; it had then been placed as a bridge over the mill-stream near Head weir, about 0.8 km. from Tavistock.[3] On 22 October 1804 Bray removed the stone for safety to what was then 'the grounds of the Abbey-house, and now within the precincts of the churchyard'.[4] Subsequently Bray ('On my quitting the Abbey-house for the Vicarage') moved the stone to the vicarage garden and had it set up 'near the drawing-room window'.[5] The stone is still in this position. This removal probably occurred in 1818; Bray became vicar of Tavistock in 1812 and according to Kempe the vicarage was built for him in 1818.[6] In 1822, Lysons and Lysons recorded the stone 'on the site of the abbey', but this probably also refers to the vicarage garden.[7]

Description

The stone is an uncarved pillar-stone, probably complete (fig. II.58). It measures 200 cm. in height, 46 to 51 cm. in width and 20 to 27 cm. in thickness. Lysons and Lysons gave the height of the stone as seven feet (c. 210 cm.).[8] This suggests that then only some 10 cm. more was visible above ground level than is today. The text is incised without framing-lines

---

1. I am most grateful to the Rev. R.T. Gilpin, vicar of Tavistock, for his help concerning all the Tavistock stones.
2. The National Grid Reference refers to Tavistock vicarage garden, not to the individual stone.
3. Bray (1836) 373.
4. Bray (1836) 374. The stone was shown there in Kempe's drawing: Kempe (1830) fig. opp. p. 489.
5. Bray (1836) 374.
6. Kempe (1830) 218-19. Kempe, being Mrs Bray's brother, was presumably a reliable witness.
7. Lysons, D. & Lysons, S. (1822) cccviii.
8. Lysons, D. & Lysons, S. (1822) cccviii.

Figure II.58   Tavistock I (photograph Bruce Sinclair).

or panels on one face of the stone. The text is legible, complete and appears to be primary. The letters, 7 to 18 cm. in height, are in two lines and read downwards facing left. The text uses a predominantly capital script.

Text

NEPRANI
F/ILICON<u>BE</u>VI

Discussion

The text reads, NEPRANI FILI CONBEVI, that is, '[the stone] of Nepranus, son of Conbevus', with FILI for FILII. The name CONBEVI is Celtic;[9] the name NEPRANI may be Latin.

The stone belongs to Category 1a, pillar-stones with a simple memorial text. Category 1 stones date from the fifth or sixth centuries to the eleventh century. If the name NEPRANI is Latin, this would suggest a sixth- to eighth-century date for the stone.

Bibliography

Lysons, D. & Lysons, S. (1822) cccviii & fig.
Kempe (1830) 219 & fig. opp. p. 489.
Bray (1836) 373-6 & fig.
Wright, T. (1852) 455.
Haigh (1858-9) 184.
Smirke *et al.* (1861) 177.
Haddan & Stubbs (1869) 162.
Bate (1873-6) 392.
Rhys (1874*b*) 333-4.
Huebner (1876) no. 27, p. 10 & fig.
Brash (1879) 405.
Crossing (1882) 189-90.
Worth, R.N. (1886) 179-80.
Alford (1890) 230-1.
Page (1890*b*) 309.
Burnard (1893) 52-4.
Holder (1896) col. 1090.
(-) (1896*b*) 234-7 & fig.
(-) (1897) 122-3.
Crossing (1902) 109-10.
Holder (1904) col. 716.
Rhys (1905) 89.
Chanter (1910) 481.
Alexander (1937) 153-4.
Macalister (1945) no. 493, p. 472 & fig.
Jackson (1953) 191, 274, 373, 646-7.
(-) (1966) 51.
Finberg (1969) 31.
Pearce (1978) 29, 71, 75, 183.
Pearce (1982) 4 & fig.
Thomas, A.C. (1985*b*) 174.
Woods (1988) 74, 76 & figs.
McManus (1991) 177n.

---

9. Jackson (1953) 191, 373.

59 Tavistock II

The stone is now in the garden of Tavistock vicarage. National Grid Reference SX 481 742.[1] Examined 27 June 1984 and 4 July 1986.

History

The stone was first noted by Polwhele in 1797: 'And there is an upright stone, by a smith's shop, near the church-yard of Buckland-Monachorum'.[2] The stone was also seen there by Bray on 28 September 1804. He described it as serving 'as a coigne to a blacksmith's shop, adjoining the entrance to the church-yard'.[3] It was seen at Buckland Monachorum by Lysons and Lysons in 1822 and by Kempe in 1830.[4] In 1831 Bray, then the vicar of Tavistock, found that 'the blacksmith's shop had recently been taken down, and the stone in question was lying with its inscription exposed towards the street, with the possibility of its being worn, if not obliterated, by every passing wheel'.[5] On application to Sir Ralph Lopez, 'as lord of the manor', Bray was given the stone and he had it erected in the vicarage garden, where it has remained.[6]

Description

The stone is a complete and uncarved pillar-stone. It measures 220 cm. in height, 38 to 44 cm. in width and 22 to 34 cm. in thickness. Bray gave the height of the stone as seven feet, two and a half inches[7] (c. 216 cm.), which suggests that some 16 cm. more is now beneath ground level than was so then. The text is incised without framing-lines or panels on the face of the stone (fig. II.59). The text is legible and complete although the final letter is now half hidden beneath the ground. The text appears to be primary and uses a predominantly capital script. The letters, 8 to 12 cm. in height, are in two lines and read downwards facing left. There is a gouged-out hole on the face of the stone, presumably made in modern

---

1. The National Grid Reference refers to Tavistock vicarage garden, not to the individual stone.
2. Polwhele (1797) I, 152.
3. Bray (1836) 361-2, quotation from p. 362.
4. Lysons, D. & Lysons, S. (1822) cccviii; Kempe (1830) 219.
5. Bray (1836) 362.
6. Bray (1836) 362.
7. Bray (1836) 363-4.

Figure II.59 Tavistock II (photograph E.N. Masson Phillips).

times. In 1896 the stone was described as having been re-cut,[8] but the evidence of early drawings suggests that the text has always been quite legible.

Text

SA[.]I<u>NI</u>:F/ILI
MA<u>CC</u>O<u>D</u>ECHETI

8. (-) (1896*b*) 236.

Discussion

The text now reads, SA[.]INI : FILI MACCODECHETI. Bray's drawing suggests that the lost letter was probably B.[9] The text can then be translated, '[the stone] of Sa[b]inus, son of Maccodechetus', with FILI for FILII. The name SA[B]INI is Latin.[10] The name SABINVS probably occurs on a Romano-British stone from Chester.[11] A name similar to MACCODECHETI occurs on a stone from Penrhos-Lligwy in Wales; Nash-Williams read this name as MACCVDECCETI.[12] Another Welsh stone, from Llanychaer but now lost, may have had a similar name.[13] Jackson discussed these names in detail, taking them all as Primitive Irish.[14] The name was also discussed by Rhys and MacNeill,[15] while Macalister recorded similar names on Irish ogham stones from Ballintaggart, Gort-nagullenagh and Coolmagort.[16]

The stone belongs to Category 1a, pillar-stones with a simple memorial text. Category 1 stones date from the fifth or sixth centuries to the eleventh century. The Primitive Irish name suggests a date from the fifth or sixth century to the eighth century for this stone. The Latin name is in accordance with such a dating and the use of horizontal I probably also corroborates it.

Bibliography

Polwhele (1797) I, 152.
Polwhele (1803) I, 146-8.
Lysons, D. & Lysons, S. (1822) cccviii & fig.
Kempe (1830) 219.
Bray (1836) 360-7 & fig.
Haigh (1858-9) 184.
Smirke *et al.* (1861) 178n.
Haddan & Stubbs (1869) 162.
Iago (1871-3) 65n.
Bate (1873-6) 392.
Rhys (1874*b*) 334.
Rhys (1875) 361.
Huebner (1876) no. 26, p. 10 & fig.
Brash (1879) 350, 404-5.
Ferguson (1879*a*) 31.
Ferguson (1879*b*) 179.

9. Bray (1836) 364-5 & fig.
10. Jackson (1953) 518n.
11. Collingwood, R.G. & Wright, R.P. (1965) no. 518, p. 172 & fig.
12. Macalister (1945) no. 326, pp. 313-14 & fig.; Nash-Williams (1950) no. 39, p. 67 & figs.
13. Macalister (1945) no. 440, p. 421; Nash-Williams (1950) no. 335, p. 191 & fig.
14. Jackson (1953) 181-2, 566.
15. Rhys (1879) 407-12; MacNeill (1908-9) 339-40.
16. Macalister (1945) no. 159, pp. 153-4 & fig.; no. 184, pp. 177-8 & fig.; no. 203, pp. 197-8 & figs.

Ferguson (1879c) 183-5.
Rhys (1879) 164-6, 170-1, 401, 407-12.
Crossing (1882) 189-90.
Worth, R.N. (1886) 179-80.
Alford (1890) 231.
Loth (1890) 46.
Page (1890b) 309.
Burnard (1893) 52-4 & fig.
(-) (1896b) 234-7 & fig.
(-) (1897) 122-3.
Crossing (1902) 62, 109-10.
Holder (1904) cols 365, 415, 1367.
MacNeill (1908-9) 339-40.
Chanter (1910) 481.
Hull (1926) 37.
Diack (1927) 232.
Macalister (1929) 193.
Alexander (1937) 153-4.
Macalister (1945) no. 492, pp. 471-2 & fig.
Jackson (1950) 211-12.
Nash-Williams (1950) 11n.
Jackson (1953) 171-2, 176-7, 181-2, 518, 566, 610, 627.
(-) (1966) 51.
Finberg (1969) 31.
Radford (1975) 5.[17]
Pearce (1978) 29, 71, 161 & fig.
Pearce (1981) 171-2 & fig.
Pearce (1982) 4 & fig.
Thomas, A.C. (1985b) 173.
Woods (1988) 74-5 & figs.
McManus (1991) 62.

17. This reference may alternatively be to Tavistock III.

60 Tavistock III

The stone is now in the garden of Tavistock vicarage. National Grid Reference SX 481 742.[1] Examined 27 June 1984, 7 July 1985, and 4 July 1986.

History

The stone was noticed around 1834 by Bray; it was then in use as a gatepost to a field on Roborough Down near Buckland Monachorum.[2] Bray applied for permission to move the stone to Tavistock vicarage garden but failed: 'the farmer was inexorable and it there remains'.[3] Alford recorded that in 1868 Mr Hastings Russell, subsequently the Duke of Bedford, had the stone moved to the vicarage garden, and *pace* Todd, it has remained there since.[4] The ogham text was first noticed by Ferguson in August 1873.[5]

Description

The stone is an uncarved pillar-stone, probably complete (fig. II.60). It measures 152 cm. in height, 39 to 43 cm. in width and 27 to 30 cm. in thickness. Text (i) is incised in three lines on the face of the stone. There are no framing-lines or panels except for traces of one incised line at the top of the stone. This text is probably complete and appears to be primary. It uses a predominantly capital script and is slightly deteriorated. The letters measure 7 to 13 cm. in height and read downwards facing left. Text (ii), the ogham text, is incised vertically on the edge of the stone between the face and the left-hand side and is probably primary. This text is incomplete and is so highly deteriorated as to be virtually illegible. It is not clear whether it reads upwards or downwards. There are two, presumably modern, letters incised on the back of the stone reading O.C.

---

1. The National Grid Reference refers to Tavistock vicarage garden, not to the individual stone.
2. Bray (1836) 367.
3. Bray (1836) 372.
4. Alford (1890) 232; Todd (1987) 250.
5. Ferguson (1874) 92.

Figure II.60 Tavistock III (photograph Bruce Sinclair).

Texts

(i)   DOBVNNI[...]
      FABRI[F]ILI[I]
      [E]NABARRI[.]
(ii) [ogham]: this text is now illegible.

Discussion

Text (i) reads, DOBVNNI [-] FABRI [F]ILI[I] [E]NABARRI[.], perhaps to be interpreted, '[the stone] of Dobunnus the smith, son of [E]nabarrus'. Alternatively, FABRI could be a Latin personal name; whether as a name or a title, it could refer to either DOBVNNI or to [E]NABARRI. The three letters following DOBVNNI are now illegible. Jackson took the name, read as ENABARRI, as Primitive Irish, derived from *Etnobarros* 'Birdhead',[6] while O'Brien described the Irish names *Barra*, *Barri*, *Barre* as hypocoristic.[7] DOBVNNI is a Celtic name; it may also be a hypocoristic form,[8] or the first element might be from Primitive Irish *dubu-* 'black'.[9]

Text (ii) has always been hard to read and is now illegible. Rhys, for example, saw only 'traces of an Ogam inscription'.[10] Nevertheless, various commentators have read on it a name from text (i), for example Ferguson who said, 'the substantial part of the name *Enabarr* is still traceable'.[11] It is possible that the ogham text originally contained a rendering of part of the roman text but this is not now demonstrable; theories built upon such a reading must be treated with great caution.[12]

The stone belongs to Category 1b, pillar-stones with a longer text. Category 1 stones date from the fifth or sixth centuries to the eleventh century. On the evidence of the ogham text, this stone is likely to date from the fifth or sixth century to the eighth century. The Primitive Irish name suggests a similar date for the stone and, if FABRI were a Latin name, this would corroborate it. The use of horizontal I is probably also in accordance with such a dating.

Bibliography

Bray (1836) 367-73 & figs.
Iago (1871-3) 61n.
(-) (1871-3*b*) 312-13.
Bate (1873-6) 392-3, 396-8 & fig.
Ferguson (1874) 92.
Rhys (1874*a*) 173.
Rhys (1874*b*) 333-4.
Rhys (1875) 361-2.
Huebner (1876) no. 25, p. 10 & fig.
Brash (1879) 350-1, 405 & fig.
Ferguson (1879*c*) 183-5.

---

6. Jackson (1953) 181, 645.
7. O'Brien (1973) 220; see also Plummer (1910) II, 344.
8. Cf. Plummer (1910) II, 344.
9. Cf. Jackson (1950-1) 106.
10. Rhys (1905) 59.
11. Ferguson (1879*c*) 185. Cf. also Chanter (1910) 481 and Macalister (1945) 468.
12. Cf. Macalister (1945) 468: 'Clearly the Ogham is a generation older than the Roman inscription. Dobunnius was the son, and when his time came his epitaph was added to his father's; but Ogham was then falling into disfavour'.

Rhys (1879) 25, 207-8, 284, 358, 400-1.
Crossing (1882) 189-90.
Worth, R.N. (1886) 179-80.
Ferguson (1887) 117.
Alford (1890) 231-3.
Loth (1890) 44-5.
Page (1890*b*) 309.
Langdon (1892*a*) 336.
Langdon (1892*b*) 251.
Langdon (1892-3) 285.
Burnard (1893) 52-4.
Burnard (1895) 228-9.
Holder (1896) cols 1297, 1435.
(-) (1896*b*) 234-7 & fig.
(-) (1897) 122-3.
Crossing (1902) 33, 62, 109-11.
Macalister (1902) 28.
Rhys (1905) 59-60.
Chanter (1910) 481.
Alexander (1937) 153-4.
Macalister (1945) no. 488, pp. 467-8 & fig.
Jackson (1950) 199, 205-6.
Nash-Williams (1950) 11n.
Jackson (1953) 171n, 181, 645.
Fox (1964) 159.
(-) (1966) 50.
Finberg (1969) 31.
Radford (1975) 5, 12-13.[13]
Pearce (1978) 26-30, 182.
Pearce (1981) 172.
Pearce (1982) 4-5, 7, 17 & fig.
Todd (1987) 250.
Woods (1988) 74, 77 & figs.
Schmidt (1990) 134.
McManus (1991) 62, 64, 89, 93, 98-9, 103, 114.

---

13. Page 5 of this work may alternatively refer to Tavistock II.

61 Tavistock IV

The stone is now lost.

History

The stone was recorded by Bray in a letter dated 10 March 1834, published in 1836: '. . . when I was a boy [it was] lying in a little plot of garden-ground over the gateway of the Abbey commonly known by the name of Betsy Grimbal's Tower'.[1] Bray moved the stone, 'several years ago',[2] to a position in front of an arch which was 'then within the grounds of the Abbey-house, and now within the precincts of the churchyard'.[3] Bray became vicar of Tavistock in 1812 and probably moved into the vicarage in 1818.[4] On moving there he replaced the stone near its original position but 'beneath instead of on the top of the gateway'.[5] The stone was shown in this position in Kempe's figure.[6] The stone disappeared at some time around 1831: 'two or three years since';[7] Bray suggested a local man took it 'to convert it into a pig's trough'.[8] In 1830 Kempe said that by then the stone was already lost.[9]

Description and Texts

The description and texts are taken from Bray's description and figure with reference also to Kempe's figure. The stone was an uncarved slab broken at the top and the right-hand side (fig. II.61). There is no evidence as to whether or not the texts were primary. Text (i) was set without panels or framing-lines in three lines on the face of the stone. It was probably

---

1. Bray (1836) 376.
2. Bray (1836) 376.
3. Bray (1836) 374.
4. See Entry 58, Tavistock I, History and fn. 6.
5. Bray (1836) 376.
6. Kempe (1830) fig. opp. p. 489. This figure does not, however, represent the situation in 1830 since it also shows Tavistock I outside Betsy Grimbal's tower and Tavistock I had been moved to the vicarage garden, probably in 1818. Either Kempe made his drawing in 1818, when all three stones may have been outside the tower, or he put together a composite picture.
7. Bray (1836) 376. The letter is dated 10 March 1834.
8. Bray (1836) 377.
9. Kempe (1830) 116n. Kempe, being Mrs Bray's brother, might have been expected to provide reliable evidence. He seems, however, to have taken Tavistock IV as being two stones, perhaps due to confusion with Tavistock V.

Figure II.61   Tavistock IV (from Bray (1836) 382).

incomplete at the beginning and text was lost from the end of each line. The letters were legible, in a predominantly capital script and read horizontally. Text (ii) was set in one line on the left-hand thickness of the stone, probably without framing-lines or panels. It was incomplete at the beginning but probably complete at the end. The letters were legible and in a predominantly capital script; they read downwards facing the back of the stone. Bray suggested the possibility that this stone and Tavistock V may have formed part of the same monument.[10]

Text (i) read:
  INDOLE[.-]
  CONDITOR[.-]
  PRESTETAM[.]N[..-]

Text (ii) read:
  [-]NDISVBIACETINTVS

10. Bray (1836) 377.

Discussion

From the two existing drawings, text (i) may be read, IN DOLE[-]
CONDITOR [-] PRESTETAM [-]. CONDITOR could be *conditor* 'maker,
founder; Creator' and PRESTETAM could be a form of *presto* 'lend; cause'
or of *praesto* 'excell' or of *prestitum* 'a loan'. The text cannot, however, be
interpreted with any certainty. Text (ii) may have read, [-]NDI SUB IACET
INTVS, perhaps '[-] within lies [-] under [-]'. Bray suggested that the wording
of text (ii) indicated 'that the stone formed the cover of the stone coffin or
sarcophagus'.[11] This is a possibility, but the fragmentary nature of these
lost texts makes any certainty about them impossible.

The stone belongs to Category 3b, undecorated slabs. Its date is uncertain. Both the complexity of the text and its layout, in part along the
thickness of the slab, suggest a late date, tenth to eleventh century or even
post-Conquest.

Bibliography

Kempe (1830) 116, 495 & fig. opp. p. 489.
Bray (1836) 376-82 & fig.
Crossing (1882) 189-90.

---

11. Bray (1836) 381-2, quotation from p. 382.

62 Tavistock V

The stone is now lost.

History

The stone was recorded by Bray in a letter dated 10 March 1834, published in 1836: '. . . when I was a boy [it was] lying in a little plot of garden-ground over the gateway of the Abbey commonly known by the name of Betsy Grimbal's Tower'.[1] Bray moved the stone, 'several years ago',[2] to a position in front of an arch which was 'then within the grounds of the Abbey-house, and now within the precincts of the churchyard'.[3] Bray became vicar of Tavistock in 1812 and probably moved into the vicarage in 1818.[4] On moving there he replaced the stone near its original position but 'beneath instead of on the top of the gateway'.[5] The stone was shown in this position in Kempe's figure.[6] Around 1831, after the disappearance of Tavistock IV, Bray moved Tavistock V into the vicarage garden 'beneath the trellised-shed before the door of my house'.[7] Bray's wording suggests that the stone was still there in 1834; by implication it was presumably lost by July 1889 when the Rev. D.P. Alford, vicar of Tavistock, described the stones in Tavistock vicarage garden without mentioning it.[8]

Description and Text

The description and text are taken from Bray's description and figure, with reference also to Kempe's figure. The stone was an uncarved slab probably broken at all four edges (fig. II.62). The text was set without framing-lines or panels in three lines on the face of the stone. There is no evidence as to whether or not it was primary. The text was legible but incomplete and read horizontally in a predominantly capital script. Bray suggested the

---

1. Bray (1836) 376.
2. Bray (1836) 376.
3. Bray (1836) 374.
4. See Entry 58, Tavistock I, History and fn. 6.
5. Bray (1836) 376.
6. Kempe did not, however, mention the stone in his text; Kempe (1830) fig. opp. p. 489. See Entry 61, Tavistock IV, fn. 6.
7. Bray (1836) 377.
8. Alford (1890) 229-33.

Figure II.62   Tavistock V (from Bray (1836) 378).

possibility that this stone and Tavistock IV might have formed part of the same monument.[9] The text read:

[-]HI[C]
[-]FRIDVSSITVSEST
[-.]VS

Discussion

From the two existing drawings the text may be read, [-]HI[C] [-]FRIDVS SITVS EST [-]VS, perhaps, '[-] here is buried [-]fridus'. The common Old English name element *-friđ* regularly appears in Latin texts as *-frid(us)*.

The stone belongs to Category 3b, undecorated slabs. Its date is uncertain. The complexity of the text suggests a late date, tenth to eleventh century or even post-Conquest. The use of an English name element is in accordance with such a dating.

---

9. Bray (1836) 377.

Bibliography

Kempe (1830) fig. opp. p. 489.
Bray (1836) 376-81 & fig.
Crossing (1882) 189-90.

63 Tawna

The stone is now at a crossroads about 0.3 km. north-west of Welltown. It is set on a grass bank at the side of the road, beside the Welltown stone. National Grid Reference SX 1361 6784. Examined 8 July 1984 and 5 July 1985.

History

At the 1881 spring meeting of the Royal Institution of Cornwall it was stated: 'The Rev. W. Iago then gave a description of a newly-discovered inscribed stone at Cardynham, ... It is used as a gate post'.[1] In 1895 it was still in use as a gatepost and was described as, 'Standing in lane leading to Tawna'.[2] In 1929 Macalister described it as 'the right-hand gatepost' of 'the third gate on the left-hand side of the road leading to Bodmin from Venn Cross Roads'.[3] It is likely that these descriptions all refer to the same place. The stone was recorded there in 1951,[4] but by 1970 it had been moved to its present position.[5]

Description

The stone is a pillar-stone, probably uncarved and probably complete, with gatepost markings on each side (fig. II.63). It measures 168 cm. in height, 25 to 27 cm. in width and 28 to 34 cm. in thickness. Comparison with Macalister's measurements shows that some 30 cm. more are now above ground than were then.[6] The text is incised without framing-lines or panels on one of the narrow faces, that is a thickness, of the stone. The text is probably complete and appears to be primary but it is now so highly deteriorated as to be virtually illegible, and it is uncertain both what script is used and whether the text reads downwards facing left or upwards facing right. The letters are in one line and measure 6 to 13 cm. in height.

---

1. Iago (1881–3a) 4.
2. Langdon & Allen, J.R. (1895) 52.
3. Macalister (1929) 190.
4. Pevsner (1951) 41.
5. Pevsner (1970) 51.
6. Macalister (1945) 437.

Figure II.63 Tawna (photograph Woolf/Greenham Collection).

Text

The text is now illegible.

Discussion

The earliest published drawing was by Langdon and showed the text reading up the stone.[7] Langdon and Allen noted, 'Reading doubtful but oni eps is clear', a statement that their drawing supports.[8] In 1929 Macalister read rather more text and included a photograph in support of his reading.[9] The photograph does not, however, altogether substantiate Macalister's reading and it gives the impression that the letters had been chalked in prior to photography. Macalister read the text upwards with the letters facing right as OR P ĒPS TITUS.[10] In view of the state of the text today, of Langdon's drawing and of Macalister's own photograph, Macalister's reading must be treated with extreme caution. A reliable text is not now recoverable.

The stone probably belongs to Category 1a, pillar-stones with a simple memorial text. Category 1 stones date from the fifth or sixth centuries to the eleventh century but this stone cannot be more closely dated.

Bibliography

Iago (1881-3a) 4.
Langdon & Allen, J.R. (1895) 52, 56, 60 & fig.
Langdon (1906) 415, *passim* & fig.
Macalister (1929) 189-90 & fig.
Hencken (1932) 242, 244, 294.
Jenkin (1934) 30.
Macalister (1945) no. 459, pp. 437-8 & fig.
(-) (1966) 50.
Pevsner (1970) 51.
Radford (1975) 7, 12.
Pearce (1978) 28.

---

7. Langdon & Allen, J.R. (1895) 52, 56, 60 & fig.
8. Langdon & Allen, J.R. (1895) 56 & fig.
9. Macalister (1929) 189-90 & fig.
10. Macalister (1929) 190 & fig.

64 Tintagel

The stone is now in the front garden of the Wharncliffe Arms Hotel, Tintagel. National Grid Reference SX 0576 8840. Examined 30 September 1965 and 10 July 1984.

History

The stone was recorded in 1879 by Maclean who stated that: 'About four years ago Mr. J.J.E. Venning, the Steward for Lord Wharncliffe's property in Tintagel, caused to be brought from Trevillet, where it was being used as a gate post, an ancient stone cross, and had it set up in front of the Wharncliffe Arms Hotel, in the village of Trevena'.[1] It is possible, but not certain, that a cross recorded by Blight in 1858 was the inscribed cross. Blight described a cross then, 'used as a post to the garden-gate at Trevillet'.[2] Blight did not show a text and illustrated his stone standing among grass, not as a gatepost, its height being given as approximately one half of that of the inscribed stone;[3] on the other hand, his description and figure (except for the lack of text) suggest that the stones, if not identical, were at least very similar.

Description

The stone is a cross, incomplete but containing carving. It is cemented into a modern base. The cross measures 109 cm. in height, 34 to 41 cm. in width and 8 to 18 cm. in thickness. Comparison with Langdon's measurements suggests that some 9 cm. of shaft are inside the base.[4] The texts are primary and both use a predominantly capital script. Text (i) is incised without framing-lines but within traces of a panel on one face of the shaft (fig. II.64(i)). Text (i) is incomplete at the end and rather deteriorated. Its letters, 6 to 7 cm. in height, are now in four lines though originally there may have been more. The letters read horizontally. Text (ii) is incised on the opposite face of the shaft (fig. II.64(ii)). It is incomplete and highly deteriorated. Traces of three lines can be made out, two reading horizontally and the third reading upwards with the letters facing right. The letters

---

1. Maclean (1879) 190. 'Trevena' refers to Tintagel village.
2. Blight (1858a) 33. Iago accepted that Blight had seen the inscribed cross without noticing the inscription; see Iago (1881-3b) 237.
3. Blight (1858a) 33 & fig.
4. Langdon (1896) 366-7 & figs. Langdon made no mention of a base.

Figure II.64(i)   Tintagel, text (i) (photograph E.N.
Masson Phillips)

measure 6 to 8 cm. in height and are set without framing-lines but within
traces of a panel. The texts are more deteriorated now than they were in
1965.

Texts

(i)   [ÆGR]
       [A]T
       [F]ECIT
       [-]

Figure II.64(ii) Tintagel, text (ii) (photograph E.N. Masson Phillips).

(ii) [MAT]
      [.US]
      [-]
      SIO[T.]

Discussion

Text (i) now appears to read, [ÆGRA]T [F]ECIT [-], although in 1965 I read it as, [.]ELNAT + FECIT [Ā]C C[-]. Maclean read, ÆLNAT + FECIT HANC CRVCEM PRO ANIMA SVA, with the abbreviations expanded, a reading to some extent supported by Iago's drawing which accompanies it.[5] Langdon's drawing of the stone, published several times, does to some extent support Langdon and Allen's reading of text (i) as, ÆLNAT + FECIT HĀC CRVCEM P A[N]IMA SŪ.[6] Elsewhere Langdon admitted that the N and part of the I of A[N]IMA had disappeared, while the letters SU were 'somewhat indistinct'.[7] Macalister read substantially the same text except for the name which he read as ÆLRIAT.[8] Using the two early drawings, my 1965 drawing and the traces remaining today, a text can be reconstructed: [ÆLNA]T + FECIT HĀC CRVCEM P A[N]IMA SŪ, that is, '[Aelnat] + made this cross for his own soul', with HĀC for HANC, P for PRO and SŪ for SUA. [ÆLNA]T, if this is the reading, is probably an English personal name. *Ael-* is a common Old English name element and -[NA]T could perhaps be a spelling of the common element *-noð*. The name *aelfnoð* is recorded on coins of Cnut as *aelnoð* and as *eelnað*.[9]

Text (ii) now reads, [MAT.US] [-]S IO[T.] and I read substantially the same text in 1965. Langdon read, MATHEUS MARCVS LUCAS IOH̄, in six lines set around the stone.[10] This reading, supported by his drawing, by Iago's drawing,[11] and by the traces remaining today, is likely to have been correct.

The stone belongs to Category 2a, inscribed cross-shafts. Category 2 stones date from the ninth to the eleventh century; if the name is English this would be in accordance with such a date.

Bibliography

Blight (1858a) 33 & fig.[12]
Maclean (1879) 190 & figs.
Iago (1878-81) 399, 401.
Iago (1881-3b) 237-8.
Langdon & Allen, J.R. (1888) 312-13, 320 & figs.
Allen, J.R. (1889) 129, 221.
Langdon (1889a) 319, 321-3.
Langdon (1889c) 239.
Langdon (1890-1) 35, 91 & *passim*.
Borlase, W.C. (1893) 184-5.
Langdon (1894b) 315.
Langdon & Allen, J.R. (1895) 52, 58, 60 & figs.
Langdon (1896) 6, 22, 366-8, *passim* & figs.
(-) (1896a) 153-5 & figs.
Reed, H. (1899) 193, 198 & figs.
Rhys (1905) 81.
Daniell (1906) 342.
Langdon (1906) 423, *passim* & figs.

---

5. Maclean (1879) 190 & fig.
6. Langdon & Allen, J.R. (1885) 58 & fig.
7. Langdon (1896) 367.
8. Macalister (1949) 187.
9. Smart (1981) 2, 9.
10. Langdon (1896) 368 & fig. on p. 366.
11. Reproduced in Maclean (1879) 190 & fig.; Maclean's reading is slightly different.
12. It is not certain that Blight was describing the inscribed cross.

Henderson, C.G. (1925) 189.
Macalister (1929) 192.
Hencken (1932) 271, 283, 309.
Macalister (1949) no. 1059, p. 187 & figs (figs numbered 1060).
Ellis, G.E. (1962-4) 275-6 & figs.
Pevsner (1970) 220.
Higgitt (1986) 141.

65 Trebyan

The stone is set vertically into the hedge at the junction where the unclassified road to Tredinnick Farm meets the B 3268 Bodmin to Lostwithiel road.[1] National Grid Reference SX 0788 6292. Examined 5 July 1985.

History

The stone was first recorded in 1870 by Polsue: 'At Tredinnick Lane are the remains of an ancient granite cross, the basement of which is built into the hedge'.[2] This is presumably the stone's present location. It is possible, but not certain, that this is the Tredinnick cross-base listed without description by Langdon.[3]

Description

The stone is a cross-base (fig. II.65). It is not clear whether it is complete since only one half of it is visible. The visible portion is not carved, unless the 'text' is really the remains of carved decoration. The visible height of the stone is 64 cm. and it measures 112 cm. in width; the visible height of the socket-hole is 17 cm. and it measures 30 cm. in width. Macalister described it as 'roughly circular, about 3 ft. 7 ins. [c. 107.5 cm.] in diameter'.[4] The text, if text it is, is incised without framing-lines or panels on the top face of the base, along the present upper edge of the socket-hole. The letters are set in one line reading horizontally and measure 3 cm. in height. The text is highly deteriorated and it is uncertain whether or not it is complete. It is not clear what script was used nor whether or not the text is primary. The modern letters R [.] RR and JA (unless the A is an Ordnance Survey mark) are incised around the socket.

Text

The text is now illegible.

---

1. I am most grateful to Cedric Coad, Tredinnick Farm, Lanhydrock, Bodmin for helping me to locate this stone.
2. Polsue (1870) 9.
3. Langdon (1896) 423.
4. Macalister (1929) 191.

Figure II.65   Trebyan (photograph Woolf/Greenham Collection).

Discussion

In 1929 Macalister read, MAVISIR, a reading substantiated by his drawing.[5] Hencken quoted C.G. Henderson as suggesting that the letters were probably modern,[6] and by 1945 Macalister was also doubtful of the text's antiquity.[7] The 'text', highly deteriorated though it is, does not look much like lettering to me. It is possible that it consists of a carved pattern, or of accidental markings, around the socket-hole.

If inscribed, the stone belongs to Category 2b, inscribed cross-bases. Category 2 stones date from the ninth to the eleventh century but this stone cannot be more closely dated.

Bibliography

Polsue (1870) 9.
Langdon (1896) 423.[8]
Macalister (1929) 190-1 & fig.

---

5. Macalister (1929) 191 & fig.
6. Hencken (1932) 224.
7. Macalister (1945) no. 464, p. 441.
8. It is not certain that Langdon was describing this cross-base.

Hencken (1932) 224, 300.
Macalister (1945) no. 464, p. 441 & fig.
Ellis, G.E. (1954–5*b*) 226-7 & fig.
Henderson, C.G. (1957-60*a*) 285.

66 Tregony

The stone is now built into the outside of St Cuby church, the parish church of Tregony. It is built into the west-facing side of the south-west corner of the church at ground level. National Grid Reference SW 9276 4526. Examined 3 July 1984.

History

The stone was first noted in 1862 when it was described as forming 'part of the foundation of the south-west angle of the Church'.[1] This is the present position of the stone. Penaluna recorded that the church, except for the tower, was rebuilt around 1828,[2] and it may be that the stone was built or rebuilt into the wall then. Daniell (or the editor, Peter) was presumably in error in describing it in 1906 as in the churchyard,[3] although local tradition asserts that the stone was once a standing stone in the churchyard.[4]

Description

The stone is an uncarved pillar-stone set into a wall (fig. II.66). It is uncertain whether or not it is complete. If it were erect its height would be 143 cm. and its width 30 to 54 cm.; c. 18 cm. of its thickness stand out from the wall. The text is incised without framing-lines or panels on the visible face of the stone. The text is legible but it is unclear whether or not it is complete. The text appears to be primary and uses a predominantly capital script. The letters, 6 to 7 cm. in height, are in four lines. They probably read downwards facing left, *see* Introduction, Section 4c.

Text

NONNITA
ERCIL/I[V]I
RICATITRISF/IL/I
ERCIL/INGI

---

1. Smirke (1862) 9.
2. Penaluna (1838) I, 140.
3. Daniell (1906) 240.
4. I am most grateful to K.O. Parsons of Tregony for this information and for his help over the history of this stone.

Figure II.66   Tregony (photograph K.O. Parsons).

Discussion

The text probably reads, NONNITA ERCILI[V]I RICATI TRIS FILI ERCIL-
INGI, that is, '[the stone] of Nonnita, of Ercili[v]us [and] of Ricatus, three
children of Ercilingus', with TRIS for TRES and FILI for FILII, presumably
in error for FILIORUM. The phrase TRES FILI (nominative) occurs on a
Gaulish stone from Narbonne.[5] NONNITA appears to be nominative,
perhaps in error for genitive NONNITAE. Jackson took NONNITA as a
Celtic feminine name,[6] but it could be Latin, cf. *Nonnus*. The same name
occurs on at least one Gaulish stone from Treves,[7] and in the form
NONNITE on a Gaulish stone from Amiens, though whether it is here
nominative or genitive is not certain.[8] An alternative word-division of the
second and third words could give the names ERCILI and [V]IRICATI.[9]
The name RICATI would be Celtic,[10] but the origin of [V]IRICATI is
unknown. The names ERCILI[V]I (or ERCILI) and ERCILINGI are also

5. Le Blant (1865) no. 621, pp. 476-80 & fig.
6. Jackson (1953) 188. On all these names see also Rhys (1879) 404-5.
7. Le Blant (1856) no. 278, pp. 385-6 & fig.; cf. no. 273, pp. 379-80 & fig.
8. Le Blant (1856) no. 326, p. 430 & fig.
9. Cf. Jackson (1953) 456-7.
10. Jackson (1953) 456-7, 459; Evans (1967) 174, 247.

Celtic. The element *erc-* occurs in Irish names,[11] and the name ERCAGNI is on a stone from St Ishmaels, Wales.[12]

The Tregony stone belongs to Category 1b, pillar-stones with a longer text. Category 1 stones date from the fifth or sixth centuries to the eleventh century but this stone cannot be more closely dated unless NONNITA is a Latin name, in which case it would suggest a sixth- to eighth-century date for the stone.

Bibliography

Smirke (1862) 9.
Barham (1866) 417-28 & fig.
Barham (1866-7) 47-55 & fig.
Paull (1866-7*a*) xi.
Polsue (1867) 280-1.
Haddan & Stubbs (1869) 163.
Iago (1871-3) 61n.
Iago *et al.* (1871-3) xlvi-xlvii.
Huebner (1876) no. 10, p. 4 & fig.
Rhys (1879) 166, 278, 359, 404-5.
Langdon & Allen, J.R. (1888) 306-8, 316.
Loth (1890) 45-6.
Borlase, W.C. (1893) 182-3.
Langdon & Allen, J.R. (1895) 50, 54, 59 & fig.
Holder (1896) cols 1458.
Langdon (1896) 23.
Holder (1904) col. 758, 1182.
Rhys (1905) 18-21.
Daniell (1906) 240.
Langdon (1906) 416, *passim* & fig.
Henderson, C.G. (1925) 51-2.
Macalister (1929) 179.
Hencken (1932) 243, 296.
Macalister (1945) no. 461, pp. 438-40 & fig.
Jackson (1953) 188, 192, 456-7, 570.
Fox (1964) 159.
(-) (1966) 50.
Evans (1967) 174, 247.
Sheppard (1968) 98.
Pevsner (1970) 61.
Radford (1975) 6.
Pearce (1978) 71, 178.
Weatherhill (1985) 46 & fig.

11. For example Macalister (1945) no. 93, p. 91 & fig.; Macalister (1945) no. 262, p. 257 & fig. Cf. MacNeill (1929-31) 38.
12. Macalister (1945) no. 376, pp. 358-9 & fig.; Nash-Williams (1950) no. 174, pp. 118-20 & figs. Cf. Rhys (1879) 359, 404.

67 Trencrom

The stone forms the top stone of the first stile on the path to Trencrom which leads to the left off the unclassified road from Lelant to Trencrom. National Grid Reference SW 5204 3640. Examined 3 July 1985.

History

The stone was recorded by C.G. Henderson some time before 1933. It was then the 'Top Stone in the Stile of the footpath that leads to Trencrom from the Lelant road'.[1] In 1976 the stone was described as 'destroyed'.[2]

Description

Pace Maxwell, the stone described by Henderson appears to be in existence today. The stone is uncarved and may be incomplete (fig. II.67). It measures 37 to 40 cm. in height, 120 cm. in length and 28 cm. in thickness. There are some incisions on the top and sides of the stone. It is possible, although by no means certain, that these were once letters. Even if they were, the text is now illegible and no further description of it is possible. Henderson described the stone as 'undoubtedly inscribed' adding that it might 'be a genuine early inscribed stone'.[3]

Text

If there ever was a text, it is now illegible.

Discussion

No interpretation of this text is possible. The stone is too deteriorated to be classifiable and cannot be dated.

---

1. Henderson C.G. (unpub. 1912-17) II, 175. This entry is one of Henderson's later additions to the volume.
2. Maxwell (1976) 10.
3. Henderson C.G. (unpub. 1912-17) II, 175.

Figure II.67   Trencrom (photograph Woolf/Greenham Collection).

Bibliography

Russell (1969) 122.
Russell (1971) 81.
Maxwell (1976) 10.
Henderson C.G. (unpub. 1912-17) II, 175.

68 Tresco

The stone is now in the ruins of St Nicholas' Priory, Tresco. It is set flat into the ground beneath a doorway, just west of the only surviving large archway. One end of the stone is built under the eastern jamb of the doorway. National Grid Reference SV 8945 1424. Examined 11 July 1985.

History

The stone was first recorded in 1869 by Bannister: 'It is partly under the eastern jamb of the south doorway of the Abbey Church'.[1] Macalister visited Tresco on 9 July 1929 but failed to find the stone since 'the floor of the meagre remains of the Abbey was covered with earth'.[2] The stone was rediscovered, however, in 1937 by Major Dorrien-Smith, the then proprietor of the island.[3] The stone has remained in the same position since 1869.

Description

The stone is uncarved and incomplete (fig. II.68). Originally it was probably an erect pillar-stone measuring 76 cm. in height and 37 cm. in width. The text is incised without framing-lines or panels on the visible face of the stone. The text is incomplete and slightly deteriorated. It is set in two lines and originally probably read downwards facing left, *see* Introduction, Section 4c. The text appears to be primary and uses a predominantly capital script.

Text

[-.]HIF/ILI
[-CO]B/I

Discussion

It is possible that the final letter I is set horizontally, ligatured to the B, and

---

1. Bannister (1869) xxxiv.
2. Macalister (1945) 463.
3. Macalister (1945) 464.

Figure II.68   Tresco (photograph E.R. Cooper).

that a vertical line below is an accidental mark. Alternatively, the horizontal 'I' may be a flaw in the stone and the vertical line below be read as I. The first legible letter is probably H, but N is also a possible reading. The text probably reads, [-]HI FILI [-CO]BI, presumably, '[the stone] of [-]hus, son of [-co]bus' with FILI for FILII. The earliest drawing of the text, by Iago, was based on a rubbing by Alford; this drawing was published by Macalister.[4] Bannister also mentioned a rubbing, although whether this was the same one or a different one is not clear.[5] Iago's drawing shows the text in a similar condition to today but suggests a reading, [-]THI FILI [-]COGI. The penultimate letter seems to me, however, to be clearly B. The origin of this incomplete name is unknown.

The stone belongs to Category 1a, pillar-stones with a simple memorial text. Category 1 stones date from the fifth or sixth centuries to the eleventh century but this stone cannot be more closely dated. If the use of horizontal I were certain, this might suggest a sixth- to eighth-century date for the stone.

---

4. Macalister (1929) 191 & fig. The figure later published by Macalister is a conflation of Iago's drawing and one by Major Dorrien-Smith: Macalister (1945) 462-4 & fig.
5. Bannister (1869) xxxiv; cf. Macalister (1929) 191.

Bibliography

Bannister (1869) xxxiv-xxxv.
Macalister (1929) 179, 191-2 & fig.
Hencken (1932) 224-6, 308.
Macalister (1945) no. 485, pp. 462-4 & fig.
O'Neil (1961) 12.
(-) (1966) 51.
Pevsner (1970) 210.
Ashbee (1974) 224.
Gill (1975) 21.
Pearce (1978) 30, 70, 182.[6]
Thomas, A.C. (1979) 30, 34-6.
Thomas, A.C. (1985*a*) 178 & fig.
Thomas, A.C. (1985*b*) 173.
Weatherhill (1985) 131.
Todd (1987) 251.
Nenk *et al.* (1991) 137.

---

6. The reference on p. 30 to an inscribed stone from Tean is presumably an error for the Tresco stone mentioned on pp. 70 and 182.

69 Treslothan

The stone is now in Treslothan church. It is set on a pedestal and is in use as an altar, at the east end of the south-east aisle. National Grid Reference SW 6506 3781. Examined 29 September 1965 and 4 July 1984.

History

The stone may be the one referred to in 1851. A chapel erected at Pendarves in 1842 was described in 1851 as on 'the site of an ancient chapel, among the ruins of which the workmen discovered an inscribed and curiously sculptured tablet of granite'.[1] A.C. Thomas concluded that this was the inscribed stone and that the ruins were St James' Chapel at Treslothan.[2] The stone may also be the one referred to in 1875 by Rhys: 'Mr. Iago told me of another altar, a fragment of which is preserved in the neighbourhood',[3] that is, the neighbourhood of Camborne. The stone was certainly recorded in 1889 by Langdon: 'This slab now forms the top of a sundial in the private grounds of Pendarves'.[4] In December 1955, after the demolition of Pendarves House, the stone was brought to the church and placed in its present position.

Description

The stone is a slab with incised margins and a T-fret within the margins (fig. II.69). The slab is slightly broken and measures 96 cm. in length, 71 to 72 cm. in width and 17 to 25 cm. in thickness. The mark left by part of the sundial is visible towards the centre of the slab. The text appears to be primary. It is incised without framing-lines in a space left by panels and margins on the face of the slab. This space measures *c.* 20 by 44 cm. The letters, 7 to 10 cm. in height, are in one line and read horizontally. The text is so highly deteriorated that it is not clear whether or not it is complete. The script appears to be predominantly insular but this is not certain either. The text has not significantly deteriorated since 1965.

1. (-) (1851*b*) 148.
2. Thomas, A.C. (1967) 64-7.
3. Rhys (1875) 366.
4. Langdon (1889*b*) 357.

Figure II.69   Treslothan (photograph Woolf/Greenham Collection).

Text

[..GU.E]

Discussion

The text is now virtually illegible and only three letters can be made out: [..GU.E]. The first drawing of the stone, by Langdon, was published in 1895 and it shows that even then the text was difficult to read.[5] Langdon and Allen then noted, 'Reading doubtful, but perhaps ÆGVRED'.[6] Macalister read AGURED but added that the R could be read as D or T 'if those interpretations would give a better reading'.[7] The text is likely to be a name but its exact form is not now recoverable.

The stone belongs to Category 3a, altar-slabs. It is dated to the tenth or eleventh century on artistic grounds, especially on the evidence of the T-fret.[8] A.C. Thomas suggested that it was later in date than the similar Camborne altar-slab.[9]

5. Langdon & Allen, J.R. (1895) 51, 58, 60 & fig.
6. Langdon & Allen, J.R. (1895) 58.
7. Macalister (1949) 177n.
8. Thomas, A.C. (1967) 104, 106.
9. Thomas, A.C. (1967) 104, 106.

Bibliography

(-) (1851*b*) 148.[10]
(-) (1856) 161.[11]
Rhys (1875) 366.[12]
Allen, J.R. (1889) 129, 213, 217.
Langdon (1889*a*) 319.
Langdon (1889*b*) 357.
Iago (1890-1) 261-2.
Langdon (1890-1) 36, 93 & *passim*.
Langdon & Allen, J.R. (1895) 51, 58, 60 & fig.
Langdon (1896) 24.
Daniell (1906) 255.
Langdon (1906) 415, *passim* & fig.
Sedding (1909) 164.
Henderson, C.G. (1925) 39.
Macalister (1929) 179.
Hencken (1932) 280, 294.
Macalister (1949) no. 1045, p. 177 & fig.
Henderson, C.G. (1953-6*a*) 69, 72.
Thomas, A.C. (1967) 64-7, 103-10, 168 & figs.
Thomas, A.C. (1970) 139.
Laing (1975) 141.
Pearce (1978) 181.
Todd (1987) 299.

---

10. It is not certain that this reference is to the Treslothan stone.
11. It is not certain that this reference is to the Treslothan stone.
12. It is not certain that this reference is to the Treslothan stone.

70 Trevarrack

The stone is now built into the front wall of the farmhouse at Trevarrack Farm, Lelant, St Ives. It is built in upside down some 4 m. from the ground. National Grid Reference SW 5192 3719. Examined 10 July 1986.

History

The stone was first noted by Matthews in 1892 in the same position in which it is now.[1] Matthews stated that the stone came from the ruins of a chapel in a nearby field called 'Chapel Field'. He continued: 'The site was ploughed up in the year 1840, and the remains of the chapel carted away'.[2] The inscribed stone was presumably built into the farmhouse wall at some time between 1840 and 1892. There are other stones in the farmhouse garden which are said to be from the same chapel. C.G. Henderson noted in particular a 'piece of 15th century window tracery'.[3]

Description

The stone is probably uncarved and is now incomplete (fig. II.70).[4] It measures 43 cm. in height and 75 cm. in width. The text is incised in three lines on the visible face of the stone. As the stone is now, the text reads horizontally and upside down. The present lowest line of text, that is, [-]BELIE, is set in a panel but the others have no panels or framing-lines. The text is legible but incomplete. It is unclear whether or not the text is primary. The letters measure 5 to 10 cm. in height and the script used is a predominantly capital one.

Text

[-]BELIE
[-]ASDI
[-]N[D]A

---

1. Matthews (1892) 38.
2. Matthews (1892) 38.
3. Henderson, C.G. (1957-60a) 301.
4. For convenience, the figure is printed so as to show the stone the right way up.

Figure II.70 Trevarrack (photograph Woolf/Greenham
Collection).

Discussion

The text reads, [-]BELIE[-]ASDI[-]N[D]A and is too fragmentary to be interpreted. In 1916 C.G. Henderson examined the stone and saw traces of a
fourth line of text,[5] but I could see no sign of this. The letters are neater
than is common in south-western inscriptions but the forms of the letters
are consistent with those of other inscriptions; there are, in particular, two
instances of horizontal I.

The stone probably belongs to Category 3b, undecorated slabs; it cannot
be dated, although the use of horizontal I might suggest a sixth- to eighth-
century date for the stone.

Bibliography

Matthews (1892) 38 & fig.
Doble *et al.* (1939) 31.
Henderson, C.G. (1957-60*a*) 301-2.
Henderson, C.G. (unpub. 1912-17) I, 125, 129 & figs.

---

5. Henderson, C.G. (unpub. 1912-17) I, 125, 129 & figs.

71 Treveneague

The stone is now built into a wall on South Treveneague Farm, St Hilary. This wall is on the right-hand side of the unclassified road from St Hilary to South Treveneague, perpendicular to the road and c. 300 m. before the farm-house. The stone is built in at ground level and is c. 5 m. from the road. National Grid Reference SW 5478 3223. Examined 10 July 1986.

History

The stone was first recorded in 1890-1 by Langdon at Treveneague in use as a gatepost.[1] In 1895 Langdon and Allen described it as: 'Standing at entrance to East Treveneague Farm, in use as gate-post'.[2] They described it as having the 'Letters obliterated'.[3] Subsequently, Langdon explained that the stone had twice been used as a gatepost, first in its original state and then later when it was 're-cut for the same purpose in a new position and entirely defaced'.[4] In 1896 Langdon said that this had been 'Within the last few years'.[5] A drawing was made of the text by Iago before it was defaced and this was reproduced by Langdon.[6] M. Henderson recorded the stone still in use as a gatepost at the farmyard entrance of South Treveneague Farm in 1960; by 1961 it had been placed in its present position.[7]

Description and Text

The stone is built lengthways into the wall at ground level and it is therefore not possible to be certain whether the visible part is a portion of a face or of a side. A small hole and some tool marks are visible but there is no sign of any lettering. The stone now measures 19 to 22 cm. in height and 134 cm. in length. The description and reading of the text are taken from Iago's drawing reproduced by Langdon.[8] This drawing was made before the re-cutting of the stone which resulted in the defacement of the text (fig. II.71). The stone was probably carved, perhaps a carved pillar-stone

---

1. Langdon (1890-1) 91.
2. Langdon & Allen, J.R. (1895) 52.
3. Langdon & Allen, J.R. (1895) 56.
4. Langdon (1906) 420.
5. Langdon (1896) 20.
6. Langdon (1906) 418, 420 & fig. See fig. II.71.
7. Henderson, M. (unpub. 1985) 464.
8. Langdon (1906) 418 & fig.

Figure II.71   Treveneague (from Langdon (1906) p. 418, fig. 27).

or possibly a cross-slab, since Langdon described a 'long and wide-limbed Latin cross in relief on the back of the stone' which had been 'obliterated at the same time as the lettering'.[9] No measurements of the letters were recorded and it is unclear whether or not the text was primary. The text appears to have been set without framing-lines or panels in two lines on the face of the stone, the letters presumably incised. The script used was a predominantly capital one and the text read downwards facing left. When

9. Langdon (1906) 420.

the drawing was made, the text may have been complete but was rather deteriorated. The text appears to have read:

NL[.]L[I.]TRC
NEMIAVS

The letters transliterated as [.]TRC, if read as a mirror image, could give F/IL[..]; in my view, however, this is probably coincidental. After the stone had been re-cut Langdon recorded: 'Nothing is now left of the inscription except portions of an N and an A'.[10]

Discussion

Iago's drawing suggests that the text originally ended -NEMIAVS which could have been part of a name; its origin is unknown although the Irish name *Nemanus* can be compared.[11] The earlier part of the text is not now recoverable.

The stone probably belongs to Category 1a, pillar-stones with a simple memorial text. Category 1 stones date from the fifth or sixth centuries to the eleventh century but this stone cannot be more closely dated.

Bibliography

Langdon (1890-1) 91.
Langdon & Allen, J.R. (1895) 52, 56, 60.
Langdon (1896) 6, 20, 22.
Langdon (1906) 420, *passim* & fig.
Macalister (1929) 179.
Hencken (1932) 265, 298.
Macalister (1945) no. 482, p. 461.
Pearce (1978) 28.
Henderson, C.G. (unpub. 1912-17) I, 162-5 & fig.
Henderson, M. (unpub. 1985) no. 232, pp. 464-5 & figs.

---

10. Langdon (1906) 420.
11. Plummer (1910) II, 367.

72 Trewint

The stone is now in the ground and partially beneath a hedge at Saw-Pits, Trewint. It lies at the junction where a track to the left leaves the A 30 Bodmin to Launceston road, at the north end of Trewint village. National Grid Reference SX 2203 8063. Examined 6 July 1986.

History

The stone was first recorded by G.E. Ellis in 1939: 'This cross-base lies, presumably "in situ", close under the hedge which marks the line of the old highway through Trewint village'.[1] The stone may or may not be *in situ* but it has remained in this position. It is possible, but not certain, that this is the Trewint cross-base listed without description by Langdon.[2]

Description

The stone is a complete cross-base with no carving (fig. II.72). Only the top face of the base is now visible and it measures 95 cm. in height by 73 cm. in width; the socket-hole measures 37 by 35 cm. There are some slight markings on one side of the visible face of the stone. It may be that these are the remaining traces of a now illegible text but, if so, no further description of it is possible.

Text

The text is now illegible.

Discussion

Ellis suggested that the stone might be inscribed in capitals but offered no reading.[3] Andrew rejected this theory: 'with a little imagination one could read "... .iri. . ." in minuscules. I feel sure, however, that this is fortuitous and not a true inscription'.[4]

---

1. Ellis, G.E. (1938-9) 221-2.
2. Langdon (1896) 422.
3. Ellis, G.E. (1938-9) 222.
4. Andrew (1938-9) 327.

Figure II.72   Trewint (photograph Woolf/Greenham Collection).

The stone, if it was inscribed, belongs to Category 2b, inscribed cross-bases. Category 2 stones date from the ninth to the eleventh century but this stone cannot be closely dated. Andrew suggested that it was in fact of late medieval date.[5]

Bibliography

Langdon (1896) 422.[6]
Andrew (1938-9) 32/-8.
Ellis, G.E. (1938-9) 221-2 & fig.
Macalister (1945) 467.
Macalister (1949) no. 1043, p. 176 & fig.
Ellis, G.E. (1950-1) 109-10 & fig.

5. Andrew (1938-9) 328.
6. It is not certain that Langdon was describing the Trewint stone.

73 Tuckingmill

The stone is now lost.

History

The stone was recorded in 1930 by Opie: 'Some years ago, during some alterations in a building near Tuckingmill . . . a stone was found with a deal of "lettering" on one side'.[1] A Mr Jim Thomas of Camborne was notified but, by the time he arrived, the stone had been placed in the foundations and was 'built up before a copy was made'.[2] The building was on the road from Redruth to Camborne, at the junction with the road to North Roskear and 'was formerly occupied by a wheelwright's shop under the name of Jenkin'.[3]

Description and Text

The only description of the stone was given by Opie: 'Part of the inscription was still visible, however, and as far as I can gather, it ran down the face of the stone'.[4]

Discussion

No further discussion of this text is possible. The stone is unclassifiable since it is lost and no adequate description or drawing exists. Such stones cannot be dated.

Bibliography

Opie (1930) 18.
Thomas, A.C. (1967) 162.
Thomas, A.C. (1970) 138.

---

1. Opie (1930) 18.
2. Opie (1930) 18.
3. Opie (1930) 18.
4. Opie (1930) 18.

74 Waterpit Down

The stone is now about 5 km. from Tintagel, on the right-hand side of the unclassified road from Tintagel to Davidstow, about 0.5 km. beyond the junction of this road with the B 3266, Boscastle to Camelford road. National Grid Reference SX 1199 8807. Examined 10 July 1984 and 4 July 1985.

History

This stone was probably the one described by Penaluna in 1838: 'On Waterpit Downs is an ancient cross, beautifully embellished with sculpture and delicate tracery'.[1] It was certainly recorded in 1873 by Maclean:

> There stood formerly on 'Waterpit Down' ... a very fine way-side cross, the base of which still remains in *situ* at the angle formed by the junction of the ancient roads from Tregaer, in St. Kew, and Tintagel to Warbstow Beacon ... The shaft itself was removed about seventeen years ago to a neighbouring farm, called Trekeek, where it forms the base upon which works the pivot of the horse-power of a threshing machine there set up.[2]

In June 1889 the stone was moved back to the roadside by Colonel S.G. Bake.[3] It was then found to be inscribed. Langdon described it then as 'in its original base, in *situ*'.[4] In 1949 Macalister described the stone in its present position, that is, not at the road junction but 'about a quarter of a mile from the cross-roads'.[5] It is not certain how this came about: Langdon may have been wrong in stating that the stone was replaced in *situ*, or the stone may have been moved again between 1889 and 1949. In view of the massive base in which the stone is fixed, it seems to me that neither of these explanations is probable and it is more likely that there has been a slight alteration in the road system.

1. Penaluna (1838) II, 111.
2. Maclean (1873) 585-6.
3. Langdon (1890-1) 38.
4. Langdon (1890-1) 38.
5. Macalister (1949) 180.

Figure II.74   Waterpit Down (photograph Woolf/Greenham Collection).

Description

The stone is a carved cross-shaft, now incomplete, set in a large, probably original base which measures approximately 130 cm. square (fig. II.74). The stone measures 204 cm. in height to the base, 46 to 66 cm. in width and 21 to 27 cm. in thickness. Langdon gave the height as seven feet, ten inches including the tenon (*c.* 235 cm.),[6] which suggests that some 31 cm. are inside the base. Traces of what was probably a text remain towards the centre of one face of the shaft. The text is now illegible and it is uncertain what script was used. The text was probably incised without framing-lines in a panel measuring 59 by 29 cm. and was probably primary. The letters, 5 to 8 cm. in height, were set in five lines reading horizontally.

Text

The text is now illegible.

Discussion

Only a few letters of the text can now be made out. Langdon first read the text as, CRUX IHS UROC, although expressing some doubt over IHS; this reading is to some extent supported by his drawing.[7] Subsequently Langdon and Allen, describing the text as 'doubtful', read, CRVX INVROC and the accompanying drawing by Langdon shows that it was then hard to read.[8] In 1896 Langdon suggested a new reading, CRVX IRCVROC.[9] Other readings are also recorded, for example one by Iago of CRVX INBVRGE,[10] and one by Macalister of CRVX MEVROC.[11] A reliable text is not now recoverable.

The stone belongs to Category 2a, inscribed cross-shafts. Category 2 stones date from the ninth to the eleventh century but this stone cannot be more closely dated.

Bibliography

Penaluna (1838) II, 111.
Maclean (1873) 585-6 & fig.
Langdon (1889*a*) 319, 335.
Langdon (1890-1) 34-41, 92, *passim* & figs.
Langdon & Allen, J.R. (1895) 52, 58, 60 & fig.
Langdon (1896) 6, 23, 374-7, *passim* & figs.
(-) (1896*a*) 150-2 & figs.
Daniell (1906) 245.
Langdon (1906) 419, *passim* & fig.
Macalister (1929) 192.
Hencken (1932) 270, 276, 304.

---

6. Langdon (1890-1) 39.
7. Langdon (1890-1) 40 & fig.
8. Langdon & Allen, J.R. (1895) 58 & fig.
9. Langdon (1896) 376.
10. Quoted in Langdon (1896) 376.
11. Macalister (1929) 192.

Macalister (1949) no. 1050, p. 180 & fig.
Ellis, G.E. (1952-3*a*) 58.
Ellis, G.E. (1959-61) 196-8 & figs.
Pevsner (1970) 120.
Todd (1987) 296.
Baird & White (unpub. 1961) vol. VIII, M.[12]

---

12. There is no page numbering in this typescript.

75 Welltown

The stone is now at a crossroads about 0.3 km. north-west of Welltown. It is set on a grass bank at the side of the road beside the Tawna stone. National Grid Reference SX 1361 6784. Examined 8 July 1984.

History

The stone was first noted in 1858 by Blight. It was then at Welltown and had 'been used as a gate-post'.[1] In 1867 Polsue stated that the stone was at Welltown, that it had been used as a gatepost, but that 'through the instrumentality of T.Q. Couch, Esq., of Bodmin, it is now enclosed with strong iron railings'.[2] Iago added that the stone, protected by iron railings, stood 'against the wall of a farm-building'.[3] This is presumably the 'waggon-shed' referred to by Langdon and Allen.[4] Subsequently Langdon said that the stone had previously been a gatepost inside this waggon-shed.[5] This sounds improbable but was repeated by Macalister.[6] In 1951 Pevsner recorded the stone still at Welltown,[7] but in his revised edition of 1970 the stone was described in its present position.[8] In 1985 Weatherhill was clearly in error in describing the stone as still against the wall of the farm building.[9] In his 1970 edition Pevsner noted four inscribed stones at Cardinham. These are Cardinham II, Tawna, Welltown and a fourth stone described as 'S of the churchyard, in the wall of a wagon shed'.[10] I could find no stone in such a position. Comparison of the two editions of Pevsner's book suggests that the description of the fourth stone, quoted above, is in fact part of his description of the Welltown stone and that this confusion probably arose during the re-editing process.

Description

The stone is an uncarved pillar-stone, probably complete. It measures 134 cm. in height, 20 to 30 cm. in width and 17 to 26 cm. in thickness.

1. Blight (1858a) 126.
2. Polsue (1867) 197.
3. Iago (1874–8) 364.
4. Langdon & Allen, J.R. (1895) 52.
5. Langdon (1906) 415–16.
6. Macalister (1945) 438.
7. Pevsner (1951) 41.
8. Pevsner (1970) 51.
9. Weatherhill (1985) 69.
10. Pevsner (1970) 51.

Figure II.75   Welltown (photograph Woolf/Greenham Collection).

Comparison with Macalister's measurements suggests that little or none of the stone has been buried in the bank.[11] The text appears to be primary; it is incised without framing-lines or panels, but beneath the incised arc of a

---

11. Macalister (1945) 438.

circle, on one face of the stone (fig. II.75). The face also contains several modern holes. The text is slightly deteriorated but is probably complete. The letters, 5 to 9 cm. in height, are in two lines and read downwards facing left. The script used is predominantly capital in form.

Text

[VA]ILAT[H]I
[F]ILIVROCH[ANI]

Discussion

The text now reads, [VA]ILAT[H]I [F]ILI VROCH[ANI]. Blight's drawing published in 1858 shows the text in substantially the same condition then as it is today; nevertheless, Blight described the text as 'nearly obliterated, the word *Filius* only being traced with certainty'.[12] Iago read, VAILATHI FILI UROCHANI, a reading supported by his drawing.[13] This text accords well with the text as it is today, except for the initial letter of the last word. The reading is likely to have been , VAILATHI FILI VROCHANI, that is, '[the stone] of Vailathus, son of Vrochanus' with FILI for FILII. Jackson suggested that the names might be Primitive Irish.[14]

The stone belongs to Category 1a, pillar-stones with a simple memorial text. Category 1 stones date from the fifth or sixth centuries to the eleventh century. If the names are Primitive Irish, this would suggest a date from the fifth or sixth century to the eighth century for this stone.

Bibliography

Blight (1858a) 126 & fig.
Polsue (1867) 197.
Haddan & Stubbs (1869) 163.
Iago (1874-8) 364-5 & fig.
Rhys (1875) 364.
Huebner (1876) no. 21, p. 8 & fig.
Rhys (1879) 216, 402.
Langdon & Allen, J.R. (1888) 308, 316.
Langdon & Allen, J.R. (1895) 52, 56, 60 & fig.
(-) (1896b) 257.
Rhys (1905) 70.
Daniell (1906) 241.
Langdon (1906) 415-16, *passim* & fig.
Holder (1907-13) cols 85, 454.

12. Blight (1858a) 126.
13. Iago (1874-8) 365 & fig.
14. Jackson (1953) 566; see also O'Brien (1973) 226.

Macalister (1929) 179.
Hencken (1932) 243, 294.
Jenkin (1934) 30.
Macalister (1945) no. 460, p. 438 & fig.
Jackson (1953) 566.
(-) (1966) 50.
Pevsner (1970) 51.
Thomas, A.C. (1985*a*) 178.
Thomas, A.C. (1985*b*) 173.
Weatherhill (1985) 69 & fig.
McManus (1991) 121.

76 Whitestile

The stone now forms the horizontal seat of the left-hand side of the stile at Whitestile. The stile is at the junction where the entrance drive to Trevince branches to the left off the B 3298, Truro to Falmouth road, about 0.8 km. after Carharrock. National Grid Reference SW 7332 4047. Examined 9 July 1985 and 5 July 1986.

History

The stone was described by Bannister in 1869: 'While writing, I would mention another *men scryfa* discovered by me, at Whitestile, in Gwennap ... Built up in the stone hedge adjoining is half of the stone in which it was set, exhibiting a section of the socket'.[1] I could not find this socketed stone but the hedge is now very overgrown. Bannister did not make clear exactly where the inscribed stone then was, but it may have been in its present position; it was certainly there by 1949.[2]

Description

There is a tenon at the left-hand end of the stone, suggesting that it may once have been a cross-shaft; the other end may also have been shaped (fig. II.76). The visible face shows no sign of carving and it seems likely that an inscribed pillar-stone was later cut to form a cross-shaft. The stone may also have been cut to fit the stile and so is probably incomplete. When erect the stone would measure 207 cm. in height, 35 cm. in width and 13 to 15 cm. in thickness. The text is incised without framing-lines or panels on the visible face of the stone. The text is highly deteriorated and may be incomplete; it is unclear whether or not it is primary. The text is set in one line and probably reads downwards facing left, *see* Introduction, Section 4c. The text uses a predominantly capital script and the letters measure 8 to 12 cm. in height.

Text

[.]N[-]A[-]

---

1. Bannister (1869) xxxv.
2. James (1949) 48.

Figure II.76   Whitestile (photograph Woolf/Greenham Collection).

Discussion

About two letters are lost from the first lacuna and about three from the second, and the text is now virtually illegible. No early drawings of it survive. In 1869 Bannister recorded that, 'Only one or two letters are decipherable',[3] suggesting that the text was in a similar condition to today. In these circumstances, no interpretation of the text is possible.

The stone probably belongs to Category 1c, pillar-stones which were later re-cut to form crosses. Category 1 stones date from the fifth or sixth centuries to the eleventh century. In their original form Category 1c stones are likely to pre-date the period of the ninth to the eleventh century since the re-cutting of the stones to form crosses may date from then.

Bibliography

Bannister (1869) xxxv.
James (1949) 48.
Baird & White (unpub. 1961) vol. IV, D-G.[4]
Henderson, M. (unpub. 1985) 439-40.

---

3. Bannister (1869) xxxv.
4. There is no page numbering in this typescript. The Whitestile stone is noted under '*Gwennap and St. Day*'.

77 Winsford Hill

The stone is now on the moor about 8 km. from Dulverton. It stands on the right-hand side of the unclassified road to Winsford which branches off to the right from the B 3223, Dulverton to Exford road. The stone is *c.* 25 m. off the road under a shelter. National Grid Reference SS 8897 3356. Examined 29 June 1984 and 3 July 1986.

History

Page recorded the stone in 1890 on Winsford Hill, on Sir Thomas Acland's land; it was then standing 'by the side of an old road cutting off the angle made by the road from Dulverton to Withypoole crossing that from Tarr's Steps to Winsford'.[1] This is its present position. A few months before Page recorded the stone, a piece had been broken off.[2] Page noted that, according to the Rev. J.J. Coleman, the stone had been known for seven or eight years and, some three years previously, two pieces had been broken off, one containing the letter N; Coleman had buried these two pieces.[3] Two pieces (whether these two, or pieces broken off in 1890, or another two is unclear) were 'carefully hidden ... close by'.[4] In 1906 James Weetch found the piece containing the letter N and, early in 1908, he cemented it into position.[5] In 1890 Acland had a fence built around the stone and in 1906 he had a shelter built over it.[6] In 1918 he leased Winsford Hill to the National Trust for 500 years. In October 1936 the stone was found to have been 'thrown down' and some digging done around it.[7] It was temporarily moved to a nearby cottage. Prior to its re-erection on 14 June 1937, a 'small excavation' was undertaken but this revealed no sign of any burial and indeed nothing of interest.[8] It is possible, but by no means certain, that this stone is the 'Langestone' mentioned in a document of 1297.[9] It is also possible, although equally uncertain, that this stone is the one referred to by Camden as being among other stones on Exmoor: 'vnum Saxonicis vel

---

1. Page (1890*c*) 82-7, quotation from p. 82.
2. Page (1890*c*) 82; Page (1890*b*) 91.
3. Page (1890*c*) 84.
4. Page (1890*c*) 87. This final sentence is initialled 'F.T.E.' and presumably refers to F.T. Elworthy.
5. Vowles (1939) 17-19.
6. Page (1890*c*) 87; Vowles (1939) 13. Grinsell was presumably in error when he gave the date of the erection of the shelter as 1923: Grinsell (1970) 104.
7. Gray (1937) 166.
8. Gray (1937) 166-7, quotation from p. 167; Vowles (1939) 19.
9. See Weaver *et al.* (1900) 26-7 and MacDermot (1973) 119.

potiùs Danicis literis inscriptum ad dirigendum eos, vt videtur, qui illac iter haberent'.[10] If Camden was not referring to this stone then Camden's stone is now lost.

Description

The stone is an uncarved pillar-stone which may or may not now be complete; certainly at least one piece has been broken off and cemented on again. It measures 129 cm. in height, 34 to 37 cm. in width and 19 to 20 cm. in thickness. Comparison with Gray's measurements indicates that some 29 cm. are now beneath the ground.[11] The text is incised without framing-lines or panels on one face of the stone (fig. II.77). The text appears to be primary. Although there are no signs of any lost letters, the reading of the text suggests that it may in fact be incomplete. The text is legible but it has been rather inaccurately recut in modern times. The letters, 5 to 10 cm. in height, are in two lines and read downwards facing left. The text uses a predominantly capital script. Some modern graffiti have been scratched on the lower part of the inscribed face of the stone.

Text

CARĀACI
NEPVS

Discussion

The text now reads, CARĀACI NEPVS. NEPVS for NEPOS might mean 'descendant', 'nephew', 'cousin' or 'grandson'. NEPVS also occurs on a stone from Whithorn, Scotland.[12] NEPOS is common as a name on Romano-British stones and NEPOS 'descendant, nephew, grandson' occurs on a Romano-British bronze plate from Colchester.[13] The exact form of the first word on the Winsford stone is uncertain. The horizontal stroke above the second A could indicate, as in manuscript abbreviation, an omitted M or N, hence CARAMACI or CARANACI. Alternatively, since the horizontal stroke touches the A, it might indicate a ligature A/T, hence CARATACI. It is possible that the horizontal stroke might indicate both of these simultaneously, hence CARANTACI. In my view, CARATACI seems

10. Camden (1594) 137. This is the earliest edition of Camden's work to contain the reference. It was repeated in all subsequent editions and translations and also appears in Speed (1676) 19. See also Chanter & Worth, R.H. (1905) 377-8.
11. Gray (1937) 167.
12. Macalister (1945) no. 520, pp. 499-501 & fig.
13. Collingwood, R.G. & Wright, R.P. (1965) no. 191, p. 63 & fig. On NEPOS as a name see Goodburn & Waugh (1983).

Figure II.77 Winsford Hill (photograph Joan Astell).

the most likely interpretation and there is a well-attested Celtic name appearing in Latinised form as *Caratacus, Caratocus*.[14] On the other hand, the name CARANTACVS probably occurs on a sixth-century stone from Egremont in Wales, although the reading of the first two letters looks doubtful to me from Nash-Williams' figure.[15] The form of the name apart, the interpretation of the text is still not certain. As it stands, CARÃACI NEPVS could mean, '[the stone of] the descendant of Caratacus' with NEPVS in the nominative instead of the genitive, assuming NEPVS to be a common noun, not a personal name. If the text is incomplete, it might have taken the usual form, '[the stone of X], descendant of Caratacus'. Macalister did indeed record traces of a further line of text: '. . . there are clear traces of a line of writing preceding *Carãaci*, which has been chipped completely away: nothing is left of it but an S, just above the third A'.[16] No such traces remain today, nor have any such been recorded by anyone else; Vowles went to look for Macalister's 'line of writing' but found nothing.[17] In view of this, Macalister's 'line of writing' cannot be accepted with any confidence and the original form of the text remains uncertain.

The stone belongs to Category 1a, pillar-stones with a simple memorial text. Category 1 stones date from the fifth or sixth centuries to the eleventh century but this stone cannot be more closely dated.

Bibliography

Page (1890*a*) 263-4.
Page (1890*b*) 80, 90-2, 309.
Page (1890*c*) 82-7 & fig.
Rhys (1890*a*) 179.
Rhys (1890*b*) 201.
Page (1891*a*) 168-9.
Page (1891*b*) 164-5.
Rhys (1891) 29-32 & fig.
Holder (1896) cols 771-3.
Greswell (1900) 125.
Rhys & Brynmor-Jones (1900) 47-8.
Weaver *et al.* (1900) 26-7.
Chanter & Worth, R.H. (1905) 382, 386.
Haverfield (1906) 369 & fig.
Macalister (1907) 123-4.
Chanter (1910) 482.
Haverfield (1913) no. 982, p. 510.
Haverfield (1918) xxxii-xxxiii, xxxviii-xxxix.
Bruton (1919) 208-10 & fig.
Gray (1924) xl-xli & fig.
Macalister (1929) 193, 195.

---

14. Jackson (1953) 290, 297.
15. Macalister (1945) no. 363, p. 347 & fig.; Nash-Williams (1950) no. 143, p. 111 & fig. See also Jackson (1953) 291, 502.
16. Macalister (1929) 195.
17. Vowles (1939) 15.

Gray (1937) 166-8.
Vivian-Neal (1937) 211-12.
Vowles (1939) *passim* & figs.
Macalister (1945) no. 499, pp. 476-7 & fig.
Fox (1964) 159, 162, 244 & fig.
(-) (1966) 51.
Evans (1967) 163.
Grinsell (1970) 104, 210 & fig.
MacDermot (1973) 119.
Radford (1975) 12-13.
Pearce (1978) 29 & fig.
Pearce (1981) 169, 172, 270 & fig.
Pearce (1985) 257-8.
Todd (1987) 249-50.

78 Worthyvale

The stone is now about 0.3 km. upstream from Slaughter Bridge, on the left-hand bank of the stream. National Grid Reference SX 1092 8568. Examined 10 July 1984 and 6 July 1986.

History

The stone was first recorded in 1602 by Carew: '... the olde folke thereabouts will shew you a stone, bearing Arthurs name, though now depraued to *Atry*'.[1] It was then apparently lost sight of, because in 1745 Pomeroy stated: 'Some years since the above inscription was discovered at a place called *Slaughter bridge*, or corruptly *Sloven's bridge*, which lies near *Worthevale*'.[2] In 1754 W. Borlase stated that the stone had been 'formerly a foot bridge near the late Lord Falmouth's seat of Worthyvale, about a mile and half from Camelford. It was call'd Slaughter Bridge'.[3] Borlase continued:

> A few years since, the present Lady Dowager Falmouth, shaping a rough kind of hill, about 100 yards off, into spiral walks, remov'd this Stone from the place where it serv'd as a bridge, and building a low piece of Masonry for it's support, plac'd it at the foot of her improvements, where it still lyes in one of the natural grotts of the hill.[4]

This stone is probably the one seen by Alfred Lord Tennyson in June 1848.[5] Rhys in 1875 was the first to record the ogham text.[6]

In 1799 a tradition was recorded that the underneath of another large stone, similar in size to the inscribed stone but lying in the stream, was also inscribed; the writer failed to examine it, due to its weight and the height of the stream.[7] The inscribed stone and the stone in the stream remain in these positions. A letter from Wrey I' Ans to the Rev. D. Lysons, dated 8 May 1812, described how a man sent to copy the inscription on the inscribed stone 'found That the present Tenant of the Premises, had

---

1. Carew (1602) 122v.
2. Pomeroy (1745) 304.
3. Borlase, W. (1754) 360.
4. Borlase, W. (1754) 360.
5. Tennyson (1897) I, 275.
6. Rhys (1875) 363.
7. (-) (1799) 571-2.

removed it – and turning the Inscription downwards – placed it as a Foot Bridge over the adjoining Brook . . .'.[8] In 1873 Maclean quoted part of this letter and said that the inscribed stone was then 'close to the stream' adding that it 'may, at some time, have been placed across it'.[9] In the summer of 1985 Daniel J. Parsons of Worthyvale Manor tried to lift the stone in the stream but managed only to feel underneath it. There was no indication of any inscription.[10] It is possible that the inscribed stone was once across the stream. It is also possible that the stone in the stream was once inscribed and that the text has been worn away by the water. It seems to me more likely, however, that the stone in the stream was never inscribed and the tradition that it was so resulted from confusion between the two stones.

Description

The stone is probably a pillar-stone, though it now lies in a recumbent position (fig. II.78). It appears to be uncarved and is probably complete. If erect, it would measure 206 cm. in height, 50 to 70 cm. in width and 28 to 37 cm. in thickness.

Text (i) is incised without framing-lines or panels on the visible face of the stone. The text is legible, probably complete and appears to be primary. The letters, 10 to 19 cm. in height, are set in two lines and are in a predominantly capital script. Originally the letters probably read downwards facing left, *see* Introduction, Section 4c.

Text (ii), the ogham text, is incised on the upper part of the edge between the visible face and the right-hand side of the stone. Originally text (ii) probably read vertically upwards. Text (ii) is incomplete and so highly deteriorated that only two letters can be made out. It is probably primary.

Texts

(i)   LATINIICIACIT
      FIL/IUSMA[...]RI
(ii) [ogham] [-]NI

Discussion

The lower part of the first A and the upper part of the L of FIL/IUS touch each other. Text (i) appears to read, LATINI IC IACIT FILIUS MA[...]RI, which can be interpreted, '[the stone] of Latinus; here lies the son of Ma[-]'

---

8. BL Add. MS 9418, fo. 114.
9. Maclean (1873) 584.
10. In a personal communication.

Figure II.78 Worthyvale (photograph Woolf/Greenham Collection).

with IC for HIC and IACIT for IACET. An alternative translation might be, '[the body] of Latinus lies here, son of Ma[-]'. W. Borlase's drawing suggests a reading, CATINI IC IACIT F/ILIUS MAGARI[.], although Borlase actually read the text as *'Catin hc jacit -- filius magari --'*.[11] Pomeroy's slightly earlier sketch is consistent with Borlase's drawing although it shows the final name less clearly.[12] In 1875 Rhys read the final name as 'MA. . .ARI', which suggests that it was as unclear then as it is today.[13] The original form of this name is not now recoverable although various suggestions have been made, for example, MAGARI, MAGIARI, MAFARI[14] and MACARI.[15] The name LATINI is Latin.[16] The name LATINVS occurs on a stone from Whithorn, Scotland.[17] It also occurred on a now lost Romano-British stone from Bath.[18]

Text (ii) reads, [-]NI and is now too incomplete to be intelligible. Rhys

---

11. Borlase, W. (1754) 360 & fig.
12. Pomeroy (1745) 304 & fig.
13. Rhys (1875) 362.
14. Rhys (1875) 362-3. Macalister also read MAGARI: Macalister (1945) 449.
15. Langdon & Allen, J.R. (1895) 56.
16. Jackson (1953) 172, 184.
17. Macalister (1945) no. 520, pp. 499-501 & fig.
18. Collingwood, R.G. & Wright, R.P. (1965) no. 158, p. 52 & fig.

read only a final I, perhaps preceded by R,[19] although Macalister recorded, LA[TI]NI.[20] It is possible, but by no means certain, that text (ii) is a rendering of part of text (i), perhaps the end of LATINI.

The stone belongs to Category 1b, pillar-stones with longer texts. Category 1 stones date from the fifth or sixth centuries to the eleventh century. On the evidence of the ogham text, this stone is likely to date from the fifth or sixth century to the eighth century. The use of a Latin name is in accordance with this dating.

Bibliography

Carew (1602) 122v.
Pomeroy (1745) 304 & fig.
Borlase, W. (1754) 360 & fig.
Gough (1789) I, 20.
(-) (1799) 571-2.
Polwhele (1803) II, 194-5.
Lysons, D. & Lysons, S. (1814) ccxxii.
Gilbert, C.S. (1817) 203.
Gilbert, C.S. (1820) 579.
Hitchins (1824) I, 394-5, 435.
Gilbert, D. (1838) III, 236.
Penaluna (1838) II, 111.
Redding (1842) 57n.
Wright, T. (1852) 456.
Polsue (1867) 191, 193.
Iago (1868-70) xxxix, 318 & fig.
Iago (1870-3) 483.
Iago (1871-3) 65n.
Polsue (1872) fig. (frontispiece).
Maclean (1873) 583-4 & fig.
Rhys (1875) 362-3.
Huebner (1876) no. 17, pp. 6, 89 & fig.
Brash (1879) 351, 403-4.
Rhys (1879) 204, 284-5, 402.
Iago (1883-5a) 278n.
Langdon & Allen, J.R. (1888) 306-8, 317 & fig.
Iago (1890-1) 237.
Langdon (1893) 107-8.
Iago (1893-5b) 172-4.
Iago et al. (1893-5) 120.
Langdon & Allen, J.R. (1895) 52, 56, 60 & fig.
(-) (1896a) 149-50 & fig.
Tennyson (1897) I, 275.
Holder (1904) cols 152, 374.
Rhys (1905) 59-61.
Daniell (1906) 25n, 242-3.
Langdon (1906) 419, passim & fig.
Macalister (1929) 192.
Hencken (1932) 242-3, 304.

---

19. Rhys (1875) 363.
20. Macalister (1945) 448-9 & fig.

Jenkin (1934) 30.
Macalister (1945) no. 470, pp. 447-9 & fig.
Jackson (1950) 199, 205, 208.
Jackson (1953) 171-2, 184.
Fox (1964) 159.
(-) (1966) 51.
Radford (1968) 190, 195 (illus. no. 156) & fig.
Pevsner (1970) 120.
Alcock (1971) 164-5 & fig.
Laing (1975) 125.
Pearce (1978) 26-7, 161-2.
Pearce (1981) 172.
Brewer & Frankl (1985) 33.
Thomas, A.C. (1985*a*) 269-70 & figs.
Thomas, A.C. (1985*b*) 174.
Weatherhill (1985) 83 & figs.
McManus (1991) 62, 64, 113.

79 Yealmpton

The stone is now in Yealmpton churchyard, on a grass bank outside the west door of the church. National Grid Reference SX 5775 5170. Examined 25 June 1984 and 3 July 1986.

History

The stone was first recorded in 1797 by Polwhele when it was described as 'lying . . . in the church-yard' and 'being somewhat sunk in the earth by its weight, its thickness does not appear'.[1] The earliest drawing, published in 1806 by Gough, shows the stone lying on its side; Gough described it as, 'In *Yalmpton* church-yard'.[2] Gough also gave the information that a Mr Jones had had 'the grave opened, but he did not find any thing but the remains of bones'.[3] It is thus possible that the stone was found in association with a grave, although it is not absolutely certain that the bones and stone belonged together. The stone was recorded at Yealmpton in 1874 and in 1910,[4] although in 1918 it was said to be lost.[5] By 1929 it was standing in front of the west end of the church.[6] This is presumably its present position. Subsequently Macalister suggested that it had been used as a gatepost.[7]

Description

The stone is a complete, uncarved pillar-stone. It measures 180 cm. in height, 27 to 47 cm. in width and 14 to 16 cm. in thickness. When the stone was prostrate, Polwhele gave its length as 'nine feet' (c. 270 cm.).[8] This suggests that some 90 cm. are now beneath the ground. The text is incised without framing-lines or panels on one face of the stone (fig. II.79). The text is legible, complete and appears to be primary. The letters, 8 to 15 cm. in height, are in one line and read downwards facing left. The text uses a predominantly capital script. Gough's drawing shows a large X at the

1. Polwhele (1797) I, 152.
2. Gough (1806) I, 47 & fig.
3. Gough (1806) I, 47.
4. Bate (1873-6) 392, paper read 19 November 1874; Chanter (1910) 481.
5. Rhys (1918) 192. This paper, dated September 1915, was published posthumously; see Rhys (1918) 181n.
6. Macalister (1929) 193.
7. Macalister (1945) 472.
8. Polwhele (1797) I, 152.

Figure II.79 Yealmpton (photograph E.N. Masson Phillips).

lower end of the face of the stone, on the part now beneath the ground.[9] As Huebner first suggested, this X may perhaps have been a later addition.[10]

Text

GOREV<u>S</u>

---

9. Gough (1806) I, 47 & fig.
10. Huebner (1876) 9.

Discussion

The text reads, GOREVS, a Celtic name.[11] The similar name GUORGORET occurs on a stone from Margam, Wales.[12]

The stone belongs to Category 1a, pillar-stones with a simple memorial text. Category 1 stones date from the fifth or sixth centuries to the eleventh century but this stone cannot be more closely dated.

Bibliography

Polwhele (1797) I, 152.
Britton & Brayley (1803) 137.
Polwhele (1803) I, 146-8.
Gough (1806) I, 47-8 & fig.
Lysons, D. & Lysons, S. (1822) cccviii.
(-) (1851a) 424.
Smirke *et al.* (1861) 177-8.
Haddan & Stubbs (1869) 162.
Bate (1873-6) 392.
Huebner (1876) no. 23, p. 9 & fig.
Worth, R.N. (1886) 179-81, 238-9.
Holder (1896) col. 2032.
Chanter (1910) 481.
Rhys (1918) 192.
Macalister (1929) 193.
Alexander (1937) 153-4.
Macalister (1945) no. 494, p. 472 & fig.
(-) (1966) 51.
Pearce (1978) 71, 183.
Bampfield & O'Flynn (1981) 8.
Pearce (1982) 7.

---

11. Holder (1896) col. 2032; Rhys (1918) 192.
12. Macalister (1949) no. 1014, p. 157 & fig.; Nash-Williams (1950) no. 231, pp. 146-8 & figs.

APPENDICES

Appendix A: Personal Names

The personal names occurring in the inscriptions are discussed in Section 6 of the Introduction and in the appropriate Entries. For convenience, the personal names are listed here in alphabetical order. The list includes both words that are certainly personal names and those that may be personal names. The names are quoted in the forms in which they occur on the stones, with the occasional restoration within brackets of a single lost letter. Where an early drawing permits the reconstruction of a name that is now largely deteriorated, the reconstructed letters are enclosed within brackets and the name is asterisked. The names on stones now lost are treated in a similar way. The only names excluded from this list are those whose form is now totally irrecoverable.

[ÆLNA]T*, Tintagel
ÆLSEL[Ð], Lanteglos
ÆLWYNEYS, Lanteglos
ANNICV, Lanivet

BO[N]EMIMORI, Rialton
BREID, Lanherne
[BROCAGNI]*, St Endellion

CARĀACI, Winsford Hill
CAVVDI, Lynton
CA[-]OCI, East Ogwell
[CI]LRORON, Biscovey
CIVI[L]I, Lynton
CLO[TUALI]*, Phillack I
[CNEGVMI]*, Mawgan
CONBEVI, Tavistock I
CONET[O]CI, Cubert
CONHINO[C], Lustleigh
CVMREGNI, Southill
[CVNATDO]* or [CVNAIDE]*, Hayle
CV[N]OMORI, Castledore
CVNOVALI, Madron I
[-CO]BI, Tresco

[D]AP[-], Buckland Monachorum
DATUIDOC, Lustleigh
DINVI, Gulval I
DOBVNNI, Tavistock III
DONIERT, Redgate
DVNO[C]ATI, Lancarffe

[ELEW], Plymstock
[E]NABARRI, Tavistock III
ERCILI or ERCILI[V]I, Tregony
ERCILINGI, Tregony
[E]VOCA[.], Boskenna

FABRI, Tavistock III
FANONI, Fardel
[-FRIDVS]*, Tavistock V

G[A]G[R]A[NV]I or G[A]G[R]A[SN]I, Fardel
[GENAIVS]*, Mawgan
GENE[REÐ], Lanteglos
GOREVS, Yealmpton
[G]U[RG]LE[S], Stowford

HEY[SEL]*, Lanteglos

IGNIOC, St Clement
[I]MAH, Lanherne
[I]N[.EN.]VI, Lewannick I
IVGDOCI, [R]IVGDOCI, IVSDOCI or [R]IVSDOCI, Bosworgey
IV[S]TI, St Kew

LATINI, Worthyvale
LEUIUT, Camborne

MACCODECHETI, Tavistock II
MAQIQICI or QICI, Fardel
MAQVIRINI or RINI, Fardel
MAVCI, Southill
ME[S]CAGNI, Lancarffe
MO[BRA]TTI, Phillack I

[NADOTTI]*, St Endellion
[NEMIAVS]*, Treveneague
NEPRANI, Tavistock I
NEPVS, Winsford Hill
[NICI]N[..]SC[I], Buckland Monachorum
NONNITA, Tregony
NOTI and NOTI, St Hilary

[PO]TIT, Lundy II

QVENATAVCI, Gulval I

RESGEVT[A], Lundy III
RIALOBRANI, Madron I
RICATI or [V]IRICATI, Tregony
RŪHOL, Lanherne
[.]R[A]H, Cardinham I

SA[B]INI, Tavistock II
SAFAQQUCI, Fardel

SELVS, SENILVS or SELNIVS, St Just II
SEVERI, Nanscow

TEGE[R]NOMALI, Cubert
[T]I[G]ERNI, Lundy I
TIMI, Lundy IV
TORRICI, St Clement
TRIBVNI, Rialton
T[..T]UEN[T] or T[..T]UER[T], Boslow

[VA]ILAT[H]I, Welltown
[VALCI]*, Bowden
VITALI, St Clement
VLC[A]GNI, U[L]CAG[.I] and [.L]CAG[.]I, Lewannick II
VLCAGNI, Nanscow
VROCH[ANI], Welltown

Appendix B: Romano-British Inscribed Stones from the South-west[1]

Collingwood and Wright noted five Romano-British 'milestones' from Cornwall:[2]

1. Breage
   Collingwood, R.G. & Wright, R.P. (1965) no. 2232, p. 696 & fig.: dated AD 258-268.
   Sedgley (1975) no. 20, p. 23.

2. Gwennap
   Collingwood, R.G. & Wright, R.P. (1965) no. 2234, p. 697 & fig.: dated AD 238-244.
   Sedgley (1975) no. 19, p. 23.

3. St Hilary
   Collingwood, R.G. & Wright, R.P. (1965) no. 2233, pp. 696-7 & fig.: dated AD 306-307.
   Sedgley (1975) no. 21, pp. 23-4.

4. Tintagel
   Collingwood, R.G. & Wright, R.P. (1965) no. 2231, pp. 695-6 & fig.: dated AD 308-324.
   Sedgley (1975) no. 18, pp. 22-3.

5. Trethevy
   Collingwood, R.G. & Wright, R.P. (1965) no. 2230, pp. 694-5 & fig.: dated AD 251-253.
   Sedgley (1975) no. 17, p. 22.

There are no Romano-British inscribed stones from Devon. The *Dumnonii* are, however, mentioned in two inscriptions from Hadrian's Wall.[3] From Somerset there is one 'milestone' from Ilchester,[4] and a series of other inscribed stones, mainly from Bath.[5]

---

1. I have not examined all these stones.
2. Cf. also Sedgley (1975) esp. p. 6, Collingwood, R.G. (1924) 101-12 and Todd (1987) 217-19. Todd pointed out that the stones were records of road maintenance, not milestones.
3. Collingwood, R.G. & Wright, R.P. (1965) nos 1843-4, pp. 570-1 & figs.
4. Collingwood, R.G. & Wright, R.P. (1965) no. 2229, pp. 693-4 & fig.; Sedgley (1975) 22.
5. Collingwood, R.G. & Wright, R.P. (1965) nos 138-78, pp. 42-58 & figs.

Appendix C: Inscribed Stones from the South-west Post-dating AD 1100

Listed below are seven stones from the south-west which have been described as dating, or possibly dating, from the early Christian period. Almost certainly, however, they date from later than AD 1100. The bibliographical references cited are chosen for their accessibility and to include, where possible, at least one illustration of each stone.

1. Hensbarrow, Cornwall.
   Iago (1883-5b) 287-91 & fig.

2. Lanteglos by Fowey, Cornwall.
   Hencken (1935) 156, 158-9 & fig.

3. Little Petherick, Cornwall.
   Barber (1890) 3.

4. Ludgvan, Cornwall.
   Maxwell (1976) 10.

5. Mabe, Cornwall.
   Whitley (1871-3) xxiii.
   It is probable but not certain that Whitley is referring to the existing stones, which are built into a wall on Church Road at Turnemere Farm, Mabe.

6. Nun's Cross, Devon.
   Phillips (1937) 297, 309 & fig.

7. St Michael Penkevil, Cornwall.
   Macalister (1949) no. 1056, p. 185 & fig. (fig. numbered 1057).

Appendix D: Comparable Inscribed Stones from outside the South-west

Listed below are eight inscribed stones comparable to those from south-west Britain but found outside the south-west area. Inscribed stones from Wales are not listed.[1] The bibliographical references cited are chosen both for their accessibility and to include at least one illustration of each stone.

1. Jersey.
   Stevens *et al.* (1975) 343-57 & figs.

2. Silchester, Hampshire.
   Macalister (1945) no. 496, pp. 473-5 & fig.
   Fulford & Sellwood (1980) 95-9 & figs.

3. Wareham I, Dorset.
   Radford & Jackson (1970) 310-11.
   (-) (1970) pt 1, pp. xlix-l; pt 2, p. 308 & figs.

4. Wareham II, Dorset.
   Radford & Jackson (1970) 310-11.
   (-) (1970) pt 1, pp. xlix-l; pt 2, p. 308 & figs.

5. Wareham III, Dorset.
   Radford & Jackson (1970) 310-12.
   (-) (1970) pt 1, pp. xlix-l; pt 2, p. 308 & figs.

6. Wareham IV, Dorset.
   Radford & Jackson (1970) 310, 312.
   (-) (1970) pt 1, pp. xlix-l; pt 2, p. 308 & figs.

7. Wareham V, Dorset.
   Radford & Jackson (1970) 310, 312.
   (-) (1970) pt 1, pp. xlix-l; pt 2, p. 308 & figs.

8. Wroxeter, Shropshire.
   Wright, R.P. & Jackson (1968) 296-300 & fig.

---

1. For the Welsh stones, see Nash-Williams (1950).

Appendix E: Stones excluded on Grounds other than those of Provenance or Date

Listed below are six stones from the south-west omitted from the corpus on grounds other than those of provenance or date. The first three stones contain markings of some sort but in my view these markings are not inscriptions. The remaining three stones are now lost but the drawings that exist suggest that they are unlikely to have been early Christian inscribed stones.

1. Brendon, Somerset.
   Unpublished; for details, refer to the Somerset County Archaeologist.

2. Combwich, Somerset.
   Dewar (1940) 131-3.
   Grinsell (1970) 105-6, 210.

3. Ilsington, Devon.
   Unpublished; for details, refer to the Devon County Archaeologist.

4. Kenegie, Cornwall.
   Russell (1971) 81.
   Henderson, C.G. (unpub. 1912-17) II, 36-7 & fig.

5. Polyphant, Lewannick, Cornwall.
   Nicholls & Dewey (1912-14) 41-2 & fig.

6. Trevellion, Luxulyan, Cornwall.
   Henderson, C.G. (unpub. 1912-17) III, 322 & fig.
   Beagrie (1981) 214.

Appendix F: Macalister's Numbering of the Stones

Many of the inscribed stones from the south-west were included by Macalister in his *Corpus* where they were assigned numbers.[1] Several subsequent scholars have referred to the stones by these numbers without the name of the stone, that is, in the form 'CIIC 457'. For convenience, Macalister's CIIC numbers are given here, with the corresponding name of the stone which I have used.

CIIC

457 : Lancarffe
458 : Cardinham II
459 : Tawna
460 : Welltown
461 : Tregony
462 : Gulval I
463 : Gulval II
464 : Trebyan
465 : Lanivet
466 : Lewannick I
467 : Lewannick II
468 : Madron I
469 : Mawgan
470 : Worthyvale
471 : Phillack I
472 : Nanscow
473 : St Clement
474 : Indian Queens
475 : St Columb Major
476 : Rialton
477 : Cubert
478 : St Endellion
479 : Hayle
480 : Lanhadron
481 : St Hilary

---

1. Macalister (1945) and Macalister (1949). Macalister (1945) includes CIIC numbers 457 to 499 inclusive, Macalister (1949) CIIC numbers 1043 to 1060 inclusive.

482   : Treveneague
483   : St Just II
484   : St Kew
485   : Tresco
486   : Southill
487   : Castledore
488   : Tavistock III
489   : Fardel
490   : Lustleigh
491   : Sourton
492   : Tavistock II
493   : Tavistock I
494   : Yealmpton
499   : Winsford Hill

1043   : Trewint
1044   : Camborne
1045   : Treslothan
1046   : Cardinham I
1047   : Lanherne
1048   : Madron II
1049   : Madron III
1050   : Waterpit Down
1051   : Penzance
1052   : Perranporth
1053   : Biscovey
1054   : Redgate
1055   : Boslow
1057   : Sancreed II
1058   : Sancreed I
1059   : Tintagel
1060   : Stowford

Appendix G: Alternative Names Assigned to Individual Stones

In choosing by which name to refer to each stone, I have taken into account both the present location of the stone and the name most frequently assigned to it in the past. There has, however, been some inconsistency in nomenclature and the following are among the most frequently occurring alternatives.

Barlowena *see* Gulval I
Bleubridge *see* Gulval I
Bosullow *see* Boslow
Buckland Monachorum *see* Tavistock III
Cape Cornwall *see* St Just I
Carnsew *see* Hayle
Chapel Close *see* Lanherne
Cuby *see* Tregony
Doniert *see* Redgate
Doyden *see* St Endellion
Fowey *see* Castledore
Lanhydrock *see* Trebyan
Lanyon *see* Madron I
Men Scryfa *see* Madron I
Pendarves *see* Treslothan
Ruan *see* Indian Queens
St Blazey *see* Biscovey
St Breock *see* Nanscow
St Cleer *see* Redgate
St Columb Minor *see* Rialton
St Erth *see* Hayle
St Ewe *see* Lanhadron
St Helen's *see* St Just I
St Michael *see* Indian Queens
Trevena *see* Tintagel
Trevillet *see* Tintagel
Wadebridge *see* Nanscow

Bibliography

The Bibliography gives in full every reference quoted in abbreviated form in the Corpus. The most recent edition of each work is used except where an early date is of significance, as in a find-report. Authors' first names are given as initials and these are made consistent; this is due to the inconsistency of usage found on occasion, especially among authors from previous centuries. Anonymous works are denoted (-) (1900) etc., but this list is kept to a minimum by using an author's name even if he/she is only mentioned in Proceedings. The dates given for periodicals are of the year to which the volume refers, failing which, the year of publication. Where the title of an article appears differently in the list of contents and heading the article, the former is used. Information concerning the bibliography given in each Entry appears in the Introduction, Section 8.

Adams, A. (1888-92): A. Adams, in 'Excursions', *Trans Penzance NHA Soc.* NS, 3 (1888-92), 201-9.

Adams, J.H. (1968-70): J.H. Adams, '144. Further Note on St. Werye Chapel, St. Blazey', *Devon & Cornwall N & Q* 31 (1968-70), 214-5.

Alcock (1971): L. Alcock, *Arthur's Britain. History and Archaeology AD 367-634* (London, 1971).

Alexander (1937): J.J. Alexander, 'Eighth Report on Early History', *Trans Devon Assoc.* 69 (1937), 151-4.

Alford (1890): D.P. Alford, 'The Inscribed Stones in the Vicarage Garden, Tavistock', *Trans Devon Assoc.* 22 (1890), 229-33.

Allen, J (1967): J. Allen, ed. W.H. Paynter, *The History of the Borough of Liskeard* (Liskeard, 1967).

Allen, J.R. (1887): J.R. Allen, *Early Christian Symbolism in Great Britain and Ireland before the thirteenth century* (London, 1887).

Allen, J.R. (1889): J.R. Allen, *The Monumental History of the Early British Church* (London, 1889).

Allen, J.R. (1892): J.R. Allen, 'Inscribed Stone at Southill, Cornwall', in 'Archaeological Notes and Queries', *Arch. Camb.* 5S, 9 (1892), 160-73.

Andrew (1932): C.K.C. Andrew, 'Excavations at the Doniert Stone Site', *Old Cornwall* 2, no. 4 (winter, 1932), 25-7.

Andrew (1933-6): C.K.C. Andrew, 'The Doniert Stone, St. Cleer', *JRIC* 24, pts 1-2 (1933-6), 112-39.

Andrew (1938-9): C.K.C. Andrew, '231. Trewint Cross-base', *Devon & Cornwall N & Q* 20 (1938-9), 327-8.

Appleby (1975): C. Appleby, 'Parochial Check-Lists of Antiquities: *Penwith* (E): 6, St Erth', *Cornish Arch.* 14 (1975), 112-16.

Ashbee (1974): P. Ashbee, *Ancient Scilly From the First Farmers to the Early Christians. . .* (Newton Abbot, 1974).

Ashbee (1982): P. Ashbee, 'Hugh O'Neill Hencken (1902-1981) and his *Archaeology of Cornwall and Scilly* and Beyond', *Cornish Arch.* 21 (1982), 179-82.

Baird & White (unpub. 1961): R.D. Baird and Lady A. White, *Cornish Crosses*, typescript in 12 volumes. RIC, Truro: MS. (Acc. 1961).[1]

Bampfield & O'Flynn (1981): G.C. Bampfield and P. O'Flynn, *St. Clement: the Church of Moresk* (Truro, 1981).

---

1. References to this work are confined to entries of particular importance.

Bannister (1869): J. Bannister, in a letter dated 28 November 1868, *Rpt RIC* no. 51 (1869), xxxiv–xxxv.

Barber (1890): S. Barber, 'The Lost Village and Ruined Church at St. Constantine, near Padstow', *Western Antiquary* 9 (1890), 1-5.

Barham (1866): C. Barham, 'The Ancient Inscribed Stones at Tregoney and Cubert, Cornwall', *Arch. Camb.* 3S, 12 (1866), 417-29.

Barham (1866-7): C. Barham, 'Ancient Inscribed Stones at Tregoney & Cubert', *JRIC* 2, no. 5 (1866-7), 47-58.

Baring-Gould (1899-1900): S. Baring-Gould, 'Cornish Dedications of Saints, Part II', *JRIC* 14, pt 1 (1899-1900), 85-172.

Baring-Gould (1918): S. Baring-Gould, 'Two Inscribed Stones in Devon', *Arch. Camb.* 6S, 18 (1918), 195-8.

Bartrum (1966): P.C. Bartrum ed., *Early Welsh Genealogical Tracts* (Cardiff, 1966).

Bate (1873-6): C.S. Bate, 'The Inscribed Stones and Ancient Crosses of Devon. Part I', *Trans Plymouth Inst.* 5 (1873-6), 392-8.

Bate (1876-8): C.S. Bate, 'The Inscribed Stones and Ancient Crosses of Devon. Part II', *Trans Plymouth Inst.* 6 (1876-8), 154-66.

Beagrie (1972): N. Beagrie, 'Parochial Check-lists of Antiquities: *Powder*: 12, St. Blazey', *Cornish Arch.* 11 (1972), 70-2.

Beagrie (1981): N. Beagrie, 'Parish Check-lists: Luxulyan', *Cornish Arch.* 20 (1981), 209-14.

Beckerlegge (1953): J.J. Beckerlegge, 'The Ancient Memorial Inscription on the Stone at Hayle', *Old Cornwall* 5, no. 4 (1953), 173-7.

Beckerlegge (1959-61): J.J. Beckerlegge, '142. The Inscribed Stone at Mawgan-in-Meneage', *Devon & Cornwall N & Q* 28 (1959-61), 281-2.

Benyon et al. (1937): E.A. Benyon et al., *Saint Ewe. The Church and Parish...* (Shipstown-on-Stour, 1937).

Bergin (1932): O. Bergin, 'Varia. II. 10. *Eochu, Eochaid.*', *Ériu* 11 (1932), 140-6.

Bernier (1982): G. Bernier, *Les Chrétientés bretonnes continentales depuis les origines jusqu'au Ixéme siècle* (Rennes, 1982).

Best (1959): W.S. Best, 'Gleanings from the Dark-Ages Map of Britain', *Old Cornwall* 5, no. 10 (1959), 436-42.

Birch (1885): W. de G. Birch, 'Notes on the Inscription of the Carew Cross, Pembrokeshire', *JBAA* 41 (1885), 405-11.

Blight (1856): J.T. Blight, *Ancient Crosses, and other Antiquities, In the West of Cornwall* (London, Penzance, 1856).

Blight (1858a): J.T. Blight, *Ancient Crosses, and Other Antiquities in the East of Cornwall* (London, Dublin, Penzance, 1858).

Blight (1858b): J.T. Blight, *Ancient Crosses, and other Antiquities in the West of Cornwall* 2nd ed. (London, Dublin, Penzance, 1858).[2]

Blight (1861): J.T. Blight, *A Week at The Land's End* (London, 1861).

Blight (1862): J.T. Blight, 'Cornish Churches. II. St. Madron - St. Paul - Sancreed - St. Just', *Gents Mag.* 212 (1862) (i), 527-39.

Blight (1865): J.T. Blight, *Churches of West Cornwall; with notes of Antiquities of the District* (Oxford, London, 1865).

Bond (1823): T. Bond, *Topographical and Historical Sketches of the Boroughs of East and West Looe...* (London, 1823).

Borlase, W. (1754): W. Borlase, *Observations on the Antiquities Historical and Monumental, of the County of Cornwall* (Oxford, 1754).

Borlase, W. (unpub. 1740): W. Borlase, *Parochial Memorandums of Cornwall*, BL MS Egerton 2657.

Borlase, W.C. (1868-70): W.C. Borlase, 'Inscribed Stone at Stowford', *JRIC* 3, no. 12 (1868-70), 236-7.

Borlase, W.C. (1869): W.C. Borlase, 'Barrows in Cornwall', *Arch. Camb.* 3S, 15 (1869), 32-8.

2. References to this work are confined to entries not appearing in Blight's first edition; see Blight (1856).

Borlase, W.C. (1893): W.C. Borlase, *The Age of the Saints. . .* (Truro, London, 1893).

Brash (1869): R.R. Brash, 'The Ogham Inscribed Stones of Wales', *Arch. Camb.* 3S, 15 (1869), 148-67.

Brash (1879): R.R. Brash, ed. G.M. Atkinson, *The Ogam Inscribed Monuments of the Gœdhil in the British Islands. . .* (London, 1879).

Bray (1836): E.A. Bray, in a letter to Mrs A.E. Bray dated 10 March 1834, in A.E. Bray, *A Description of the Part of Devonshire bordering on the Tamar and the Tavy. . .* I (London, 1836), 360-84.[3]

Brewer & Frankl (1985): D. Brewer and E. Frankl, *Arthur's Britain: the Land and the Legend* (Cambridge, 1985).

Britton & Brayley (1801): J. Britton and E.W. Brayley, *The Beauties of England and Wales. . .* II (London, 1801).

Britton & Brayley (1803): J. Britton and E.W. Brayley, *The Beauties of England and Wales. . .* IV (London, 1803).

Bromwich (1954): R. Bromwich, 'The Character of the Early Welsh Tradition', in H.M. Chadwick *et al.*, *Studies in Early British History* (Cambridge, 1954), 83-136.

Bromwich (1955): R. Bromwich, 'Some Remarks on the Celtic Sources of "Tristan"', *Trans Hon. Soc. Cymmrodorion* vol. for 1953 (1955), 32-60.

Bromwich (1961): R. Bromwich ed., *Trioedd Ynys Prydein. The Welsh Triads* (Cardiff, 1961).

Brown (1921): G.B. Brown, *The Arts in Early England* V (London, 1921).

Bruton (1919): F.A. Bruton, 'The Caratacus Stone on Exmoor (plate xv)', *J Roman Stud.* 9 (1919), 208-10.

Buchner (1955): R. Buchner ed., *Gregorii Episcopi Turonensis Historiarum Libri Decem*, I *Libri I-V* (Berlin, 1955).

Buckley *et al.* (1885*a*): W.E. Buckley *et al.*, 'Inscribed Stone at Hayle', *Western Antiquary* 4 (1885), 267.

Buckley *et al.* (1885*b*): W.E. Buckley *et al.*, 'Inscribed Stone at Hayle', *N&Q* 6S, 11 (1885), 335-6.

Buller (1842): J. Buller, *A Statistical Account of the Parish of Saint Just in Penwith in the County of Cornwall. . .* (Penzance, 1842).

Bu'lock (1956): J.D. Bu'lock, 'Early Christian Memorial Formulae', *Arch. Camb.* 105 (1956), 133-41.

Burnard (1893): R. Burnard, *Dartmoor Pictorial Records* III (Plymouth, 1893).

Burnard (1895): R. Burnard, 'The Inscribed Stone at Stowford, Devon', *Reliquary* NS, 1 (1895), 228-9.

Camden (1594): W. Camden, *Britannia. . .* (London, 1594).[4]

Camden (1600): W. Camden, *Britannia. . .* (London, 1600).

Camden (1607): W. Camden, *Britannia. . .* (London, 1607).

Carew (1602): R. Carew, *The Survey of Cornwall* (London, 1602).

Chadwick (1963): N.K. Chadwick, *Celtic Britain* (London, 1963).

Chadwick (1965): N.K. Chadwick, 'The Colonization of Brittany from Celtic Britain', *PBA* 51 (1965), 235-99.

Chanter (1910): J.F. Chanter, 'Christianity in Devon, before A.D. 909', *Trans Devon Assoc.* 42 (1910), 475-502.

Chanter (1913): J.F. Chanter, 'A Romano-British Inscribed Stone between Parracombe and Lynton', *Trans Devon Assoc.* 45 (1913), 270-5.

Chanter (1924-5): J.F. Chanter, '281. Romano-British Inscription on Lundy Island', *Devon & Cornwall N & Q* 13 (1924-5), 308-9.

Chanter & Worth, R.H. (1905): J.F. Chanter and R.H. Worth, 'The Rude Stone Monuments of Exmoor and its Borders. Part I', *Trans Devon Assoc.* 37 (1905), 375-97.

---

3. The Rev. E.A. Bray's letter of 10 March 1834 to Mrs A.E. Bray was reprinted with small omissions in, A.E. Bray, *The Borders of the Tamar and the Tavy. . .* I (London, Plymouth, 1879), 313-37.

4. Only those editions and translations of this work which add significantly to the material in earlier editions are cited. See below, Gough (1789), and Gough (1806).

Collingwood, R.G. (1924): R.G. Collingwood, 'Roman Milestones in Cornwall', *Antiq. J* 4 (1924), 101-12.

Collingwood, R.G. & Wright, R.P. (1965): R.G. Collingwood and R.P. Wright, *The Roman Inscriptions of Britain.* I *Inscriptions on Stone* (Oxford, 1965).

Collingwood, W.G. (1927): W.G. Collingwood, *Northumbrian Crosses of the Pre-Norman Age* (London, 1927).

Collins (1851): W.W. Collins, *Rambles Beyond Railways; or, Notes in Cornwall taken a-foot* (London, 1851).

Coppard (1851): W.J. Coppard, in 'Proceedings at the Meetings of the Institute', *Arch. J* 8 (1851), 187-214.

Coppard (1853): W.J. Coppard, in 'Proceedings of the Plymouth Local Committee', 9 July 1850, *Trans Exeter Dioc. Archit. Soc.* 4 (1853), 73-8.

Cornish (1880-4): T. Cornish, in 'Meetings of the Society', *Trans Penzance NHA Soc.* NS, 1 (1880-4), 172-85.

Cornish (1884-8): T. Cornish, in 'Excursions', *Trans Penzance NHA Soc.* NS, 2 (1884-8), 311-24.

Cornish *et al.* (1892-8): T. Cornish *et al.*, in 'Meetings and Excursions. 1894-5', *Trans Penzance NHA Soc.* NS, 4 (1892-8), 79-91.

Courtney (1845): J.S. Courtney, *A Guide to Penzance and its Neighbourhood. . . .* (Penzance, 1845).

Courts (unpub. 1785): T. Courts, 'a Third part of LESCROW TENEMENT . . .', single sheet plan, in the County Record Office, Cornwall County Council, ref. no. DD. TF 858.

Cressy (1668): S. (born, H.P.) Cressy, *The Church-History of Brittany from the Beginning of Christianity to the Norman Conquest. . .* (? Rouen, 1668).

Crossing (1882): W. Crossing, 'Inscribed Stones at Tavistock', *Western Antiquary* 1 (1882), 189-90.

Crossing (1902): W. Crossing, *The Ancient Stone Crosses of Dartmoor and its Borderland* rev. ed. (Exeter, 1902).

Cuissard (1881-3): C. Cuissard, 'Vie de saint Paul de Léon en Bretagne', *Revue Celt.* 5 (1881-3), 413-60.

Dalton (1921): O.M. Dalton, *British Museum: A Guide to the Early Christian and Byzantine Antiquities in the Department of British and Mediaeval Antiquities* 2nd ed. (London, 1921).

Daniell (1906): J.J. Daniell, ed. T.C. Peter, *A Compendium of the History and Geography of Cornwall* 4th ed. (Truro, London, 1906).

Davies (1979): W. Davies, *The Llandaff Charters* (Aberystwyth, 1979).

Davies (1982): W. Davies, *Wales in the Early Middle Ages* (Leicester, 1982).

Dewar (1940): H.S.L. Dewar, 'A Romano-British Settlement at Combwich', *Proc. Som. ANH Soc.* 86 (1940), 129-33.

Dexter, T.F.G. & Dexter, H. (1938): T.F.G. Dexter and H. Dexter, *Cornish Crosses Christian and Pagan* (London, 1938).

Diack (1927): F.C. Diack, 'The Dumnoqeni Inscription at Yarrow, and the Lociti Inscription at Whithorn', *Scottish Gaelic Stud.* 2 (1927), 221-32.

Doble (1927): G.H. Doble, *Saint Docco & Saint Kew,* 'Cornish Saints' Series No. 12 (Truro, 1927).

Doble *et al.* (1939): G.H. Doble *et al.*, *A History of the Church and Parish of Saint Euny-Lelant. . .* (Shipston-on-Stour, 1939).

Dodd (1864): S. Dodd, in 'Proceedings at Meetings of the Archaeological Institute', *Arch. J* 21 (1864), 86-102.

Dowson (1966): E. Dowson, 'Parochial Check-Lists of Antiquities: *Kerrier:* 5, Mawgan in Meneage', *Cornish Arch.* 5 (1966), 78-9.

Edmonds (1844): R. Edmonds, 'Sepulchral Monument at Carnsew', *Rpt R Cornwall Polytech. Soc.* 12 (1844), 69-71.

Edmonds (1845): R. Edmonds, 'Sepulchral Monument at Carnsew', in J.S. Courtney, *A Guide to Penzance and its Neighbourhood. . .* (Penzance, 1845), Appendix, pp. 56-8.

Edmonds (1858a): R. Edmonds, 'The Celtic and other Antiquities of the Land's End District of Cornwall', *Arch. Camb.* 3S, 4 (1858), 173-83.

Edmonds (1858*b*): R. Edmonds, 'Inscribed Stone at Hayle, St. Erth, Cornwall', *Arch. Camb.* 3S, 4 (1858), 426.

Edmonds (1862): R. Edmonds, *The Land's End District. . .* (London, Penzance, 1862).

Ellis, G.E. (1938-9): G.E. Ellis, '160. Trewint Cross-base', *Devon & Cornwall N & Q* 20 (1938-9), 221-2.

Ellis, G.E. (1950-1): G.E. Ellis, '99. Cornish Crosses', *Devon & Cornwall N & Q* 24 (1950-1), 105-11.

Ellis, G.E. (1952-3*a*): G.E. Ellis, '54. Cornish Crosses', *Devon & Cornwall N & Q* 25 (1952-3), 57-61.

Ellis, G.E. (1952-3*b*): G.E. Ellis, '156. Cornish Crosses', *Devon & Cornwall N & Q* 25 (1952-3), 177-84.

Ellis, G.E. (1954-5*a*): G.E. Ellis, '60. Cornish Crosses', *Devon & Cornwall N & Q* 26 (1954-5), 65-70.

Ellis, G.E. (1954-5*b*): G.E. Ellis, '177. Cornish Crosses', *Devon & Cornwall N & Q* 26 (1954-5), 225-8.

Ellis, G.E. (1956-8*a*): G.E. Ellis, '1. Cornish Crosses', *Devon & Cornwall N & Q* 27 (1956-8), 1-5.

Ellis, G.E. (1956-8*b*): G.E. Ellis, '97. Cornish Crosses', *Devon & Cornwall N & Q* 27 (1956-8), 129-34.

Ellis, G.E. (1959-61): G.E. Ellis, '97. Cornish Crosses (*continued. . .*)', *Devon & Cornwall N & Q* 28 (1959-61), 196-9.

Ellis, G.E. (1962-4): G.E. Ellis, '164. Cornish Crosses', *Devon & Cornwall N & Q* 29 (1962-4), 273-6.

Ellis, P.B. (1974): P.B. Ellis, *The Cornish Language and its Literature* (London, Boston, 1974).

Etherton & Barlow (1950): P.T. Etherton and V. Barlow, *Tempestuous Isle. The Story of Lundy* (London, 1950).

Evans (1967): D.E. Evans, *Gaulish Personal Names. . .* (Oxford, 1967).

Feilitzen (1937): O. v. Feilitzen, *The Pre-Conquest Personal Names of Domesday Book*, Nomina Germanica 3 (Uppsala, 1937).

Ferguson (1874): S. Ferguson, 'Oghams', in 'Miscellaneous Notices', *Arch. Camb.* 4S, 5 (1874), 91-5.

Ferguson (1879*a*): S. Ferguson, 'On the Difficulties attendant on the Transcription of Ogham Legends, and the Means of Removing them', *PRIA* 2S, 1: *Polite Literature and Antiquities* (1879), 30-64.[5]

Ferguson (1879*b*): S. Ferguson, 'On the Completion of the Biliteral Key to the Values of the Letters in the South British Ogham Alphabet', *PRIA* 2S, 1: *Polite Literature and Antiquities* (1879), 176-80.[6]

Ferguson (1879*c*): S. Ferguson, 'On the Collateral Evidences corroborating the Biliteral Key to the South British Ogham Alphabet', *PRIA* 2S, 1: *Polite Literature and Antiquities* (1879), 181-5.[7]

Ferguson (1887): S. Ferguson, *Ogham Inscriptions in Ireland, Wales, and Scotland* (Edinburgh, 1887).

Finberg (1969): H.P.R. Finberg, *Tavistock Abbey: A Study in the Social and Economic History of Devon* 2nd ed. (Newton Abbot, 1969).

Fox (1964): A. Fox, *South West England* (London, 1964).

Fulford & Sellwood (1980): M. Fulford and B. Sellwood, 'The Silchester ogham stone: a reconsideration', *Antiquity* 54 (1980), 95-9.

Gardner (1960): K.S. Gardner, 'Dark Age Remains on Lundy', *Rpt Lundy Field Soc.* 13 (1959-60), 53-64.

Gardner (1962): K.S. Gardner, 'Archaeological Investigations on Lundy 1962', *Rpt Lundy Field Soc.* 15 (1962), 22-33.

Gardner (1984): K.S. Gardner, 'The Archaeology of Lundy', in A. Langham and M. Langham, *Lundy* 2nd ed. (Newton Abbot, 1984), 121-34.

---

5. Read in five instalments between 14 November 1870 and 13 February 1871.
6. Read on 29 November 1873.
7. Read on 8 December 1873.

Gilbert, C.S. (1817): C.S. Gilbert, *An Historical Survey of the County of Cornwall. . .* I (Plymouth-Dock, London, 1817).

Gilbert, C.S. (1820): C.S. Gilbert, *An Historical Survey of the County of Cornwall. . .* II (Plymouth-Dock, London, 1820).

Gilbert, D. (1838): D. Gilbert, *The Parochial History of Cornwall, founded on the Manuscript Histories of Mr. Hals and Mr. Tonkin. . .* (London, 1838).

Gill (1975): C. Gill, *The Isles of Scilly* (Newton Abbot, 1975).

Godwin (1853): E.W. Godwin, 'Examples of Church Architecture in Cornwall', *Arch. J* 10 (1853), 317-24.

Goodburn & Waugh (1983): R. Goodburn and H. Waugh eds., *Inscriptions on Stone. Epigraphic Indexes* (Gloucester, 1983).[8]

Gough (1789): R. Gough ed., *Britannia . . . By William Camden* (London, 1789).

Gough (1806): R. Gough ed., *Britannia . . . By William Camden* 2nd ed. (London, 1806).

Graham (1966): F. Graham ed., J. Norden, *Speculi Britanniæ Pars. A Topographical & Historical description of Cornwall. . .* (Newcastle-upon-Tyne, 1966).[9]

Gray (1924): H. St G. Gray, 'Caratacus Stone', *Proc. Som. ANH Soc.* 69 (1924), xl-xli.

Gray (1937): H. St G. Gray, 'Rude Stone Monuments of Exmoor (Somerset portion, Pt V)', *Proc. Som. ANH Soc.* 83 (1937), 166-70.

Greenbank (1906a): Greenbank, 'Is it the Tomb of St. Levan?', in P. Penn ed., *Cornish Notes & Queries. (First Series)*, reprinted from *The Cornish Telegraph* (London, 1906), 183.[10]

Greenbank (1906b): Greenbank, 'Carnsew Sepulchral Monument', in P. Penn ed., *Cornish Notes & Queries. (First Series)*, reprinted from *The Cornish Telegraph* (London, 1906), 187-8.

Greene (1968): D. Greene, 'Some Linguistic Evidence Relating to the British Church', in M.W. Barley and R.P.C. Hanson eds., *Christianity in Britain, 300-700* (Leicester, 1968), 75-86.

Grein (1872): C.W.M. Grein ed., *Bibliothek der Angelsächsischen Prosa* I (Cassel, Goettingen, 1872).

Greswell (1900): W.P. Greswell, 'The Quantocks and their Place-Names', *Proc. Som. ANH Soc.* 46, pt 2 (1900), 125-48.

Gribble (1884): H. Gribble, 'Plymstock Priory', *Western Antiquary* 3 (1884), 42.

Grinsell (1970): L.V. Grinsell, *The Archaeology of Exmoor: Bideford Bay to Bridgwater* (Newton Abbot, 1970).

Grover (1867): J.W. Grover, 'Pre-Augustine Christianity in Britain', *JBAA* 23 (1867), 221-30.

Haddan & Stubbs (1869): A.W. Haddan and W. Stubbs eds., *Councils and Ecclesiastical Documents relating to Great Britain and Ireland* I (Oxford, 1869).

Hague (1982): D.B. Hague, *The Early Christian Memorials Lundy* (1982).[11]

Haigh (1858-9): D.H. Haigh, 'Cryptic Inscriptions on the Cross at Hackness, in Yorkshire', *J Kilkenny SE Ireland A Soc.* 2S, 2 (1858-9), 170-94.

Halle (1851): H.F. Halle, *Letters, historical and botanical. . .* (London, 1851).

Halliwell (1861): J.O. Halliwell, *Rambles in Western Cornwall by the Footsteps of the Giants. . .* (London, 1861).

Hals (?1750): W. Hals, *The Compleat History of Cornwal, General and Parochial*, pt 2 (Truro, ?1750).

Hamlin (1972): A. Hamlin, 'A Chi-rho-carved Stone at Drumaqueran, Co. Antrim . . .', *Ulster J Arch.* 3S, 35 (1972), 22-8.

Hammond (1897): J. Hammond, *A Cornish Parish: Being an Account of St. Austell. . .* (London, 1897).

8. These indexes are to Collingwood, R.G. & Wright, R.P. (1965).
9. This work is a reprint of Norden (1728), with an introduction by Graham.
10. No initials are given for Greenbank in this or the following work.
11. This pamphlet mentions no place of publication and contains no page numbering.

Harding (1856): W. Harding, 'On the Churches of Lustleigh and Ilsington, Devon', *Trans Exeter Dioc. Archit. Soc.* 5 (1856), 77-94.

Harding (1867): W. Harding, 'Some Observations on Crosses and Pillar Stones', *Trans Exeter Dioc. Archit. Soc.* 2S, 1 (1867), 16-23.

Harvey (1987): A. Harvey, 'The Ogam Inscriptions and their Geminate Symbols', *Ériu* 38 (1987), 45-71.

Haslam (1845): W. Haslam, 'On the Crosses of Cornwall', *Rpt RIC* no. 27 (1845), 26-32.

Haslam (1846a): W. Haslam, 'Ancient Oratories of Cornwall', *Arch. J* 2 (1846), 225-39.

Haslam (1846b): W. Haslam, in 'Proceedings of the Committee', *Arch. J* 2 (1846), 383-404.

Haslam (1847): W. Haslam, 'An Account of some Monumental and Wayside Crosses, still remaining in the West of Cornwall', *Arch. J* 4 (1847), 302-13.

Haverfield (1906): F.J. Haverfield, 'Romano-British Somerset', *VCH Somerset* I (London, 1906), 207-371.

Haverfield (1913): F.J. Haverfield, 'Addimenta Qvinta ad Corporis Volumen VII', *Ephemeris Epigraphica* 9 (Berlin, 1913), 509-690.

Haverfield (1914): F.J. Haverfield, *Roman Britain in 1913*, British Academy Supplemental Papers II (Oxford, 1914).

Haverfield (1918): F.J. Haverfield, 'The Character of the Roman Empire as seen in West Somerset', Presidential Address, *Proc. Som. ANH Soc.* 64 (1918), xxiii-xlii.

Hencken (1932): H. O'N. Hencken, *The Archaeology of Cornwall and Scilly* (London, 1932).

Hencken (1935): H. O'N. Hencken, 'Inscribed Stones at St. Kew and Lanteglos by Fowey, Cornwall', in 'Miscellanea', *Arch. Camb.* 90 (1935), 144-62.

Henderson, C.G. (1925): C.G. Henderson, *The Cornish Church Guide and Parochial History of Cornwall* (Truro, 1925).

Henderson, C.G. (1930): C.G. Henderson, *St. Columb Major Church & Parish Cornwall* (Long Compton, Shipston-on-Stour, 1930).

Henderson, C.G. (1935): C.G. Henderson, eds. A.L. Rowse and M.I. Henderson, *Essays in Cornish History* (Oxford, 1935).

Henderson, C.G. (1936): C.G. Henderson, 'Rialton', *Old Cornwall* 2, no. 12 (winter, 1936), 1-10.

Henderson, C.G. (1953-6a): C.G. Henderson, 'The 109 Ancient Parishes of the four Western Hundreds of Cornwall (Part I)', *JRIC* NS, 2, pt 3 (1953-6), 1-104.[12]

Henderson, C.G. (1953-6b): C.G. Henderson, 'The Ecclesiastical History of the Four Western Hundreds of Cornwall, Part 2', *JRIC* NS, 2, pt 4 (1953-6), 105-210.

Henderson, C.G. (1957-60a): C.G. Henderson, 'The Ecclesiastical Antiquities of the 109 Parishes of West Cornwall', *JRIC* NS, 3, pt 2 (1957-60), 211-382.

Henderson, C.G. (1957-60b): C.G. Henderson, 'The Ecclesiastical History of the Four Western Hundreds. Part IV', *JRIC* NS, 3, pt 4 (1957-60), 383-497.

Henderson, C.G. (unpub. 1912-17): C.G. Henderson, *Antiquities of the Deaneries of Penwith, Kirrier and Carnmouth*, MS in 5 volumes. RIC, Truro.[13]

Henderson, M. (unpub. 1985): M. Henderson, *A Survey of Ancient Crosses of Cornwall 1952-1983*, typescript in 4 volumes. RIC, Truro.[14]

Higgitt (1986): J. Higgitt, 'Words and Crosses: The Inscribed Stone Cross in Early Medieval Britain and Ireland', in J. Higgitt ed., *Early Medieval Sculpture in Britain and Ireland*, BAR British Series 152 (Oxford, 1986), 125-52.

Hingston (1850): F.C. Hingston, *Specimens of Ancient Cornish Crosses, Fonts, etc.* (London, Oxford, Truro, 1850).[15]

---

12. This work and the three following were compiled between 1910 and 1924, written between 1923 and 1924, and published posthumously.
13. References to this work are confined to entries of particular importance.
14. References to this work are confined to entries of particular importance.
15. There is no page numbering in this work.

Hitchins (1824): F. Hitchins, ed. S. Drew, *The History of Cornwall, from the earliest records and traditions, to the present time* (Helston, 1824).

Hogg (1960-1): A.H.A. Hogg, 'A lost inscription at Porthgwarra, St. Levan', *Proc. W Cornwall Field Club* 2, no. 5 (1960-1), 246-7.

Holder (1896): A. Holder, *Alt-Celtischer Sprachschatz* I (Leipzig, 1896).

Holder (1904): A. Holder, *Alt-Celtischer Sprachschatz* II (Leipzig, 1904).

Holder (1907-13): A. Holder, *Alt-Celtischer Sprachschatz* III (Leipzig, 1907-13).

Huebner (1876): Ae. Huebner, *Inscriptiones Britanniae Christianae* (Berlin, London, 1876).

Hughes (1980): K. Hughes, *Celtic Britain in the Early Middle Ages. . .*, Stud. Celt. Hist. II (Woodbridge, 1980).

Hull (1926): E. Hull, *A History of Ireland and her People. . .* I (London, 1926).

Iago (1868-70): W. Iago, 'Slaughter-Bridge Inscribed Stone', letter to the Editor, *JRIC* 3, no. 12 (1868-70), xxxix, 318.

Iago (1870-3): W. Iago, in 'Proceedings' 20 March 1873, *Proc. Soc. Ant.* 2S, 5 (1870-3), 481-9.

Iago (1871-3): W. Iago, 'Inscribed Stones in Cornwall', *JRIC* 4, no. 13 (1871-3), 59-71.

Iago (1874-8): W. Iago, 'Cardinham Inscribed Stones, etc.', *JRIC* 5, no. 19 (1874-8), 358-65.

Iago (1878-81): W. Iago, 'The Lanhadron Inscribed Stone', *JRIC* 6, no. 23 (1878-81), 397-401.

Iago (1881-3a): W. Iago, in 'Spring Meeting, May 10th, 1881', *JRIC* 7, no. 24 (1881-3), 1-6.

Iago (1881-3b): W. Iago, 'The Annual Excursion of the Society, 1882, described and illustrated', *JRIC* 7, no. 26 (1881-3), 223-39.

Iago (1883-5a): W. Iago, 'Mawgan Cross, the Inscribed Stone of Meneage', *JRIC* 8, no. 30 (1883-5), 276-84.

Iago (1883-5b): W. Iago, 'Inscribed Stones at Stairfoot, St. Erme; and on Hensbarrow Hill, St. Austell', *JRIC* 8, no. 30 (1883-5), 285-91.

Iago (1883-5c): W. Iago, 'The Inscribed Stone at Bleu-Bridge, Gulval', *JRIC* 8, no. 31 (1883-5), 366.

Iago (1888-92): W. Iago, in 'Meetings of the Society', *Trans Penzance NHA Soc.* NS, 3 (1888-92), 383-95.

Iago (1890-1): W. Iago, 'Recent Archaeological Discoveries in Cornwall . . .', *JRIC* 10 (1890-1), 185-262.

Iago (1891-2): W. Iago, in 'Notices of Recent Archaeological and Historical Publications: The Antiquary', *Trans Bristol & Gloucester A Soc.* 16 (1891-2), 157-61.

Iago (1891-3): W. Iago, in 'Proceedings' 24 November 1892, *Proc. Soc. Ant.* 2S, 14 (1891-3), 214-15.

Iago (1892-8): W. Iago, '"The Noti-Noti Stone" in St. Hilary Churchyard', *Trans Penzance NHA Soc.* NS, 4 (1892-8), 35-9.

Iago (1893): W. Iago, 'Inscribed Stone at Cubert', *Western Antiquary* 11 (1893), 192.

Iago (1893-5a): W. Iago, 'Inscribed Stones of Cornwall', *JRIC* 12, pt 1 (1893-5), 109-14.

Iago (1893-5b): W. Iago, 'Notes on Three Ogham Stones in Cornwall', *JRIC* 12, pt 2 (1893-5), 172-4.

Iago *et al.* (1871-3): W. Iago *et al.*, in 'Conversazione', *JRIC* 4, no. 14 (1871-3), xliv-xlvii.

Iago *et al.* (1893-5): W. Iago *et al.*, in 'Spring Meeting (1894)', *JRIC* 12, pt 2 (1893-5), 119-23.

Jackson (1946): K.H. Jackson, review of R.A.S. Macalister, *Corpus Inscriptionum Insularum Celticarum* I (Dublin, 1945), *Speculum* 21 (1946), 521-3.

Jackson (1950): K.H. Jackson, 'Notes on the Ogam Inscriptions of Southern Britain', in C.F. Fox and B. Dickins eds, *The Early Cultures of North-West Europe (H.M. Chadwick Memorial Studies)* (Cambridge, 1950), 197-213.

Jackson (1950-1): K.H. Jackson, 'Primitive Irish $\underset{\times}{u}$ and $\underline{b}$', *Études Celt.* 5 (1950-1), 105-15.

Jackson (1953): K.H. Jackson, *Language and History in Early Britain. . .* (Edinburgh, 1953).

Jackson (1955): K.H. Jackson, 'The Pictish Language', in F.T. Wainwright ed., *The Problem of the Picts* (Edinburgh, 1955), 129-66.

James (1949): C.C. James, *A History of the Parish of Gwennap in Cornwall* (Penzance, 1949).

Jenkin (1934): A.K.H. Jenkin, *The Story of Cornwall* (London, Edinburgh, 1934).

Jenner (1917): H. Jenner, 'The Irish Immigrations into Cornwall in the late Fifth and Early Sixth Centuries', *Rpt R Cornwall Polytech. Soc.* NS, 3, pt 3 (1917), 38-85.

Jenner (1919): H. Jenner, 'The Royal House of Damnonia', *Rpt R Cornwall Polytech. Soc.* NS, 4, pt 2 (1919), 114-42.

Jenner (1922-5): H. Jenner, 'The Men Scrifa', *JRIC* 21, pt 1 (1922-5), 56-62.

Jenner (1924-5): H. Jenner, '250. Romano-British Inscription on Lundy Island', *Devon & Cornwall N & Q* 13 (1924-5), 274-5.

Jenner (1929): H. Jenner, 'New inscription near Bodmin', *Antiq. J* 9 (1929), 378-9.

Jenner & Henderson, C.G. (1929-32): H. Jenner and C.G. Henderson, in 'Report of Spring Meeting (1929)', *JRIC* 23, pt 2 (1929-32), 207-14.

Jennings (1936): H.R. Jennings, *Historical Notes on Madron, Morvah and Penzance* (Penzance, 1936).

Jones (1862): H.L. Jones, 'Early British Inscribed Stones. The Fardel Stone, Devonshire', *Arch. Camb.* 3S, 8 (1862), 134-42.

Jones (1863): H.L. Jones, 'Early Inscribed Stones of Cornwall', *Arch. Camb.* 3S, 9 (1863), 286-90.

Keast (1950): J. Keast, *The Story of Fowey (Cornwall)* (Exeter, 1950).

Kempe (1830): A.J. Kempe, 'Notices of Tavistock and its Abbey', *Gents Mag.* 100 (i) (1830), 113-18, 216-21, 409-12, 489-96.

Kempe (1838): A.J. Kempe, 'British Sepulchral Pillars at Llandawke, Carmarthenshire, and Stowford, Devon . . .', *Gents Mag.* NS, 9 (1838) (i), 43-5.

Kent (1858): T. Kent, 'Antiquities in the Neighbourhood of Padstow', letter to Dr Barham dated 8 May 1858, *Rpt RIC* no. 40 (1858), 24-5.

Kent *et al.* (1846a): T. Kent *et al.*, in 'Proceedings of the Central Committee', *JBAA* 1 (1846), 43-67.

Kent *et al.* (1846b): T. Kent *et al.*, in 'Proceedings of the Committee', *Arch. J* 2 (1846), 71-92.

Kermode (1907): P.M.C. Kermode, *Manx Crosses. . .* (London, 1907).

Kerslake (1884): T. Kerslake, 'Inscribed Stone at Lustleigh', *Western Antiquary* 3 (1884), 109.

Lach-Szyrma (1883-5): W.S. Lach-Szyrma, 'Notes on the Excursion of 1885', *JRIC* 8, no. 31 (1883-5), 374-7.

Lach-Szyrma (1886-9): W.S. Lach-Szyrma, 'Christian Remains in Cornwall, anterior to the Mission of Saint Augustine to Kent', *JRIC* 9 (1886-9), 55-7.

Laing (1975): L. Laing, *The Archaeology of Late Celtic Britain and Ireland c. 400-1200 AD* (London, 1975).

Langdon (1889a): A.G. Langdon, 'Celtic Ornament on the Crosses of Cornwall', *JBAA* 45 (1889), 318-47.

Langdon (1889b): A.G. Langdon, 'Inscribed Slab at Camborne, Cornwall', in 'Archaeological Notes and Queries', *Arch. Camb.* 5S, 6 (1889), 347-60.

Langdon (1889c): A.G. Langdon, 'Celtic Ornament on the Crosses of Cornwall', *Builder*, 30 March 1889, 61 (i) (1889), 238-40, 243.

Langdon (1890-1): A.G. Langdon, 'Ornament on the Early Crosses of Cornwall', *JRIC* 10 (1890-1), 33-96.

Langdon (1892a): A.G. Langdon, 'An Ogam Stone at Lewannick; in Cornwall', *JBAA* 48 (1892), 336-9.

Langdon (1892b): A.G. Langdon, 'An Ogam Stone at Lewannick, Cornwall', in 'Archaeological Notes and Queries', *Arch. Camb.* 5S, 9 (1892), 239-56.

Langdon (1892-3): A.G. Langdon, 'Ogam Stone at Lewannick, (illustrated)', *JRIC* 11, pt 2 (1892-3), 285-8.

Langdon (1893): A.G. Langdon, 'The Chi-Rho Monogram upon Early Christian Monuments in Cornwall', *Arch. Camb.* 5S, 10 (1893), 97-108.

Langdon (1893-5a): A.G. Langdon, 'Description of a Second Ogam Stone at Lewannick', *JRIC* 12, pt 2 (1893-5), 169-71.

Langdon (1893-5*b*): A.G. Langdon, in 'Proceedings' 24 January 1895, *Proc. Soc. Ant.* 2S, 15 (1893-5), 279-82.

Langdon (1894*a*): A.G. Langdon, 'Discovery of a Second Ogam Inscribed Stone at Lewannick, in Cornwall', *Illustrated Archaeologist* 2 (1894), 108-11.

Langdon (1894*b*): A.G. Langdon, 'The Inscribed and Ornamented Cross-Shaft at Biscovey, St. Blazey, Cornwall', *Arch. Camb.* 5S, 11 (1894), 308-15.

Langdon (1896): A.G. Langdon, *Old Cornish Crosses* (Truro, 1896).

Langdon (1902): A.G. Langdon, 'A Newly-Discovered Inscribed Stone in Cornwall', *Reliquary* NS, 8 (1902), 50-3.

Langdon (1906): A.G. Langdon, 'Early Christian Monuments', *VCH Cornwall* I (London, 1906), 407-49.

Langdon & Allen, J.R. (1888): A.G. Langdon and J.R. Allen, 'The Early Christian Monuments of Cornwall', *JBAA* 44 (1888), 301-25.

Langdon & Allen, J.R. (1895): A.G. Langdon and J.R. Allen, 'Catalogue of the Early Christian Inscribed Monuments in Cornwall', *Arch. Camb.* 5S, 12 (1895), 50-60.

Langham, A. & Langham, M. (1984): A. Langham and M. Langham, *Lundy* 2nd ed. (Newton Abbot, 1984).

Le Blant (1856): E. Le Blant, *Inscriptions Chrétiennes de la Gaule, antérieures au viii*[e] *Siècle* I (Paris, 1856).

Le Blant (1865): E. Le Blant, *Inscriptions Chrétiennes de la Gaule, antérieures au viii*[e] *Siècle* II (Paris, 1865).

Leland (*c.* 1540), ed. Smith, L.T. (1907): L.T. Smith ed., *The Itinerary of John Leland in or about the years 1535-1543 Parts I to III* (London, 1907).

Lhwyd (1700*a*): E. Lhwyd, letter to T. Tonkin dated 15 October 1700, letter I in W. Pryce, *Archæologia Cornu-Britannica. . .* (Sherborne, 1790).[16]

Lhwyd (1700*b*): E. Lhwyd, letter to T. Tonkin dated 29 November 1700, letter II in W. Pryce, *Archæologia Cornu-Britannica. . .* (Sherborne, 1790).

Lhwyd (1702): E. Lhwyd, in letter to the Rev. H. Foulkes dated 20 December 1702, in *Arch. Camb.* 3S, 5 (1859), 246-9.

Lindsay (1915): W.M. Lindsay, *Notae Latinae. . .* (Cambridge, 1915).

Lot (1896): F. Lot, 'Études sur la provenance du cycle arthurien (*fin*)', *Romania* 25 (1896), 1-32.

Loth (1890): J. Loth, *Chrestomathie bretonne (armoricain, gallois, cornique). . .* (Paris, 1890).

Loth (1912): J. Loth, *Contributions à l'étude des Romans de la Table Ronde* (Paris, 1912).

Loyd (1925): L.R.W. Loyd, *Lundy. Its History and Natural History* (London, 1925).

Lukis (1885): W.C. Lukis, *The Prehistoric Stone Monuments of The British Isles. Cornwall* (London, 1885).

Lysons, D. & Lysons, S. (1814): D. Lysons and S. Lysons, *Magna Britannia . . . III Cornwall* (London, 1814).

Lysons, D. & Lysons, S. (1822): D. Lysons and S. Lysons, *Magna Britannia. . . VI Devonshire* (London, 1822).

Macalister (1897): R.A.S. Macalister, *Studies in Irish Epigraphy. . . Part I. . .* (London, 1897).

Macalister (1902): R.A.S. Macalister, *Studies in Irish Epigraphy. . . Part II. . .* (London, 1902).

Macalister (1907): R.A.S. Macalister, *Studies in Irish Epigraphy. . . Part III. . .* (London, 1907).

Macalister (1929): R.A.S. Macalister, 'The Ancient Inscriptions of the South of England', *Arch. Camb.* 84 (1929), 179-96.

Macalister (1945): R.A.S. Macalister, *Corpus Inscriptionum Insularum Celticarum* I (Dublin, 1945).

Macalister (1949): R.A.S. Macalister, *Corpus Inscriptionum Insularum Celticarum* II (Dublin, 1949).

---

16. There is no page numbering in this work or in the following.

McClure (1907): E. McClure, 'The Wareham Inscriptions', *Eng. Hist. Rev.* 22 (1907), 728-30.

MacDermot (1973): E.T. MacDermot, rev. R.J. Sellick, *The History of the Forest of Exmoor* rev. ed. (Newton Abbot, 1973).

McGovern (1904): J.B. McGovern, 'Concerning the "Chi-Rho" Monogram', *Antiquary* 40 (1904), 5-9.

Maclean (1873): J. Maclean, *The Parochial and Family History of the Deanery of Trigg Minor in the County of Cornwall* I (London, Bodmin, 1873).

Maclean (1876): J. Maclean, *The Parochial and Family History of the Deanery of Trigg Minor in the County of Cornwall* II (London, Bodmin, 1876).

Maclean (1879): J. Maclean, *The Parochial and Family History of the Deanery of Trigg Minor in the County of Cornwall* III (London, Bodmin, 1879).

McManus (1991): D. McManus, *A Guide to Ogam* (Maynooth, 1991).

MacNeill (1908-9): J. MacNeill, 'Notes on the Distribution, History, Grammar, and Import of the Irish Ogham Inscriptions', *PRIA* 27, Section C (1908-9), 329-70.[17]

MacNeill (1929-31): E. MacNeill, 'Archaisms in the Ogham Inscriptions', *PRIA* 39, Section C (1929-31), 33-53.

MacNeill (1932): E. MacNeill, 'Varia. I. 4. *Fannuci, Fanoni, Svaqquci.*', *Ériu* 11 (1932), 133-5.

Madan (1905): F. Madan, *A Summary Catalogue of Western Manuscripts in the Bodleian Library at Oxford. . .* V (Oxford, 1905).

Mandach (1972): A. de Mandach, 'Aux portes de Lantïen en Cornouailles: une tombe du VIᵉ siècle portant le nom de Tristan', *Le Moyen Age* 78 (4S, 27) (1972), 389-425.

Mandach (1975): A. de Mandach, 'Aux portes de Lantïen en Cornouailles: une tombe du VIᵉ siècle portant, outre le nom de Tristan, celui d'Iseut', *Le Moyen Age* 81 (4S, 30) (1975), 3-35.

Mandach (1978): A. de Mandach, 'The shrinking tombstone of Tristan and Isolt', *J Med. Hist.* 4 (1978), 227-42.

Matthews (1892): J.H. Matthews, *A History of the Parishes of Saint Ives, Lelant, Towednack and Zennor. . .* (London, 1892).

Maxwell (1976): I.S. Maxwell, *Historical Atlas of West Penwith.* University of Sheffield (Sheffield, 1976).

Mildren (1977): J. Mildren, 'Professors seek truth behind the Tristan enigma', *Western Morning News* 3 September 1977, p. 3.

Millett (1884-8): G.B. Millett, 'The Cross of St. Ia', *Trans Penzance NHA Soc.* NS, 2 (1884-8), 145-6, 202.

Millett (1888-92): G.B. Millett, 'Penzance Market Cross', *Trans Penzance NHA Soc.* NS, 3 (1888-92), 350-1.

Morris, J. (1966): J. Morris, 'The Dates of the Celtic Saints', *J Theol. Stud.* NS, 17 (1966), 342-91.

Morris, R. (1983): R. Morris, *The church in British archaeology*, The Council for British Archaeology Research Report 47 (London, 1983).

Moyle (1726): W. Moyle, ed. T. Sergeant, *The Works of Walter Moyle Esq; None of which were ever before Publish'd* I (London, 1726).

Nance (1933a): R.M. Nance, 'The Other Halfstone: A Suggestion', *Old Cornwall* 2, no. 5 (summer, 1933), 36.

Nance (1933b): R.M. Nance, 'The Other Half Stone', *Old Cornwall* 2, no. 6 (winter, 1933), 10.

Nance (1936): R.M. Nance, 'The Otherhalf Stone', *Old Cornwall* 2, no. 11 (summer, 1936), 15-16.

Nash-Williams (1950): V.E. Nash-Williams, *The Early Christian Monuments of Wales* (Cardiff, 1950).

Nenk *et al.* (1991): B.S. Nenk *et al.*, 'Medieval Britain and Ireland in 1990', *Med. Arch.* 35 (1991), 126-238.

---

17. J. (= John) MacNeill in this work is the same person as E. (= Eoin) MacNeill in the following two works.

Nicholas (1968): E.M. Nicholas, *A Short Guide to St. Just and Pendeen* (Penzance, 1968).

Nicholls & Dewey (1912-14): F. Nicholls and H. Dewey, 'On some Antiquities at Lewannick, Cornwall (illustrated)', *JRIC* 19 (1912-14), 40-5.

Norden (1728): J. Norden, *Speculi Britanniæ Pars. A Topographical & Historical description of Cornwall...* (London, 1728).

Norway (1897): A.H. Norway, *Highways and Byways in Devon and Cornwall* (London, 1897).

O'Brien (1973): M.A. O'Brien, ed. R. Baumgarten, 'Old Irish Personal Names', *Celtica* 10 (1973), 211-36.

Okasha (1971): E. Okasha, *Hand-list of Anglo-Saxon Non-runic Inscriptions* (Cambridge, 1971).

Olson & Padel (1986): B.L. Olson and O.J. Padel, 'A Tenth-Century List of Cornish Parochial Saints', *Camb. Med. Celt. Stud.* 12 (winter, 1986), 33-71.

O'Neil (1961): B.H. St J. O'Neil, *Ancient Monuments of the Isles of Scilly.* HMSO 2nd ed. (London, 1961).

Opie (1930): S.A. Opie, 'Recent Discoveries in the Redruth District', *Old Cornwall* 1, no. 12 (winter, 1930), 17-20.

Padel (1981): O.J. Padel, 'The Cornish Background of the Tristan Stories', *Camb. Med. Celt. Stud.* 1 (summer, 1981), 53-81.

Page (1890a): J.L.W. Page, '364. Inscribed Stone on Winsford Hill', *N & Q Somerset & Dorset* 1 (1890), 263-4.

Page (1890b): J.L.W. Page, *An Exploration of Exmoor and the Hill Country of West Somerset...* (London, 1890).

Page (1890c): J.L.W. Page, 'Inscribed Stone on Winsford Hill', *Proc. Som. ANH Soc.* 36, pt 2 (1890), 82-7.

Page (1891a): J.L.W. Page, 'The Ancient Inscribed Stone on Winsford Hill, Exmoor', letter dated 9 February 1891, *Academy* 39 (1891), 168-9.

Page (1891b): J.L.W. Page, '136. Inscribed Stone on Winsford Hill', *N & Q Somerset & Dorset* 2 (1891), 164-5.

Parfitt (1884): E. Parfitt, 'The Inscribed Stone at Lustleigh', *Western Antiquary* 3 (1884), 82.

Paris (1824): J.A. Paris, *A Guide to the Mount's Bay and the Land's End...* 2nd ed. (London, 1824).

Pascoe (1976): W.H. Pascoe, 'Parochial Check-Lists of Antiquities: *Penwith (E)*: 7, Phillack', *Cornish Arch.* 15 (1976), 95-102.

Paull (1866-7a): A. Paull, in 'Report of Spring Meeting, May 25, 1866', *JRIC* 2, no. 6 (1866-7), iii-xvii.

Paull (1866-7b): A. Paull, in 'Royal Institution of Cornwall', meeting of 16 August 1867, *JRIC* 2, no. 8 (1866-7), 363-5.

Pearce (1978): S.M. Pearce, *The Kingdom of Dumnonia...* (Padstow, 1978).

Pearce (1981): S.M. Pearce, *The Archaeology of South West Britain* (London, 1981).

Pearce (1982): S.M. Pearce, 'Presidential Lecture: Church and Society in South Devon, AD 350-700', *Proc. Devon Arch. Soc.* 40 (1982), 1-18.

Pearce (1985): S.M. Pearce, 'The Early Church in the Landscape: The Evidence from North Devon', *Arch. J* 142 (1985), 255-75.

Pedler (1864-5): E.H. Pedler, 'Antiquities in East Cornwall', *JRIC* 1, pt 2 (1864-5), 12-18.

Penaluna (1819): W. Penaluna, *The Circle or Historical Survey of Sixty Parishes & Towns in Cornwall* (Helston, 1819).

Penaluna (1838): W. Penaluna, *An Historical Survey of the County of Cornwall etc.* (Helston, 1838).

Peter (1899-1900): T.C. Peter, 'Notes on the Church of S. Just-in-Penwith', *JRIC* 14, pt 1 (1899-1900), 173-90.

Pettigrew (1861): T.J. Pettigrew, 'On Ogham Inscriptions', *JBAA* 17 (1861), 293-310.

Pevsner (1951): N. Pevsner, *The Buildings of England. Cornwall* (Harmondsworth, 1951).[18]

---

18. References to this edition are confined to those entries which contain different information from Pevsner's second edition; see Pevsner (1970).

Pevsner (1952*a*): N. Pevsner, *The Buildings of England. North Devon* (Harmondsworth, 1952).

Pevsner (1952*b*): N. Pevsner, *The Buildings of England. South Devon* (Harmondsworth, 1952).

Pevsner (1970): N. Pevsner, rev. E. Radcliffe, *The Buildings of England. Cornwall* 2nd ed. (Harmondsworth, 1970).

Phillips (1937): E.N.M. Phillips, 'The Ancient Stone Crosses of Devon: Part I', *Trans Devon Assoc.* 69 (1937), 289-342.

Phillips (1938): E.N.M. Phillips, 'The Ancient Stone Crosses of Devon: Part II', *Trans Devon Assoc.* 70 (1938), 299-340.

Phillips (1939): E.N.M. Phillips, 'Supplementary Notes on the Ancient Stone Crosses of Devon', *Trans Devon Assoc.* 71 (1939), 231-41.

Phillips (1950): E.N.M. Phillips, in A. Fox, 'Seventeenth Report on Early History', *Trans Devon Assoc.* 82 (1950), 103-6.

Phillips (1954): E.N.M. Phillips, 'Supplementary Notes on the Ancient Stone Crosses of Devon (4th paper)', *Trans Devon Assoc.* 86 (1954), 173-94.

Phillips (1979): E.N.M. Phillips, 'Supplementary Notes on the Ancient Stone Crosses of Devon', *Trans Devon Assoc.* 111 (1979), 139-44.

Plummer (1910): C. Plummer ed., *Vitae Sanctorum Hiberniae. . .* (Oxford, 1910).

Polsue (1867): J. Polsue, *A Complete Parochial History of the County of Cornwall. . .* I (Truro, London, 1867).

Polsue (1868): J. Polsue, *A Complete Parochial History of the County of Cornwall. . .* II (Truro, London, 1868).

Polsue (1870): J. Polsue, *A Complete Parochial History of the County of Cornwall. . .* III (Truro, London, 1870).

Polsue (1872): J. Polsue, *A Complete Parochial History of the County of Cornwall. . .* IV (Truro, London, 1872).

Polwhele (1797): R. Polwhele, *The History of Devonshire* (London, 1797).

Polwhele (1803): R. Polwhele, *The History of Cornwall. . .* (Falmouth, 1803).

Pomeroy (1745): J. Pomeroy, letter dated 28 May 1745, *Gents Mag.* 15 (1745), 304.

Pool (1974): P.A.S. Pool, *The History of the Town and Borough of Penzance* (Penzance, 1974).

Pool (1977): P.A.S. Pool, 'Cornish Drawings by Edward Lhuyd in the British Museum', *Cornish Arch.* 16 (1977), 139-42.

Pool (undated): P.A.S. Pool, *Antiquities of Penwith. . .* (Penzance).[19]

Preston-Jones & Rose (1986): A. Preston-Jones and P. Rose, 'Medieval Cornwall', *Cornish Arch.* 25 (1986), 135-86.

Quinnell & Harris (1985): H. Quinnell and D. Harris, 'Castle Dore: the Chronology Reconsidered', *Cornish Arch.* 24 (1985), 123-32.

Radford (1946-52): C.A.R. Radford, 'Report on the Excavations at Castle Dore', *JRIC* NS, 1 (1946-52), Appendix, pp. 1-119.

Radford (1953): C.A.R. Radford, 'The Dumnonii', *JRIC* NS, 2, pt 1 (1953), 12-24.

Radford (1968): C.A.R. Radford, 'Romance and Reality in Cornwall', in G. Ashe ed., *The Quest for Arthur's Britain* (London, 1968), 75-100.

Radford (1969): C.A.R. Radford, 'An Early Christian Inscription at East Ogwell', *Proc. Devon Arch. Soc.* 27 (1969), 79-81.

Radford (1971): C.A.R. Radford, 'Christian origins in Britain', *Med. Arch.* 15 (1971), 1-12.

Radford (1975): C.A.R. Radford, *The Early Christian Inscriptions of Dumnonia*, The 1974 Holbeche Corfield Lecture. Cornwall Arch. Soc. (Redruth, 1975).

Radford & Jackson (1970): C.A.R. Radford and K.H. Jackson, 'Early Christian Inscriptions', in *An Inventory of Historical Monuments in the County of Dorset*, II South-East. RCHM (England) (London, 1970), pt 2, pp. 310-12.

Rahtz (1971): P. Rahtz, 'Castle Dore - A Reappraisal of the Post-Roman Structures', *Cornish Arch.* 10 (1971), 49-54.

---

19. This booklet has no date of publication; it was published at some time between 1976 and 1984.

Ranken (1888-92): F.S. Ranken, in 'The Annual Excursion', *Trans Penzance NHA Soc.* NS, 3 (1888-92), 305-14.

Rashleigh (1887): E.W. Rashleigh, *A Short History of the Town and Borough of Fowey* (Plymouth [printed], 1887).

Redding (1842): C. Redding, *An Illustrated Itinerary of the County of Cornwall* (London, 1842).

Reed, H. (1899): H. Reed, 'The Churches of Boscastle, Trevalga, and Tintagel, Cornwall', *Trans Exeter Dioc. Archit. Soc.* 3S, 1 (1899), 186-99.

Reed, J. & Reed, B. (1971): J. Reed and B. Reed, 'Parochial Check-Lists of Antiquities: *Pydar*: 3, St. Breoke', *Cornish Arch.* 10 (1971), 106-7.

Rhys (1873a): J. Rhys, 'On some of our British Inscriptions', *Arch. Camb.* 4S, 4 (1873), 74-7.

Rhys (1873b): J. Rhys, in 'Correspondence', *Arch. Camb.* 4S, 4 (1873), 197-205.

Rhys (1874a): J. Rhys, 'Note 32. - The Dobunni Inscription', in 'Archaeological Notes and Queries', *Arch. Camb.* 4S, 5 (1874), 173-5.

Rhys (1874b): J. Rhys, 'Ancient British Inscriptions', in 'Correspondence', *Arch. Camb.* 4S, 5 (1874), 330-5.

Rhys (1875): J. Rhys, 'On some of our Inscribed Stones', *Arch. Camb.* 4S, 6 (1875), 359-71.

Rhys (1879): J. Rhys, *Lectures on Welsh Philology* 2nd ed. (London, 1879).

Rhys (1880): J. Rhys, 'Inscribed Stone at Lustleigh in Devon', *Arch. Camb.* 4S, 11 (1880), 161-3.

Rhys (1882): J. Rhys, 'The Lustleigh Stone', *Arch. Camb.* 4S, 13 (1882), 50.

Rhys (1890a): J. Rhys, 'An Ancient Inscribed Stone on Exmoor', letter dated 21 August 1890, *Academy* 38 (1890), 179.

Rhys (1890b): J. Rhys, 'The Exmoor and Ballaqueeny Inscriptions', letter dated 30 August 1890, *Academy* 38 (1890), 201.

Rhys (1890-1): J. Rhys, 'The Early Irish Conquests of Wales and Dumnonia', *Proc. R Soc. Ant. Ireland* 5S, 1 (1890-1), 642-57.

Rhys (1891): J. Rhys, 'Notice of newly discovered Inscribed Stone on Winsford Hill, Exmoor', *Arch. Camb.* 5S, 8 (1891), 29-32.

Rhys (1896): J. Rhys, 'Early Goidelic Sentences', letter dated 10 October 1896, *Academy* 50 (1896), 285.

Rhys (1901): J. Rhys, *Celtic Folklore Welsh and Manx* (Oxford, 1901).

Rhys (1905): J. Rhys, 'The Origin of the Welsh Englyn and Kindred Metres', *Y Cymmrodor* 18 (1905), 1-185.

Rhys (1905-6): J. Rhys, 'The Celtic Inscriptions of France and Italy', *PBA* 2 (1905-6), 273-373.

Rhys (1911-12): J. Rhys, 'The Celtic Inscriptions of Gaul. Additions and Corrections', *PBA* 5 (1911-12), 261-360.

Rhys (1913-14). J. Rhys, 'The Celtic Inscriptions of Cisalpine Gaul', *PBA* 6 (1913-14), 23-112.

Rhys (1918): J. Rhys, 'Notes on Some of the Early Inscribed Stones of Wales, Devon and Cornwall', *Arch. Camb.* 6S, 18 (1918), 181-94.

Rhys & Brynmor-Jones (1900): J. Rhys and D. Brynmor-Jones, *The Welsh People...* (London, 1900).

Rickard (1978-81): W.J.C. Rickard, '79. Lanherne Cross, Mawgan in Pydar', *Devon & Cornwall N & Q* 34 (1978-81), 168-9.

Rowe, J.H. (1926-8): J.H. Rowe, 'Tristram, King Rivalen and King Mark', *JRIC* 22, pt 3 (1926-8), 445-64.

Rowe, L. (1973): L. Rowe, *Granite Crosses of West Cornwall* (Truro, 1973).[20]

Russell (1958-9): V. Russell, 'Check-list of the antiquities of West Penwith', *Proc. W Cornwall Field Club* 2, no. 3 (1958-9), 95-103.

Russell (1959-60): V. Russell, 'List of the Antiquities of West Penwith: 2. Parish of St. Buryan', *Proc. W Cornwall Field Club* 2, no. 4 (1959-60), 139-44.

---

20. There is no page numbering in this book.

Russell (1962): V. Russell, 'Parochial Check-Lists of Antiquities: Hundred of Penwith (West): 5, Sancreed', *Cornish Arch.* 1 (1962), 109-13.

Russell (1964): V. Russell, 'Parochial Check-Lists of Antiquities: Hundred of Penwith (West): 7, Penzance and Madron', *Cornish Arch.* 3 (1964), 90-5.

Russell (1965): V. Russell, 'Parochial Check-Lists of Antiquities: Hundred of Penwith (West): 8, Gulval', *Cornish Arch.* 4 (1965), 70-4.

Russell (1969): V. Russell, 'Parochial Check-Lists of Antiquities: *Penwith (W)*: 14, Lelant', *Cornish Arch.* 8 (1969), 120-3.

Russell (1971): V. Russell, *West Penwith Survey*, Cornwall Arch. Soc. (Truro, 1971).

Schmidt (1990): K.H. Schmidt, 'Late British', in A. Bammesberger and A. Wollmann eds., *Britain 400-600: Language and History* (Heidelberg, 1990), 121-48.

Sedding (1909): E.H. Sedding, *Norman Architecture in Cornwall. . .* (London, Truro, 1909).

Sedgley (1975): J.P. Sedgley, *The Roman Milestones of Britain: their Petrography and probable Origin*, BAR 18 (Oxford, 1975).

Sharrock (1893): H. Sharrock, 'Inscribed Stone at Cubert', *Western Antiquary* 11 (1893), 166.

Sheppard (1967): P. Sheppard, 'Parochial Check-Lists of Antiquities: *Powder*: 5, St. Ewe', *Cornish Arch.* 6 (1967), 98-101.

Sheppard (1968): P. Sheppard, 'Parochial Check-Lists of Antiquities: *Powder*: 7, Cuby with Tregoney St. James', *Cornish Arch.* 7 (1968), 97-8.

Sheppard (1978): P. Sheppard, 'Parochial Check-Lists of Antiquities: *Pydar*: 5, St Mawgan in Pydar', *Cornish Arch.* 17 (1978), 119-24.

Smart (1981): V. Smart, *Sylloge of Coins of the British Isles, 28 Cumulative Index of volumes 1-20* (London, 1981).

Smirke (1861a): E. Smirke, 'An Account of an ancient inscribed Stone found at Fardel, near Ivybridge, in Devon', *Rpt RIC* 43, no. 1 (1861), 20-33.

Smirke (1861b): E. Smirke, 'An Account of an Ancient Inscribed Stone found at Fardel, near Ivybridge, in Devon', *Arch. Camb.* 3S, 7 (1861), Supplement, pp. 3-16.

Smirke (1862): E. Smirke, in 'The Spring Meeting, May 23rd, 1862', *Rpt RIC* 44, pt 1 (1862), 7-20.

Smirke (1866-7): E. Smirke, in 'Report of Spring Meeting, May 25, 1866', *JRIC* 2, no. 6 (1866-7), iii-xviii.

Smirke *et al.* (1861): E. Smirke *et al.*, in 'Proceedings at Meetings of the Archaeological Institute', *Arch. J* 18 (1861), 146-93.

Smith, R.A. (1923): R.A. Smith, *British Museum. A Guide to the Anglo-Saxon and Foreign Teutonic Antiquities in the Department of British and Mediaeval Antiquities* (London, 1923).

Smith, W. & Cheetham (1880): W. Smith and S. Cheetham eds., *A Dictionary of Christian Antiquities. . .* II (London, 1880).

Soulsby (1885a): B.H. Soulsby, 'Inscribed Stone at Pencliff Castle, Cornwall', *Western Antiquary* 4 (1885), 76.

Soulsby (1885b): B.H. Soulsby, 'Inscribed Stone at Hayle', *N & Q* 6S, 11 (1885), 248.

Speed (1676): J. Speed, *The Theatre of the Empire of Great-Britain. . .* (London, 1676).

Spence (1849): C. Spence, '"Iter Cornubiense", a relation of certain passages which took place during a short tour in Cornwall', *Trans Exeter Dioc. Archit. Soc.* 3 (1849), 205-23.

Stephens, G. (1884): G. Stephens, *The Old-Northern Runic Monuments of Scandinavia and England. . .* III (London, Edinburgh, Copenhagen, 1884).

Stephens, G. (1901): G. Stephens, ed. S.O.M. Söderberg, *The Old-Northern Runic Monuments of Scandinavia and England. . .* IV (London, Edinburgh, Lund, 1901).

Stephens, W.J. (1939): W.J. Stephens, 'Inscribed Stone at Indian Queens', *Old Cornwall* 3, no. 6 (winter, 1939), 247.

Stevens *et al.* (1975): C.G. Stevens *et al.*, 'The Roman pillar in St Lawrence's Church, Jersey; a stocktaking', *Ann. Bulletin Soc. Jersiaise* 21, pt 3 (1975), 343-57.

Swanton & Pearce (1982): M. Swanton and S.M. Pearce, 'Lustleigh, South Devon: its Inscribed Stone, its Churchyard and its Parish', in S.M. Pearce ed., *The Early Church in Western Britain and Ireland*, BAR British Series 102 (Oxford, 1982), 139-43.

Tangye (1985): M. Tangye, 'A New Inscribed Stone and Churchyard Cross, St. Euny's Church, Redruth', *Cornish Arch.* 24 (1985), 171-2.

Teague *et al.* (1892-8): A.H. Teague *et al.*, in 'Meetings and Excursions. 1897-8', *Trans Penzance NHA Soc.* NS, 4 (1892-8), 116-29.

Tennyson (1897): H. Tennyson, *Alfred Lord Tennyson: A Memoir. . .* (London, 1897).

Thomas, A.C. (1953): A.C. Thomas, 'The Carnsew Inscription', *Old Cornwall* 5, no. 3 (summer, 1953), 125-30.

Thomas, A.C. (1954): A.C. Thomas, *The Principal Antiquities of the Land's End District*, West Cornwall Field Club: Field Guide No. 2 (1954).

Thomas, A.C. (1957-8): A.C. Thomas, 'Cornwall in the Dark Ages', *Proc. W Cornwall Field Club* 2, pt 2 (1957-8), 59-72.

Thomas, A.C. (1958): A.C. Thomas, *Gwithian. Ten Years' Work (1949-1958).* West Cornwall Field Club (Gwithian, 1958).

Thomas, A.C. (1961): A.C. Thomas, *Phillack Church. An Illustrated History of the Celtic, Norman, and Medieval Foundations* (Gloucester, 1961).

Thomas, A.C. (1963): A.C. Thomas, 'The Rediscovery of St. Ia's Chapel, Camborne', *Cornish Arch.* 2 (1963), 77-8.

Thomas, A.C. (1967): A.C. Thomas, *Christian Antiquities of Camborne* (St Austell, 1967).

Thomas, A.C. (1968): A.C. Thomas, *Christian Sites in West Penwith. Excursion Guide. . ..* The Society for Medieval Archaeology (Truro, 1968).

Thomas, A.C. (1969-72): A.C. Thomas, 'Irish Settlements in Post-Roman Western Britain', *JRIC* NS, 6, pt 4 (1969-72), 251-74.

Thomas, A.C. (1970): A.C. Thomas, 'Parochial Check-Lists of Antiquities: Penwith (E): 5, Camborne', *Cornish Arch.* 9 (1970), 136-44.

Thomas, A.C. (1971a): A.C. Thomas, *Britain and Ireland in Early Christian Times AD 400-800* (London, 1971).

Thomas, A.C. (1971b): A.C. Thomas, *The Early Christian Archaeology of North Britain* (Oxford, 1971).

Thomas, A.C. (1978): A.C. Thomas, 'Ninth Century Sculpture in Cornwall: a note', in J. Lang ed., *Anglo-Saxon and Viking Age Sculpture*, BAR British Series 49 (Oxford, 1978), 75-9.

Thomas, A.C. (1979): A.C. Thomas, 'Hermits on Islands or Priests in a Landscape?', (Marett Memorial Lecture, 1979), *Cornish Stud.* 6 (1979), 28-44.

Thomas, A.C. (1980): A.C. Thomas, 'An Early Christian Inscribed Stone from Boskenna, St Buryan', *Cornish Arch.* 19 (1980), 107-9.

Thomas, A.C. (1981): A.C. Thomas, *Christianity in Roman Britain to AD 500* (London, 1981).

Thomas, A.C. (1985a): A.C. Thomas, *Exploration of a drowned Landscape. Archaeology and History of the Isles of Scilly* (London, 1985).

Thomas, A.C. (1985b): A.C. Thomas, 'St. Euny's Church, Redruth: a Note on the Inscription', *Cornish Arch.* 24 (1985), 173-4.

Thomas, A.C. (1986): A.C. Thomas, *Celtic Britain* (London, 1986).

Thomas, A.C. *et al.* (1969): A.C. Thomas *et al.*, 'Lundy', *Current Arch.* 16 (September, 1969), 138-42.

Thomas, I. (1947): I. Thomas, 'Isthmus of Penwith', *Stud. Cornish Geography* I (Redruth, 1947), 41-90.

Thornton (1862): Thornton, in 'Proceedings of the Exeter Congress', *JBAA* 18 (1862), 333-46.[21]

Thurneyson (1918): R. Thurneyson, 'Miszellen', *Zeits. f Celt. Phil.* 12 (1918), 408-14.

Todd (1987): M. Todd, *The South West to AD 1000* (London, New York, 1987).

Vendryes (1937): J. Vendryes, 'Sur les hypocoristiques celtiques précédés de "mo-" ou de "to-(do-)"', *Études Celt.* 2 (1937), 254-68.

Vivian-Neal (1937): A.W. Vivian-Neal, 'St. Carantoc at Carhampton', *Proc. Som. ANH Soc.* 83 (1937), 211-14.

---

21. Thornton is referred to as 'the Rev. Dr.' but no initials are given. This was probably the Rev. W.H. Thornton of North Bovey.

Vosper (1964): D.C. Vosper, 'St. Just in Penwith', *Old Cornwall* 6, no. 6 (spring, 1964), 255-62.

Vowles (1939): A. Vowles, *Exmoor. The History of the Caratacus Stone Winsford Hill* (Minehead, 1939).

Wall (1968): J. Wall, 'Christian evidences in Roman south-west Britain', *Trans Devon Assoc.* 100 (1968), 161-78.

Warner (1963): R. Warner, 'Parochial Check-Lists of Antiquities: Hundred of Pydar: 2, Perranzabuloe', *Cornish Arch.* 2 (1963), 67-72.

Weatherhill (1981): C. Weatherhill, *Belerion. Ancient Sites of Land's End* (Penzance, 1981).

Weatherhill (1985): C. Weatherhill, *Cornovia. Ancient Sites of Cornwall and Scilly* (Penzance, 1985).

Weaver et al. (1900): F.W. Weaver *et al.*, 'Torr Steps', *Proc. Som. ANH Soc.* 46, pt 1 (1900), 25-7.

Westwood (1858): J.O. Westwood, 'Inscribed Stone at Hayle, St. Erth, Cornwall', *Arch. Camb.* 3S, 4 (1858), 318.

Whitley (1871-3): N. Whitley, in 'Report of Spring Meeting, May 18, 1872', *JRIC* 4, no. 14 (1871-3), ix-xxvi.

Whitley (1874-8): N. Whitley, 'Roman occupation of Cornwall', *JRIC* 5, no. 17 (1874-8), 199-205.

Whitley *et al.* (1856): N. Whitley *et al.*, in 'Evening Meetings', 29 April 1856, *Rpt RIC* no. 38 (1856), 23-7.

Wilkinson (1862): J.G. Wilkinson, 'On British Remains at Dartmoor. Part I', *JBAA* 18 (1862), 22-53.

Williams (1860): J. Williams ab Ithel ed., *Annales Cambriæ.* Rolls Series (London, 1860).

Willmott (1933): H.J. Willmott, 'Long Cross restored to Long Cross', *Old Cornwall* 2, no. 6 (winter, 1933) 17-18.

Wills (1891): S.J. Wills, 'Inscribed Stone at Southill, Cornwall', in 'Archaeological Notes and Queries', *Arch. Camb.* 5S, 8 (1891), 303-28.

Wilson (1964): D.M. Wilson, 'Medieval Britain in 1962 and 1963: I. Pre-conquest', *Med. Arch.* 8 (1964), 231-41.

Woods (1988): S.H. Woods, *Dartmoor Stone* (Exeter, 1988).

Worth, R.N. (1886): R.N. Worth, *A History of Devonshire. . .* 2nd ed. (London, 1886).

Wright, R.P. & Jackson (1968): R.P. Wright and K.H. Jackson, 'A Late Inscription from Wroxeter', *Antiq. J* 48 (1968), 296-300.

Wright, T. (1852): T. Wright, *The Celt, the Roman, and the Saxon. . .* (London, 1852).

(-) (1799): (-), letter signed 'Viator', dated 11 June 1799, *Gents Mag.* 69 (ii) (1799), 571-2.

(-) (1807): (-), letter initialled 'D.D.S.', dated 18 May 1807, *Gents Mag.* 77 (ii) (1807), 717-18.

(-) (1849): (-), letter initialled 'H.P.', dated 8 October 1849, *Gents Mag.* NS, 32 (1849) (ii), 494.[22]

(-) (1851a): (-), 'Proceedings at the Meetings of the Institute', 7 November 1851, *Arch. J* 8 (1851), 414-27.

(-) (1851b): (-), *Hand-book for Travellers in Devon & Cornwall* pub. John Murray (London, 1851).

(-) (1856): (-), *A Handbook for Travellers in Devon and Cornwall* 3rd ed. pub. John Murray (London, 1856).

(-) (1869): (-), 'The Autumn Excursion', *Rpt RIC* no. 51 (1869), xxi-xxviii.

(-) (1871-3a): (-), 'Autumn Excursion . . .', *JRIC* 4, no. 14 (1871-3), xxvii-xxxi.

(-) (1871-3b): (-), 'Chronological Memoranda, 1873', *JRIC* 4, no. 15 (1871-3), 308-13.

(-) (1873): (-), initialled 'J.H.H.', *New Guide to Penzance, St. Michael's Mount, Land's End. . .* (Penzance, 1873).

(-) (1874-8): (-), 'The Autumn Excursion, 1874', *JRIC* 5, no. 16 (1874-8), 138-42.

---

22. 'H.P.' is probably H. Pidgeon.

(-) (1880-4*a*): (-), 'An Account of the Fifth Excursion of the Penzance Natural History and Antiquarian Society', *Trans Penzance NHA Soc.* NS, 1 (1880-4), 14-21.

(-) (1880-4*b*): (-), 'An Account of the Annual Excursion', *Trans Penzance NHA Soc.* NS, 1 (1880-4), 87-100.

(-) (1883-5): (-), 'Annual Meeting (1885)', *JRIC* 8, no. 31 (1883-5), 317-23.

(-) (1884*a*): (-), initialled 'P.F.R.', 'Inscribed Stone at Lustleigh Church', *Western Antiquary* 3 (1884), 70.[23]

(-) (1884*b*): (-), initialled 'P.F.R.', 'The Inscribed Stone at Lustleigh Church (652)', *Western Antiquary* 3 (1884), 104.

(-) (1884*c*): (-), 'Notes to the Illustrations, Etc.', *Western Antiquary* 3 (1884), 204.

(-) (1884-8): (-), 'Annual Excursion of the Society, August 25th, 1886', *Trans Penzance NHA Soc.* NS, 2 (1884-8), 223-30.

(-) (1886-9): (-), 'Annual Excursion, 1886', *JRIC* 9 (1886-9), 107-11.

(-) (1888-92): (-), 'Excursions. Madron', *Trans Penzance NHA Soc.* NS, 3 (1888-92), 18-29.

(-) (1892): (-), 'Notes of the Month', *Antiquary* 25 (1892), 1-6.

(-) (1893-5): (-), 'Annual Excursion (1894)', *JRIC* 12, pt 2 (1893-5), 141-5.

(-) (1895): (-), 'Antiquarian News Items & Comments', *Reliquary* NS, 1 (1895), 55-64.

(-) (1896*a*): (-), 'Report of the Forty-Ninth Annual Meeting held at Launceston (continued)', *Arch. Camb.* 5S, 13 (1896), 145-64.

(-) (1896*b*): (-), 'Report of the Forty-Ninth Annual Meeting held at Launceston (continued)', *Arch. Camb.* 5S, 13 (1896), 233-57.

(-) (1897): (-), 'Périodiques analysés: Archaeologia Cambrensis', *Revue Celt.* 18 (1897), 121-4.

(-) (1903-5): (-), 'Annual Excursion (Penzance, Chysauster, Madron, 1905)', *JRIC* 16, pt 3 (1903-5), 329-32.

(-) (1906*a*): (-), signed 'Ygrec', 'And the "Chi-Rho" Monogram.', in P. Penn, ed., *Cornish Notes & Queries. (First Series)*, reprinted from *The Cornish Telegraph* (London, 1906), 181-2.

(-) (1906*b*): (-), initialled 'T.W.S.', 'Silus, the Presbyter of St. Just.', in P. Penn ed., *Cornish Notes & Queries. (First Series)*, reprinted from *The Cornish Telegraph* (London, 1906), 182-3.

(-) (1906*c*): (-), signed 'Ygrec', in P. Penn ed., *Cornish Notes & Queries. (First Series)*, reprinted from *The Cornish Telegraph* (London, 1906), 183.[24]

(-) (1906*d*): (-), initialled 'T.W.S.', 'The "Old Stone of Silus."', in P. Penn ed., *Cornish Notes & Queries. (First Series)*, reprinted from *The Cornish Telegraph* (London, 1906), 183-4.

(-) (1910-11*a*): (-), 'Annual Excursion (Sancreed, St. Just, Levant Mine, 1909)', *JRIC* 18, pt 1 (1910-11), 35-42.

(-) (1910-11*b*): (-), 'Annual Excursion (Liskeard, Phoenix Mine, St. Cleer, 1910)', *JRIC* 18, pt 2 (1910-11), 276-85.

(-) (1922-5): (-), 'Report of Summer Excursion (1924)', *JRIC* 21, pt 4 (1922-5), 348-55.

(-) (1923): (-), 'Ancient gravestone in Lundy', *Antiq. J* 3 (1923), 372-3.

(-) (1961): (-), 'The Tristan Stone. Unveiling of Plaque by Miss Foy Quiller Couch', *Old Cornwall* 6, no. 1 (autumn, 1961), 35-8.

(-) (1966): (-), *Map of Britain in the Dark Ages* 2nd ed.. Ordnance Survey (Chessington, 1966).

(-) (1968): (-), 'Lundy', *Current Arch.* 8 (May, 1968), 196-202.

(-) (1970): (-), *An Inventory of Historical Monuments in the County of Dorset,* II *South-East.* RCHM (England) (London, 1970).

---

23. 'P.F.R.' in this work and in the following may be P.F. Rowsell.
24. This article has no title.

Abbreviations of Journal and Series Titles

Where 'the' is the first word of a title it is ignored; 'ae' and 'æ' are not differentiated.

Ann. Bulletin Soc. Jersiaise	Annual Bulletin of the Société Jersiaise
Antiq. J	Antiquaries Journal
Arch. Camb.	Archaeologia Cambrensis
Arch. J	Archaeological Journal
BAR	British Archaeological Reports
CBA	Council for British Archaeology
Camb. Med. Celt. Stud.	Cambridge Medieval Celtic Studies
Cornish Arch.	Cornish Archaeology
Cornish Stud.	Cornish Studies
Cornwall Arch. Soc.	Cornwall Archaeology Society
Current Arch.	Current Archaeology
Devon & Cornwall N & Q	Devon and Cornwall Notes and Queries
Eng. Hist. Rev.	English Historical Review
Études Celt.	Études Celtiques
Gents Mag.	Gentleman's Magazine
JBAA	Journal of the British Archaeological Association
JRIC	Journal of the Royal Institution of Cornwall
J Kilkenny SE Ireland A Soc.	Journal of the Kilkenny and South-east of Ireland Archaeological Society
J Med. Hist.	Journal of Medieval History
J Roman Stud.	Journal of Roman Studies
J Theol. Stud.	Journal of Theological Studies
Med. Arch.	Medieval Archaeology
N & Q	Notes and Queries
N & Q Somerset and Dorset	Notes and Queries for Somerset and Dorset
PBA	Proceedings of the British Academy
PRIA	Proceedings of the Royal Irish Academy
Proc. Devon Arch. Soc.	Proceedings of the Devon Archaeological Society
Proc. R Soc. Ant. Ireland	Proceedings and Papers of the Royal Society of Antiquaries of Ireland
Proc. Soc. Ant.	Proceedings of the Society of Antiquaries of London
Proc. Som. ANH Soc.	Proceedings of the Somersetshire Archaeological and Natural History Society

Proc. W Cornwall Field Club	Proceedings of the West Cornwall Field Club
RCHM	Royal Commission on Historical Monuments
Revue Celt.	Revue Celtique
Rpt Lundy Field Soc.	Annual Report of the Lundy Field Society
Rpt R Cornwall Polytech. Soc.	Report of the Royal Cornwall Polytechnic Society
Rpt RIC	Annual Report of the Royal Institution of Cornwall
Scottish Gaelic Stud.	Scottish Gaelic Studies
Stud. Celt. Hist.	Studies in Celtic History
Stud. Cornish Geography	Studies in Cornish Geography
Trans Bristol & Gloucester A Soc.	Transactions of the Bristol and Gloucestershire Archaeological Society
Trans Devon Assoc.	Transactions of the Devonshire Association for the Advancement of Science, Literature, and Art
Trans Exeter Dioc. Archit. Soc.	Transactions of the Exeter Diocesan Architectural Society
Trans Hon. Soc. Cymmrodorion	Transactions of the Honourable Society of Cymmrodorion
Trans Penzance NHA Soc.	Transactions of the Natural History and Antiquarian Society of Penzance
Trans Plymouth Inst.	Transactions of the Plymouth Institute
Ulster J Arch.	Ulster Journal of Archaeology
VCH	Victoria History of the Counties of England
Zeits. f Celt. Phil.	Zeitschrift für Celtische Philologie

List of Figures

I.1	Distribution map	4
I.2	The *chi-rho* symbol	17
I.3	The ogham alphabet	19
I.4	Gaulish stones (1)	34
I.5	Gaulish stones (2)	35
I.6	Gaulish stones (3)	36
I.7	Dating model for the south-western inscribed stones	56
II.1(i)	Biscovey, text (i)	64
II.1(ii)	Biscovey, text (ii)	65
II.2	Boskenna	69
II.3	Boslow	71
II.4	Bosworgey	74
II.5	Bowden	77
II.6	Buckland Monachorum	80
II.7	Camborne	83
II.8	Cardinham I	86
II.9	Cardinham II	89
II.10	Castledore	93
II.11	Cubert	98
II.12(i)	East Ogwell, stone (i)	101
II.12(ii)	East Ogwell, stone (ii)	101
II.13(i)	Fardel, texts (i), (iii), (iv)	104
II.13(ii)	Fardel, text (ii)	105
II.14	Gulval I	110
II.15	Gulval II	114
II.16(i)	Hayle	117
II.16(ii)	Hayle	118
II.17	Indian Queens	123
II.18	Lancarffe	127
II.19(i)	Lanhadron	130
II.19(ii)	Lanhadron	131
II.20(i)	Lanherne, text (i)	134
II.20(ii)	Lanherne, text (ii)	135
II.21	Lanivet	139
II.22(i)	Lanteglos, face	142
II.22(ii)	Lanteglos, left-hand side	143
II.23	Lewannick I	147
II.24	Lewannick II	151
II.25-8	A general view of the Lundy stones	154
II.25	Lundy I	155
II.26	Lundy II	159
II.27	Lundy III	162
II.28	Lundy IV	165
II.29	Lustleigh	168

II.30	Lynton	172
II.31	Madron I	175
II.32	Madron II	180
II.33	Madron III	183
II.34	Mawgan	186
II.35	Nanscow	190
II.37(i)	Penzance, text (i)	196
II.37(ii)	Penzance, text (ii)	197
II.39	Phillack I	202
II.40	Phillack II	206
II.41	Plymstock	209
II.42	Porthgwarra	211
II.43	Redgate	214
II.44	Redruth	219
II.45	Rialton	221
II.46	St Clement	225
II.47	St Columb Major	230
II.48	St Endellion	233
II.49	St Hilary	237
II.50	St Just I	240
II.51(i)	St Just II, text (i)	244
II.51(ii)	St Just II, text (ii)	245
II.52	St Kew	249
II.53	Sancreed I	252
II.54(i)	Sancreed II, text (i)	256
II.54(ii)	Sancreed II, text (ii)	257
II.55	Sourton	261
II.56	Southill	265
II.57	Stowford	269
II.58	Tavistock I	272
II.59	Tavistock II	275
II.60	Tavistock III	279
II.61	Tavistock IV	283
II.62	Tavistock V	286
II.63	Tawna	289
II.64(i)	Tintagel, text (i)	292
II.64(ii)	Tintagel, text (ii)	293
II.65	Trebyan	297
II.66	Tregony	300
II.67	Trencrom	303
II.68	Tresco	305
II.69	Treslothan	308
II.70	Trevarrack	311
II.71	Treveneague	313
II.72	Trewint	316
II.74	Waterpit Down	319
II.75	Welltown	323
II.76	Whitestile	327
II.77	Winsford Hill	330
II.78	Worthyvale	335
II.79	Yealmpton	339